DISCARD

Divine Disobedience

FRANCINE du PLESSIX GRAY

Divine Disobedience:
Profiles in Catholic Radicalism

VINTAGE BOOKS
A Division of Random House
New York

To CLEVE GRAY

I have been sent to prison more often,
and whipped so many times more,
often almost to death . . . Constantly traveling,
I have been in danger from rivers and in danger
from brigands, in danger from my own people and
in danger from pagans; in danger in the towns,
in danger in the open country, in danger at sea,
in danger from so-called brothers.

—Saint Paul, II Corinthians

The horrors which we have seen,
the still greater horrors which we shall
presently see, are not signs that rebels, insubordinate,
untameable men, are increasing in constant numbers,
but rather that there is a constant increase,
a stupendously rapid increase,
in the number of obedient, docile men.

—Georges Bernanos

Introduction

This is a book about the conscience of dissent and about the role it has played in shaping the destinies of several extraordinary men. Of all the forces that have forged the upheaval within the Roman Catholic Church in the past decade—the revolutionary vision of Pope John XXIII, the liberation brought about by the Second Vatican Council, the crisis of authority which ensued from it—one phenomenon has interested me the most: the character of those Catholics who have remained deeply dedicated to their faith while rebelling against the Church's traditional structure and who, in the course of their rebellion, have also become some of the most militant critics and reformers of secular society. I have tried to explore the character of the new Catholic radical; to examine the tension in his conscience between his understanding of the Gospel and the rigidities of the institutional Church; and to consider his impact upon the secular world.

The phenomenon of the new Catholic radicalism has been particularly ironic in the United States, where the Catholic community has always been the most chauvinistic and conservative segment of the nation. Its most succinct explanation, if one dare put it in a single sentence, is that repression breeds radicalism. Thus, in a time of profound social and political crisis such as we have lived through in the past decade, it is the men bred in the strongest climate of repression and of moral absolutism, the men brought up in that most rigorously authoritarian of all families—the Catholic Church—who may become some of the most committed leaders of that dissident minority which is the leaven of reform.

I wish to make it clear, however, that my understanding of radicalism, both in its semantic and historical senses, implies a return to roots. The non-violent revolutionaries such as the men I write about wish to return to ancient ideological principles—be they principles of the Gospel or of the Constitution—which they feel have been sullied by time and by the blind obedience of docile majorities. In this sense the rebel heroes of this book are deeply traditional, deeply conservative men.

Before all else I want to thank my mother and father, Tatiana and Alexander Liberman, for the love and support they have offered me over the years. Anything I do will always be bettered by their trust in me, and by the standards which they have set in their own work and in their lives.

My interest in the Roman Catholic Church was rekindled by an Episcopalian minister, Reverend Otis Charles, of Washington, Connecticut, who inspired me to start this book. I thank Father Charles for his friendship and advice, and for the warmth and wisdom which he offers to all who seek his help.

I am indebted to my husband, Cleve Gray, for this book getting written and finished. It could not have been done without his love and his enthusiasm, and his patient penciling of drafts.

I am deeply grateful to the four editors—William Maxwell, William Shawn, Judith Jones, and Robert Silvers—who have given me the confidence to be a writer.

Introduction

Among the many persons who have helped me in the execution of this book I particularly thank Fathers Daniel and Philip Berrigan, whose vision has transformed my view of the world beyond recognition, and whose friendships I treasure; His Excellency Sergio Mendez Arceo, Bishop of Cuernavaca, Mexico, who I believe senses and conveys what the Holy Spirit is about more clearly than any other bishop in the Church; Ivan Illich, who has helped me to understand the complex simplicity of the Christian faith; and David Kirk, Richard Mann, and Lyle Young of Emmaus House, whose style of ministry is symbolic of the change in character of the American Church in the past decade. All have been patient and kind sitters for a very inquisitive portraitist.

I am also indebted to Jerome Berrigan and his wife, Carol, for their warm friendship and their generous help in researching the Berrigan family's biography; to William O'Connor and Brendan Walsh for their assistance in documenting the history of the Baltimore Peace Mission; to all of the Catonsville Nine, particularly Tom Lewis and George Mische, for helping me to document the background of their trial; to the Catonsville Nine's lawyers, William Kunstler and Harold Buchman, for elucidating many legal points; to Tom Cornell and John Grady for their aid in studying the background of the Catholic Resistance; to Vincent McGee, Jr., for a perceptive job of copy editing. And I am particularly indebted to James Forest of the Catholic Peace Fellowship, whose generous loan of clippings, letters, and other documents made the writing of the Berrigan profile possible, and whose committedness and sacrifices remain a source of inspiration to many of us.

Others whom I wish to thank for giving me their time to discuss some of the issues touched upon in this book are: Martin Corbin, David Eberhardt, Dr. Harvey Cox, Betty Bartelme, Reverend William Sloane Coffin, Jr., Pastor

Richard Neuhaus, Father Alden Stevenson, S.J., Reverend James Mengel, Father Joseph Fitzpatrick, S.J., Father Joseph Connolly, Monsignor Robert Fox, Father Robert Stern, Father Edmund Burke, John Heidbrink, and Tarsicio Ocampo and Father Julio Torres, both of the CIDOC staff in Cuernavaca, Mexico.

I dedicate the middle section of this book—about the Berrigans and the Catonsville Nine—to the memory of Christian Brother David Darst, who died tragically in an automobile accident in the fall of 1969.

Contents

Emmaus House:

THE BREAD IS RISING

While there is a lower class,
I am in it . . . while there is a soul
in prison, I am not free.
—Eugene Debs

"Welcome to Emmaus House!" Father Mann said. "Shall we begin? Let's gather around."

Father Richard Mann was a dapper young man with angelically blond hair, dressed in gray trousers, a striped shirt, and a fastidious paisley tie. He set a bottle of Chianti and a loaf of Italian bread on the table. Waving small sheets of typewritten paper, he walked among the forty people who sat chatting in the living room of an East Harlem brownstone.

"Who wants to help with the Agape?" he asked. "I need three people to read parts of the service."

Several hands were raised. Father Mann distributed the papers to three members of his congregation. He clapped his hands and the Sunday service at Emmaus House began.

The crowd rose cheerfully and carried their teacups and cigarettes into the adjoining room, where several dozen folding chairs had been placed around the table on which the bread and wine were set. It was a neat, brightly lit room whose furnishings had clearly been assembled out of charity. One wall was plastered with photographs of Teilhard de Chardin, Bertrand Russell, the Beatles, and Pope John receiving African pilgrims. A mural had been recently painted on the opposite wall, under the motto, "Fly the Friendly Skies of United," in that post-Matisse floral style which characterizes the art of progressive nuns. The congregation was of varied ages, scholarly in appearance, neatly and modestly dressed. A bearded young man seated under an enormous photograph of Gandhi strummed on a guitar. Father Mann lit a narrow cigar and said: "Our kappellmeister has to fill us in on the tunes. What's on the program?"

"We'll sing 'A Little Help from My Friends' at the Offertory," the guitarist said softly. "And as a recessional we'll sing 'Pack Up Your Sorrows.'"

"That fills me with Christmas cheer," Father Mann said. "As usual on Sundays, we'll start with announcements. I want to say that the new issue of our Emmaus House magazine—*The Bread is Rising*—is out. It's swinging. Help yourself to a copy. Also, I hear that there's a peace vigil at the UN Plaza on Tuesday from five to nine. It'll be bloody cold, but let's all try to get there and pray or picket or something. Any other announcements?"

"Over here on the bulletin board," said a young girl with long black hair, "I've posted up a list of names of boys who are in prison for refusing to fight in Vietnam." She pointed to a leaflet titled, "Send a Christmas Card to Jail." "Please let's all try to give them our sympathy by writing them a note."

The congregation clapped enthusiastically. Another girl of student age stood up and said, "At four o'clock every day this week, at Marymount Manhattan College, Father Roman Verosko, from Saint Vincent's Abbey, a way-out Benedictine poet, painter, musician, et cetera, will put on a performance of multi-media art. I recommend it to all."

"Wild," Father Mann said, flicking a bit of ash from his cigar. "I guess that's all the announcements, so let's get on with the Agape. Joyce, will you take over?"

Every few weeks at Emmaus House, a radical Catholic community in East Harlem that includes many non-Catholics, a different member of the congregation prepares the Agape, an ecumenical celebration which includes prayers, songs, readings, and the breaking of bread. This Sunday, Joyce Richardson, a pretty black social worker, had been asked by Father Mann to prepare the readings. She spoke in a low, gentle voice, holding a sheaf of notes on her lap.

"Christmas is just a week away," she said, "so I want to talk about how hard birth is, how hard it is for all of us to get out of the womb. By that I mean that once we are born we re-create wombs for ourselves—we limit our identities by our race, our religious denominations, our homes, the street we live on, the social class we belong to. True Christian rebirth would mean to break through these definitions."

She waved impatiently at a reproduction of a Raphael Nativity scene that had been tacked up on the wall and went on, "We're all fed up with that conception of Christmas, as we're fed up with the impersonal traditional liturgy that's been imposed on us since we were children—the coldness, the separatism of it all. Christmas and rebirth really mean being with people who help us get out of our own identities, who help us create a sense of true community. Well, I've chosen a set of readings about this theme of rebirth. Our first reading is from Henry Miller's *Tropic of Capricorn*."

She nodded to a middle-aged, schoolteacherish woman, who read:

> *Everything that happened to me happened too late to mean much to me. It was even so with my birth. Slated for Christmas I was born half an hour too late. It always seemed to me that I was meant to be the sort of individual that one is destined to be by virtue of being born on the 25th day of December. Admiral Dewey was born on that day and so was Jesus Christ . . . perhaps Krishnamurti too, for all I know. Anyway, that's the sort of guy I was meant to be. But due to the fact that my mother had a clutching womb, that she held me in her grip like an octopus, I came out under another configuration—with a bad set-up, in other words. They say—the astrologers, I mean—that it will get better and better for me as I go on: the future, in fact, is supposed to be quite glorious. But what do I care about the future? It would have been better if my mother had tripped on the stairs on the morning of the 25th of December and broken her neck . . .*

The worshippers laughed uneasily. Without prompting, the guitarist said that he was going to read an excerpt from a book called *The Politics of Experience*, by R. D. Laing.

> *Most people most of the time experience themselves and others in a way that I shall call egoic. That is, centrally or peripherally, they experience the world and themselves in terms of a consistent identity, a me-over-here against a you-over-there . . .*

The guitarist cleared his throat.

With the consensual and interpersonal confirmation it offers, this identity-anchored experience gives us a sense of ontological security, whose validity we experience as self-validating, although metaphysically-historically-ontologically-socio-economically-culturally we know its apparent validity as an illusion . . .

"Ouch," Father Mann moaned, cradling his head in his arms. The guitarist went on imperturbably:

A veil, a film of Maya, a dream to Heraclitus—and to Lao Tzu, the fundamental illusion of all Buddhism: a state of sleep, of death, of socially accepted madness, a womb state to which one has to die, from which one has to be reborn.

"Whew!" said Father Mann.
"Don't fuss, Dick, we have a light touch from *The Village Voice*," Joyce said.
The girl who had been concerned with writing postcards to jail held up a copy of *The Village Voice* and read in a declamatory tone:

Several years ago when an artist showed various foam rubber contraptions including one you could crawl into, many people wished they could own one of these pseudo-wombs for times of stress. Now they can. The new creator of pseudo-wombs, Ted Briedenthal, says: "The idea originated in my own brain-damaged skull." Constructed to individual body measurements, foam rubber inside and paisley fabric outside, it supports the body in a semi-fetal position and has white sound and circulated air as part of its total environmental effect. Six hundred dollars plus shipping from Lizzard Galleries, 515 East Main, Santa Maria, California.

The congregation laughed. Father Mann smiled and nibbled on crumbs from the loaf of bread. Several latecomers, not finding any free chairs, stood attentively at the doorsill of the room. The readings ended with a poem of e. e. cummings:

> *May my mind stroll about fearless and supple*
> *and even if it's sunday may I be wrong*
> *for whenever men are right they are not young.*

Joyce looked at her sheaf of notes again and said, "I would like to end the readings with the Roman Catholic collect for the Vigil of Christmas. 'O God you fill us with gladness each year as we look forward to our redemption. We joyfully receive your only-begotten son as our redeemer.' And also I would like to end with one of the wildest of Jesus' many wild sayings, from the Gospel of Saint John: 'A little while, and ye shall not see me; and again, a little while, and ye shall see me. Verily I say unto you, that ye shall weep and lament, but the world shall rejoice; and ye shall be sorrowful, but your sorrow shall be turned into joy. A woman when she is in travail has sorrow . . . but as soon as she is delivered of the child she remembers no more the anguish, for joy that a man is born into the world.'"

Joyce bowed her head. A silence fell upon the congregation and lasted for some fifteen minutes, broken by random expressions of sentiment. A middle-aged woman gave a sad little talk about how hard it had been to spend Christmas alone until she found Emmaus House. "Here we reveal our true identities," she said. "People of different faiths breaking bread together. It's wonderful. The disciples did not recognize Christ at Emmaus, until they had broken bread with Him."

A young man in blue jeans said angrily: "And what does it mean to 'go home for Christmas'? Usually it means just crawling back into the same old womb. With parents who don't understand us, who make a big commercial fuss over Christmas."

"I guess we're all disgusted with the goods in the front window," the guitarist said. "We're more concerned with stopping all church-building and trying to feed the hungry. Poverty's in."

"Poverty's in," Father Mann repeated thoughtfully, blowing small clouds of cigar smoke into the room. "That's good, Jim. Joyce, thanks for the fine readings." He rose and clapped his hands authoritatively. "Let's proceed with the Agape! Fold up your chairs, kids, push them against the wall, and let's gather around the table, nice and crowded."

There was a scramble as chairs were folded and stacked. Father Mann broke the loaf of bread in two and everybody sang lustily: "I'll Get By with a Little Help from My Friends, I'll Get High with a Little Help from My Friends . . ." Father Mann, clapping out the rhythm, led the chorus with a powerful tenor voice. The congregation swayed to the music with revivalist fervor.

Three persons took turns reading the free verse poem which Father Mann had written for the occasion. Holding his hands outstretched, Father Mann read the last part of the service himself: "Celebrate, let us celebrate every upset, confusion, imprudence, foolishness, joy . . . Celebrate Jesus the light, life, the gadfly . . . He Who is always annoyance, wisdom, power, meaning, absurdity, confusion, harmony, Who is alive wherever there are people . . ."

Father Mann poured the Chianti into two large chalices. The members of the congregation gave each other the kiss of peace. Accompanied by the guitarist, the worshippers sang a calypso version of the Lord's Prayer. Baskets of bread and the chalices of wine were passed around the room. The service ended with a hearty rendition of a Joan Baez song that goes "But if somehow you could pack up your sorrows and give them all to me, You would lose them, I know how to use them, Give them all to me."

"Peace be with you!" Father Mann exclaimed. He lit another cigar. Sunday-night service at Emmaus House was over. The congregation rose and milled about the room.

A girl with the puzzled air of a newcomer said to the young man she had sat next to, "I guess this is about as modern as liturgy gets."

"Mercy, no," the young man said, with a jaded air. "I've seen equally advanced ones in Holland, Germany, even France."

"I guess the underground is international," the girl said.

"And the bread is rising," the young man murmured.

"The bread is rising," a password whispered by insurgent peasants at the time of the French Revolution, is the motto of Emmaus House, which describes itself in the literature that it sends to some six thousand on its mailing list as "an experiment in Christian living," "a supra-ecumenical community," "a venture in community encounter," "a center for radical social change." Emmaus House is only one of many insurgent religious cadres pinpointed throughout the United States which have incited a remarkable phenomenon of the past decade: the revolution in American Catholicism. The uprising has been as successful as it was unpredictable. The American Catholic community, after several centuries of arch-conservatism, has become one of the world's most radical.

The year Emmaus House crystallized as a vanguard of the religious New Left—1967—was a turbulent one for American Catholics. In that year, three members of the nation's foremost missionary group were called back from their assignments for participating in a revolution in Guatemala; a Catholic priest in Milwaukee led the nation's most militant campaign for open housing; more than three thousand American clerics indicated in a survey that they wanted the Holy See to change its laws on compulsory celibacy; innumerable copies of a controversial new Dutch catechism were circulated in the United States without the Vatican's authorization; in four large cities centers were established to give guidance to the unprecedented number of American priests who were leaving their vocations; hundreds of Catholic clergymen, several of whom faced indictments for encouraging draft resistance or for destroying draft files, urged their communities to protest the Administration's policy in Vietnam; a former priest, James Kavanaugh, wrote a bestseller denouncing the medieval power structure of the Church and told a cheering crowd at Notre Dame University that "Canon Law can go into the Tiber"; and hundreds of experimental-worship groups began to thrive, from New Jersey to California. Emmaus House flourished in this turbulent atmosphere under the guidance of a nucleus of Christian laymen and priests: Richard Mann, a member of the Congregation of the Blessed Sacrament; Lyle Young, a former missionary in New Guinea; Robert Lowe, an East Harlem community organizer; James and Linda Forest, one of several Emmaus families; and David Kirk, founder and coordinator of the Emmaus community. At thirty-four, Father Kirk is one of the most provocative leaders of a movement which has been called the "Underground Church," the "Free Church," the "Liberated Church."

On my first visit to Father Kirk, he was sitting at a cluttered desk in his office on the ground floor of Emmaus House. Dressed in blue jeans and a turtleneck sweater, dark and hulking of frame, courteous but guarded, he had more the style of a student organizer than of a clergyman. His desk was covered with sheafs of paper and he was preoccupied with contacting a well-known rabbi whose good will he seemed eager to retain. As he made his phone calls in a grave and gentle Southern voice, I studied his office.

Photographs of Martin Luther King, Jr., Gandhi, Cesar Chavez, Malcolm X, Thomas Merton, Sister Mary Corita, Daniel Berrigan, Harvey Cox, and W. C. Fields were taped to the wall above his desk. On the door of the office was pinned a poster advertising a series of Sunday-night lectures scheduled to be held at Emmaus House in the following months: "An Evening with Paul Goodman," "Poverty and Powerlessness," "Revolution and the Christian," "Che Guevara as I Knew Him," "Clues for a White Radical Life-Style," "Theology of Fun City," "The Rights of Protest in the Church." The literature scattered around Father Kirk's office also championed a variety of religious and political causes. One pamphlet, Ivan Illich's "The Vanishing Clergyman," urged Catholic priests to support themselves by secular work in order to be independent of "Curial conservatism and outdated Roman hierarchies." An article by David Kirk advocated a return to the "House Church," the small, informal, early Christian type of religious community that Emmaus patterns itself upon. Experimental education, East Harlem tutorial programs, counseling of drug addicts, social injustice in Latin America, Black Power, draft resistance, Zen meditation, the Cuban Revolution were the themes of other pamphlets stacked on the desks of Father Kirk's office. The tone of dissent had even spread to the walls of the room, which were decorated with a variety of aphorisms painted on in a bold graffiti hand:

> *The modern generation has been brought to bay at the extremity of all things.* (Leon Bloy)

> *I am a human being—Do not fold, tear or manipulate.* (Berkeley students)

God is not a spectacle. (Jacques Paliard)

Whenever we say NO we imply that on a deeper level
there is a YES which provokes and originates it.
Rebellion always implies an acquiescence
which is both deeper and more free. (Henri de Lubac)

Another symbol of independence dominated the room, a large Byzantine icon hanging in a corner of the office. It reminded me that Emmaus's existence is made possible by a unique sort of freedom from Rome. I had heard that when Father Kirk was converted to Catholicism a decade ago, he had been uneasy with the reactionary character of the Roman Church. He had joined instead the Melkite rite, one of several Eastern churches that are in communion with Rome, but are responsible to their own Patriarchs. "David Kirk made a shrewd prediction of the Catholic uproar," a friend of his told me. "He's reaping the benefits of his foresight."

Father Kirk hung up the phone. He leaned back in his chair and folded his hands behind his head. A blue-and-white "The Bread is Rising" button was pinned on his sweater. "A very influential rabbi wants to resign from our board of sponsors," he said, "because we ran a picture of Che Guevara in an issue of our magazine."

"What kind of caption did you run under the picture?" I asked.

"I wrote: 'The death of Che Guevara is a tragic loss to the revolutionary movement. We mourn his death.'"

"Aren't you going to lose some Catholic sponsors, too?"

He stretched his arms over his head in a slow bearish motion and looked serene. "I don't think so. The fact is, when the Council of Catholic Laymen met in Rome last November, one of the first things they did was to say a Mass in memory of Che Guevara; Guevara, therefore, must have had some kind of spiritual meaning to thousands of

Catholics all over the world. When the Latin American poor are as exploited as they are, when such violence is done to them by the corporate structure, it is their right to revolt—even within the most traditional limits of our Just War theory. But the real revolution is the change of values which such an uprising implies. A revolution in morality, in culture, a negation of the entire Establishment—church and social, a struggle for the right to build a new society in which poverty is terminated. The revolution is to create a new environment, step by step, level by level, and new incentives for creative work. Christianity, since Constantine, has always blessed the establishment. It is only now waking up to the fact that its true message is revolution, the personal and social transformation of man."

The words came out gently in an Alabama drawl. Father Kirk leaned back in his chair, looking increasingly benign. His eyes were kind and blue, very deep-set. The loose contemporary use of the word *revolution* had been puzzling me and I asked him what his sense of the word was.

"Revolution is a *rejection* of existing institutions, lifestyles, and value systems to clear the ground for a new conception of society, of man, of power. To become revolutionary is to take an active stand in this re-evaluation."

"But that's not the usual sense of the word," I said. "*Revolution* has always meant *overthrowing* the existing order. What would you say about the element of violence associated with the word?"

"I think that's just been the narrow, secular, limited use of the word. I want to use it in a religious sense, in the sense of a radical change of values, the way Christianity was revolutionary. Jesus was a cultural revolutionary. He turned society upside down. He was rough on property—remember the destruction of property in the Temple? The confrontation with Pilate? The demonstration for him on his entrance into Jerusalem? Note his guerrilla-theatre tactics: the poor king, truth riding on a donkey, parading without a permit. His non-cooperation with the structure of evil, his solidarity with the oppressed. Chairman Jesus stirring up the people."

Father Kirk pointed to a photograph of Dorothy Day, the co-founder of the Catholic Worker Movement and of its newspaper, the *Catholic Worker*. "You see, my use of the word 'revolution' has been around for a long time. I am a spiritual stepchild of Dorothy Day, and Emmaus is a stepchild of the Catholic Worker Movement, which was the cradle of Catholic radicalism in this country. Since the thirties, the *Catholic Worker* has used the word 'revolution' in its non-violent sense. The Catholic Worker Movement brought about social change by forming little groups within society that strived to ameliorate such crucial problems as schooling, minority rights, unemployment pay, strikes, migrant problems of Mexican workers. Emmaus is trying to bring the same kind of activism into the problems of ghetto education, peace, white racism, human organizations. The *Catholic Worker* always used the word 'revolution' when it talked about its method of changing society by the media of small communities that challenged the values of the existing order."

Father Kirk began to raise his voice as from a pulpit. "It is crucially important to me that people understand that Christianity is political. A religious ideology *must* lead to a political ideology. Christianity, Christ, and the Gospels are all political. God becoming man is a political act—it creates a whole new force for reshaping man, and this is a political, a revolutionary, act. What I mean by 'revolution' is the Christianizing of a people that has never yet been fully Christian. Christianity, after all, presents an ideal state of society toward which one must always strive, according to which we must constantly reform present conditions."

The doorbell rang. Father Kirk pressed an answering buzzer and an unhappy-looking young man of college age came into the office, suitcase in hand.

"Well, Harry," Father Kirk said gently, "What are you up to now?"

"I simply don't know, David," the boy said.

"Take your bag upstairs and we'll talk later. You can take the upper bunk in the second-floor bed; there's a C.O. leaving for Canada tomorrow who's sleeping in the lower one."

The boy walked slowly out of the office and Father Kirk looked after him with concern. "It's unbelievable how few places there are in town for kids in trouble to go to. The cheapest bed in town is at the Salvation Army—$1.50—but it seems to do permanent damage to one's dignity to go there. We can only give hospitality to two or three people at a time, and it breaks my heart. My dream is to have a whole brownstone next door with thirty or forty beds in it, a real house of hospitality as we had at the Catholic Worker. I'm particularly eager to give hospitality to people coming out of hospitals and mental institutions, and to young priests who're leaving their vocation. They go through tough phases—oh my, I need a lot of money to do what I want to do."

The door opened, and a chubby, benign-looking man with thick spectacles peeked into the room. This was Father Young. "A man who just got divorced in Mexico keeps phoning and asking for someone to perform a marriage ceremony for him," he said. "Dear me, I simply don't know what to think of marriage anymore."

A few seconds later, Father Mann came into the office, wearing paint-spattered blue jeans. "Should I put on my white collar for the Community Center party?" he asked.

"A white collar is always nice, Richard," Father Kirk said. Father Mann dashed out of the room, and Father Kirk explained, "It's so hard for priests to know what to wear these days."

Father Kirk looked at his watch, but I asked him one more question:

"America's Catholicism has become almost as radical as Holland's in the past two years. How do you explain it?"

Father Kirk's voice dropped to a gentle monotone. He answered automatically, as if the question was all too familiar to him: "First there was the Catholic Worker Movement that prepared the ground for us—I cannot overstress its importance. No other country has had that tradition of Socialist anarchism. Then there was Pope John. And then came the civil rights movement, which was a training school for most of us. It is natural that my generation, which had learned to disobey unfree structures in society, would sooner or later apply the same principles and tactics to the unfree church. When the political young left of my generation crystallized at the lunch-counter sit-ins in the South, the Christian Young Left was ignited by this same movement for justice and by a sense of guilt about the Church's racist life-style. Today, there is another New Left militancy—which does not merely protest but is building up a free society within the shell of the old. Just as we learned from Paul Goodman and Staughton Lynd in the 50's, so we learn today from Cohn-Bendit, Eldridge Cleaver and Woodstock. The future of Christianity is with the young people in revolt, with the great game of freedom."

Father Kirk rose from his desk. As we walked toward the door, he said, with an ingenuous smile, "It's an exciting time to be a Christian. The most exciting time since the first century. Particularly if you're a Catholic."

. . .

I had a longer talk with Father Kirk a few days later in his own quarters—an airy room on the third floor of Emmaus House. It was furnished in an inexpensive but clean-cut modern style that revealed a strong sense of order, an aristocratic sense of comfort. A Vivaldi record was playing on the hi-fi. The bookshelves were filled with volumes on political science, sociology, and theology. By the record player stood a small, orderly desk shelf with an ice bucket, bottles of scotch, gin, and California wine. A few Byzantine icons and family photographs hung on the walls. Leaning back in a chair, his arms locked behind his head, and looking straight at me with his deep-set blue eyes, he spoke modestly and deliberately in his grave and musical Southern voice, of the events that led him to priesthood and rebellion.

"I was born in Mississippi. My father was a large-scale cotton farmer, a very just man. He went bankrupt, in the forties, because he tried to instill justice into the share-cropping system. My parents had no religious affiliation but we occasionally read from scripture at home. They were about as liberal as Southern whites can be. The first surges of emotion I felt as a child, both towards religion and towards revolt, were caused by witnessing acts of brutality against blacks. I particularly remember being horrified—I must have been about seven—by seeing a cousin of mine kill a starving black man because he had stolen a chicken. Of course there was no legal reprisal whatsoever against my cousin. It was the sporting thing for white men to do.

"I became a Catholic while I was a student at the University of Alabama. I was doing my major in history, and I was overwhelmed by the continuity of the Catholic Church throughout European history. I had always been passionately interested in the concept of Christian unity. I kept staring at those charts which show all the schisms which broke off from the Mother Church—Rome—

throughout the centuries, and I admired that Mother Church, so powerful and unified throughout time. Of course some of the intellectual arguments that converted me then—the stability, the power—would horrify me now. There was a personal incident that led to my conversion: I had a Catholic roommate who was one of the big football stars on the University of Alabama team. I watched him kneel down for prayers every night. I was impressed by a man who saw no contradiction between masculinity and prayer, who recognized a force beyond and within himself.

"In my sophomore year in college I asked to join an instruction class. But even in the full fervor of my conversion, I was uneasy with the reactionary character of the Roman Catholic Church. The Roman Church in my part of Alabama was ridden with racial and political conservatism of the familiar Irish sort, and I guess I've been a radical since birth. I became a Socialist, probably the only one in southern Alabama, when I was seventeen through correspondence with Norman Thomas. It happened that there was a Melkite Church right near the University, and this is where I chose to take instruction. The Melkite rite is not familiar to most Americans. It is one of several Eastern churches which are in full communion with Rome, but are responsible to their own Patriarch, not to the Roman Pope. The official title of our head prelate is very exotic— he is 'Patriarch of Antioch, Jerusalem, Alexandria and the Whole East.' The Melkites are the most radical wing of the Catholic clergy—for many decades the most liberal views on divorce, birth control, liturgy, and social action have been expressed by Melkite bishops. There are some 55,000 Melkites in the United States, most of them of Arabic background. I was impressed by the liberal character of this Melkite Church near my university. It had a sung Mass in the vernacular and a warm, concerned priest who was enormously active in social problems, unlike the materialistic Irish who ran the Roman church next door. So I joined the Melkite rite instead of the Roman one.

"I graduated in 1954, and then I taught for two years in Alabama public schools while getting a Master's degree in sociology. I was immersed, from the start, in the interracial movement throughout the South. I was involved in the first sit-ins in Atlanta, where we tried to integrate buses. In Mobile I worked with the NAACP; they used me as a front man since I was white. Every few weeks I invited black leaders to talk to my students. The only reason I had to stop is that the Ku Klux Klan was threatening my family. The Klan burned a cross on my family's lawn; they kept writing letters threatening to burn the house down and to kill my brothers if I was not removed from the public school system. So I decided to come North. I was too much of a threat to my family's safety.

"I came to New York, and supported myself by teaching school while I finished my Master's at Columbia. I often went to the Catholic Worker. I opened a house of hospitality on Mott Street which accommodated the overflow from the Worker center nearby. During all that time I was thinking of becoming a priest. I'd been thinking of the priesthood for years, trying to figure out how I could fit into the Church. I knew I couldn't last through a regular seminary because they're made for children, not men. Finally I applied to Beda College in Rome. It's the freest, most flexible of the institutions there; it gives you a great deal of time to just read and do social work. They wrote back saying they had a five-year waiting list. I went to Rome anyway. Going to Rome was an act of faith. I had no money, no sponsors. . . . My act of faith bore results.

"An extraordinary coincidence occurred the very first day I got to Rome. I met a Melkite priest, a Syrian, right in Saint Peter's Square. He said: 'The Melkite Patriarch is always home, come to see him.' And that same day the Patriarch sponsored me to enter Beda College. He was a wonderfully liberal man, who often said, 'We're not afraid of experimenting . . . what possible evil would you do, as a priest, by experimenting?'

"My first impression of Rome was one of scandal, outrageous scandal . . . the abundance, the wealth of the Church! It seemed all wrong. Priesthood is service, after all, before it is anything else.

"My first year at Beda was the year before the Council started—the winter of '61 to spring of '62. I had trouble that first year because I was a strong agitator for vernacular liturgy. Some of the teachers accused me of heresy on that count. They had to change their minds of course the following year, when the Council came out with its first decrees on the use of the vernacular! During my studies at Beda I was a correspondent for several Catholic magazines. There was a great deal to write home during those council years. I had a press card, I went to all the Council press conferences, and that's where I learned most of my theology.

"I was ordained in August 1964, in the Basilica of Saint Ann in Jerusalem, which stands near the pool of Bethesda. I chose to be ordained in Jerusalem rather than in Rome because I have always been deeply involved in the Ecumenical Movement, and Jerusalem, rather than Rome, is the focal point of Christianity. I was not ordained to any diocese but for the work of the Church as a whole. The day of my ordination was the Feast of the Transfiguration; it was also the anniversary of Hiroshima. For my first Mass, which I celebrated the following day, I had written a special liturgy on urban man and urban life—tying up the idea of Hiroshima, the city destroyed, and the Feast of the Transfiguration—Christ transfiguring the city.

"After my term at Beda was over I came back to the

United States with Lyle Young, who had been my closest friend in Rome. Lyle and I had many interests in common, our conceptions of social work and of service were very close. The idea of Emmaus House evolved during our days together as seminarians. We wanted to form an ecumenical community which would be a setting for change, for service to others. We wanted to express love of the poor with solidarity—no long-distance service. We wanted to build a realm of freedom not provided by present structures. While we raised and saved money for Emmaus, we worked in East Harlem parishes—we taught school and counseled delinquents. In 1966, when our plan became feasible, we went to the new American Bishop of the Melkite rite, who resides in Boston, and proposed Emmaus to him. Bishop Justin was enthusiastic, and that fall we started Emmaus in a modest way. But a few months later the New York Chancery started complaining about us. Do you know how the New York Chancery wrote off the idea of Emmaus House? They said that work among the poor is for the Roman rite only . . . that's a curious interpretation of the Sermon on the Mount!"

David Kirk stood up and started laughing. His ingenuous laugh interrupted his next few sentences as he continued to talk, pacing up and down the room.

"They actually implied that New York belongs to the Roman rite . . . I can see them saying that to the Episcopalian Bishop. Then Bishop Cooke, Spellman's vicar, made a precise list of accusations against me. He said he wanted me removed—one, because I was inviting Marxists to dialogue with Christians at Emmaus House conferences. Two, because I was participating in peace marches. Three, because I was involved in liturgical experimentation. Four, because I was giving hospitality to priests who were leaving the vocation. So in September '67, under pressure of the Roman authorities, Bishop Justin wrote that he wanted to transfer me to Rochester to be pastor of the Melkite Church there. I wrote back that I did not intend doing anything here that any bona fide ecumenical group anywhere else in the world wouldn't sanction . . . and good Bishop Justin canceled the transfer. Thanks to Bishop Justin, we have moved into a period of détente with Archbishop Cooke."

David Kirk sat down. He stretched his arms over his head and looked grateful. "That's the wonderful thing about the Eastern Church—I doubt if the average Roman Catholic or Protestant is aware of the amount of freedom it offers. They can't stand transgressing on your individuality, or hurting your feelings in any way. It's nice, human, like a family. The Eastern Church has kept a superb spirit of pre-Constantinism, an early-church quality, a democratic character that is true to the Bible. There is no codified Canon Law. There is no cultic or magic notion of the priesthood. The Eastern Church has its own brand of medieval fossilization in vestments and gestures, but the spirit is infinitely freer. The Roman Church, in comparison, has paralyzed itself in its exaggeration of liturgical observance, in its caste system, its autocracy."

Standing up, David Kirk raised his voice again, and addressed me in his stern, sermonizing manner.

"The biggest problem in the Church now—I can not stress this enough—the biggest point of friction between Rome and the new generation of religious radicals is that we are working on a different theology of authority. Newman reflected on this long ago: 'The *community* is the final authority, the voice of God is in the *people*.' We must create a loyal opposition. We must practice what A. J. Muste used to call 'Holy Disobedience.' By that I mean a faithfulness to the Church as she ought to be. I do not mean to abolish structures. Since the Church is not aloneness but community, it will always have to have structures. But the structures have to be revolutionized for the Church to survive. An *aggiornamento*, an updating, is not only inadequate but dangerous. Authority has to be radically redefined. It must be redefined as a democratic, coordinating, tying-together force, rather than an infallible, didactic one. The new generation of religious radicals will not be satisfied until parish priests can be elected by the people, until bishops can be elected by priests and laymen, until the Pope can be elected by a Synod representative of all bishops. The greatest corruption of the Church has been its refusal to recognize that the Holy Spirit works through the people.

"We also have to redefine our notion of ministry. You know, Peter has been overemphasized by the Church at the expense of Paul. Peter left his fishing nets for the priesthood. Paul went on being a laborer—a tentmaker, to be precise—while acting as a priest. I think that the only way to reform the Church is through a self-supporting ministry, composed of what Ivan Illich calls 'ordained laymen.' The main instrument of Christian mission is no longer the professional clergyman, but the *secular* minister. I visualize a structure in which the priest will be a self-supporting family man, a factory worker, dentist, lawyer, or teacher —married of course; compulsory celibacy will be out before the decade's over—who will fulfill his pastoral tasks in his free time. Not only will the administrative details of the priesthood be looked after by qualified laymen but also the teaching, the preaching, the celebration of the Eucharist. A part-time ministry is the only system that makes sense in the leisure society coming to us. Only a part-time ministry can rid the Church of its benefice system and recapture its spiritual roots. I've never been paid by a Church, not once, since I've been a priest. I've always earned my living. I am repelled by the very idea of being paid a stipend for saying a Mass!

"In the Church of the future," David Kirk went on, "the worshipping community will be structured around house-churches such as Emmaus, and the big, geographically determined parish will become obsolete. The worship groups must remain small—not more than sixty or so—there is a leavening action in small groups. Only small groups can offer a liturgy that relates to *your* intimate life problems, that increases *your* sense of social action, *your* sense of responsibility towards others. The large parish is a pre-industrial concept. Let the churches crumble! We must depropertize, renounce the material of power. The Church as a corporate structure will always remain reactionary—She has too much to protect. She must divest Herself of property to return to the spiritual roots of the Gospel!"

David Kirk took out of his pocket a button that said THE BREAD IS RISING, which he had distributed by the hundreds at the last peace march in Washington.

"Civil disobedience is very much in the air," he said. "Well, to create a meaningful Church for the future we must commit acts of civil disobedience against the traditional Church, we must develop a theology of civil disobedience. Which hinges on a new theology of authority. If the Church is the people, our true obedience is to them."

Father Lyle Young, at forty-six the oldest of the three priests at Emmaus House, is an Australian who was brought up in the Roman Catholic Church, ordained into the Anglican Church, reordained into the Roman Church, and once applied for a transfer to the Melkite rite. The owner of this rich religious background describes himself as "a pragmatic, untheological man, moved more by instinct than by any rational system." It is he who has directed many of the counseling and hospitality services that Emmaus House offers to the East Harlem community. Lyle Young, whose favorite worldly possession, according to his friends, is a copy of *Alice in Wonderland*, often reminds one of a Lewis Carroll personage. "Dear me, I shall be late to the baptism," he will say as he bustles about Emmaus House. "Dear me, I forgot to invite that rabbi to our tree-trimming party."

Lyle Young was born into a wealthy Australian sheep-ranching family. After graduating from the University of Sydney at sixteen, he spent three years teaching blind children. And he was struck by the fact that most of his students were blind because of poverty—from poor hygiene and parental ignorance. After those three years—moved, he says, by "an extraordinarily passionate sermon given by the Anglican bishop of New Guinea"—he decided to become a priest. He was ordained into the Anglican Church instead of the Church in which he had been baptized partly because he considered the Roman Church "clergy-ridden." He also objected to praying and worshipping in a dead language. After his ordination, he spent five years as the director of Anglican Mission Work in Port Moresby, New Guinea. He seldom talks about his past without recalling the impact of his missionary years on his vocation. "Much of my faith, and much of my understanding of what religion is about, I received from the faith of the native people I worked with in New Guinea," he told me. "It is from them I understood that the Church is, first and above all, the community of mankind, and not the community of the baptized."

Missionary work intensified Lyle Young's impatience with traditional religious practices at the same time that it augmented his faith. At the age of thirty-eight, he decided to rejoin the Roman Catholic Church, because of its "increasing vitality and change." He was admitted to Beda College, where he met David Kirk. Their friendship and their conception of Emmaus House grew out of their common involvement in ecumenism and in social work. Once the initial money had been raised to open Emmaus House, Lyle Young's first assignment was to provide its furnishings. He spent six months begging for furniture and office equipment, borrowing trucks to pick up donations from all over the city, in an effort to realize a dream that had originated during his years in New Guinea: a dream of a true urban mission, a house of hospitality open to all those in need. But he looked sad as he told me about the problems of a hospitality house, for his ambition to keep doors open around the clock had been somewhat thwarted by the realities of East Harlem.

"The one aspect of the priesthood that has always interested me most is that of service," he said. "And it had been my ambition for years to run an absolutely open house of hospitality for people suffering from contemporary urban problems—delinquency, mental illness, drug addiction. It's the kind of vision one has as a missionary. When we first opened Emmaus House, I tried to realize this ambition, but dear me, dear me, I have had my troubles."

Lyle sighed, and reminisced.

"I'm thinking in particular about one man who lived with us for our first few months who had an extraordinary complex about never touching money. He was a very religious man. He was trying, like the rest of us here, to be a truly primitive and very pure Christian. He used to sit on the floor praying for hours, mumbling over his beads, or else strumming a single string on a guitar. He said that his work in life was to watch, to observe, but *not* to do. He said we must go out into the street, keep our doors open perpetually. However, he did not want to do any of that himself, he wanted to observe *us* doing. He was not troublesome, he had a most beautiful and gentle character, but the poor man was almost totally insane. He would eat our bread and turn on our lights but he would not touch money. Every few days he would say to me, 'Can you put me on the subway; I have to see a friend downtown but I can't get on the subway by myself because I can't touch money, and you have to buy the subway token for me.' I tried to be very strict with him. I looked very black as I walked him to the subway and I said to him, 'I am indulging your selfish eccentricities.' Another unnerving thing he did was to blackmail us into giving liturgies. He had an insomnia problem and he said that he could only sleep if we gave him Communion. So after we had heard him prowling about the house two or three nights in a row we felt sorry for him and we'd work up a liturgy. It takes a little time and spiritual preparation to compose a Mass, you know, but he'd dragoon us into it. The evenings we gave him a liturgy he'd go to sleep quiet as a lamb, so we found ourselves saying Mass for him every two evenings. He spent three months with us, then one day he left us and we haven't heard from him since."

Lyle rattled his keys, and looked downcast. "We had many other exhausting guests that first year . . . I'll never forget the time I walked in from my counseling job and saw a man with a beard sitting on the kitchen table, crying his heart out. He was saying, 'I've searched for years for this place, a community of love! I love you all'—he was weeping as he said this—'I love you all so much, this is *my* place.' Richard Mann was still very wide-eyed about our hospitality program. He was standing by the man saying, 'We love you too, we love you too, of course you can live with us.' We've always had this terrible problem about screening: it's so hard to turn them away . . . anyhow we had a little meeting and we took this man in. His name was Chris Jones, and his mission in life was to have a ministry of total availability. 'The street is our altar,' he said. And he had us open a store-front counseling office on our ground floor so that he could be available to the local kids round the clock. He would literally pick them off the streets at three a.m. and bring them in for counseling. At first we fell for this, we thought that this would be a true service to the community which we could perform with him. The trouble was that he was very emotional; after a half-hour of counseling some teenager, he would start weeping and the boy would be weeping too. Also he overdid it, to our disappointment, with the open-door business. The boys came in smoking pot; within a month they had stolen Richard's organ, my electric shaver, three typewriters, our electric carving knife, all the valuable things that had been given us out of charity. And one night we found a few of the boys lying in our cellar dead drunk on beer and clutching David Kirk's last typewriter. So we had to lock our doors and tone down on our counseling program. It killed me having to lock the doors, but we had to to remain alive."

There is a bright-red sign inside the entrance of Emmaus House. It says, "We Love You, But Please Close the Door."

"I haven't given up. The ministry of service interests me more than liturgical experiment. The freedom to explore real problems of life in this country is more important than liturgy. Worship of God is a very good and strengthening thing; what better thing can Christians do than get beyond themselves and worship? But if you worship in this new radical way, grabbing guitars and newspaper clippings all the time, that's as satiating as the old Latin Mass. David Kirk and I don't think that liturgical avant-gardism is enough to keep a worshipping community together. There must be a political, social ideology to bind any religious community together. Many groups in this country have gone underground for reasons of liturgical experiment, and we're not sure they'll survive. It's not enough. What we really need to concentrate on is the creation of a new class of working priests who can be efficient in social reform, who can earn their living by secular, worldly work rather than living off the alms of the people. The kind of priesthood that the early Church had, that France had in the forties, that the Eastern Church makes possible."

He gave a shudder, and went on—

"The idea of being paid for doling out sacraments is repulsive . . . That kind of money makes me feel like the man who couldn't touch the coin to buy a subway token. Evidently the self-supporting ministry is the best answer. In its present form the Roman Church is drowning in the worship of its own institutions; it has become a group of functionaries. And nowhere in the Gospel have I yet seen that Christ created a group of functionaries. The biggest thing going on in religion is the realization that the Church is the world, and that the world is political, and that the true Gospel of the poor is better housing, and that priests should be the poor's picketers, and that picketing is a form of praying . . ."

He added: "Praying, after all, is a form of picketing."

If the New Church had an iconography, its image of Christ would not be modeled on the passive, saccharine figure portrayed in children's catechism books. Its cultic image would more likely be a photograph of the angry Fathers Berrigan going to jail in protest against racism or war. The theology of the New Church feeds with new appetite upon an old paradox: the disparity between the social radicalism of the Gospels and the Church's resistance to social change; the negation of Christ's original message by despotic power structures, big business, institutionalism. Like most movements of religious reform—Wycliffe's,

Hus's, Luther's—the New Church has a nostalgic longing
for the free and unstructured Evangelism of the first
Christian centuries. The phenomenon of the 1960's is that
the insurgent group took the form of a loyal opposition:
in previous centuries, men disillusioned with religious structures either left religion altogether or pioneered new sects;
in the mid-sixties, the same kind of men were building
substructures beneath official Church institutions, creating
a genuine underground.

This religious underground has tried to bring to
the Church the same democratization that men have
brought to secular governments in the past two centuries.
"Wooden shoes going up the stairs of history pass the velvet slippers coming down" has been a favorite quotation of
David Kirk's. It is from an essay by Anatole France on the
French Revolution, but in David Kirk's context it is clear
that the wooden shoes are those of underground Christians
passing the velvet slippers of the Roman Curia.

The theology of the wooden-shoed, the religious New
Left, has had many parallels with the principles of the secular New Left. Both have tended to be collectivist, pacifist,
unstructured, utopian, obsessed with community, cen-
tered on a style of life rather than on any systematic ideology. Both in politics and in religion, the New Left has expressed disgust with traditional institutions, agitated for a
nebulously defined "participatory democracy," and considered middle-of-the-road liberals to be the archenemies
who sell out on radical reform. Both movements have
worked for radical reform by dropping out of traditional
structures—be it the two-party system or the parish system
—and by forming cells that "prick at the institution," as
David Kirk put it, with ideological guerrilla warfare.

Even the documents of the two movements have fed
upon each other with friendly plagiarism. The following
passage is excerpted from Emmaus's first manifesto, dated

1967. Its second and third paragraphs occur, word for word, in Tom Hayden's influential "Port Huron Statement" of 1962, the first position paper published by the SDS (Students for a Democratic Society) during its early, more pacificist phase.

> *Our calling is to go the way of social revolution . . . we are guided by the radical implications of the Gospel and its modern applications, particularly the writings of Pope John.*
>
> *He regarded men as <u>infinitely</u> <u>precious</u> <u>and</u> <u>possessed</u> <u>of</u> <u>unfulfilled</u> <u>capacities</u> <u>for</u> <u>reason</u>, <u>freedom</u>, <u>love</u>, creativity, <u>self-direction</u>, <u>self-understanding</u>.*
>
> *Like Pope John, <u>we</u> <u>would</u> <u>replace</u> <u>power</u> <u>rooted</u> <u>in</u> <u>possession</u>, <u>privilege</u> <u>and</u> <u>circumstance</u> <u>by</u> <u>power</u> <u>and</u> <u>uniqueness</u> <u>rooted</u> <u>in</u> <u>love</u>, <u>reason</u>, <u>reflectiveness</u> <u>and</u> <u>creativity</u>.*

(The underlined words, in turn, occur word for word in Pope John XXIII's encyclical *Pacem in Terris*, written in 1961.)

David Kirk said that he had read the "Port Huron Statement" the year he came back from Rome; that it had made him join the SDS immediately. The New Left in general, he said, and the SDS in particular, offered then the best political vision that a Christian could have.

David Kirk's and Lyle Young's schedules were consistent with the social activism of the New Left. They taught, lectured, met with Black Power leaders and Urban Housing commissions, counseled narcotics addicts, sheltered draft resisters, and organized tutorial programs for East Harlem youngsters. Some seventy East Harlem children daily attended the Emmaus School which they had opened in a nearby store front, where learning-through-theatre was stressed alongside basic reading skills. Emmaus House's Breakfast Program, which was organized with the cooperation of the Black Panthers and the Puerto Rican Young Lords, provided a daily, hot, free breakfast for some thirty East Harlem children. The Emmaus Problem Clinic assisted people with "self-actualizing therapy." The Emmaus–Camillo Torres Center offered information, hospitality, adult education and emergency assistance to the Latin American community. Another project called "Alternatives" offered vocational advice to young people searching for "alternative life-styles."

Emmaus's third and youngest member, Richard Mann, saw social action in broader terms. His chief concern was to compose startling layouts for Emmaus's magazine, *The Bread is Rising,* of which he was the editor, and to prepare lively experimental liturgies, some of them in Central Park, which might involve dancing, paper masks, light effects, and readings from James Joyce. He seemed to lead an owlish night life, and would come downstairs, dressed in a corduroy jumpsuit, in the late hours of the morning. He put on a recording of the Beatles or the Supremes and started toying with a layout for his next issue. He worked on the floor of a small room adjoining the office, large scissors in hand, slicing violently through photographs of Pope John, U Thant, and Vietnamese monks. There was a fervid originality about him. He seemed to be thoroughly enjoying the flowering of a long-suppressed individualism.

I cornered Richard Mann one evening as he was leaving Emmaus House for a downtown engagement, impeccably attired in a double-breasted gray wool suit, and we made an appointment for three o'clock the following afternoon. When I arrived at Emmaus House the next day, I found him standing on the kitchen table, fitting an enormous piece of aluminum over a light bulb in the ceiling. David

Kirk was sitting below him, sipping a cup of coffee. They were arguing about a talk that Richard Mann was scheduled to give, entitled "Dropping Out Creatively."

"You see, I think the hippie type of dropping out is wrong," David Kirk was saying. "I don't think you should stress the value of that type of dropping out. The flower people's dropout was always narcissistic, sensation-centered, passive."

"I don't agree with you at all," Richard Mann said.

"But it's just the kind of dropping out I've been fighting here," David Kirk said edgily. "The whole point is that there's a kind of dropping out that *is* creative—like the Quaker groups that drop out to be faithful to their moral values, like the new farmers' cooperatives in the South that are creating fairer ways of distribution—"

"Well, I still think the flower people were lovely," Richard Mann said. He saw me standing in the doorway, and told me impatiently, "You're ten minutes late. I wanted you to see my room in just the proper light, and it's waning fast. I'll take this piece of metal up with me. I'm making a sculpture to hide that monstrous ceiling bulb."

We rushed upstairs and entered a stark white room on the fourth floor. The furnishings consisted of sofa cushions covered with white towels, a low homemade table, a mattress covered with white linen lying directly on the floor. A narrow bottle holding a single daffodil stood on the table. There were white-painted bookcases along the wall. By the bed lay a metal paint box, its brushes stacked in tidy rows. And above the bed hung a large Abstract Expressionist canvas, painted in the sweet colors and violent forms of the Willem de Kooning style, signed by Richard Mann. He fidgeted with a wooden screen by the window, carefully letting the last rays of afternoon sun filter into the room. "You missed the best light effect," he complained. "Well, let's sit on the floor and talk."

He sat cross-legged on the mattress. His handsome face, grown a bit puffy, framed by long blond sideburns, reminded one of Donatello's John the Baptist. He has catlike gestures, quick-moving blue eyes, a soft, indulgent mouth. He smoked from a pack of small cigars, and as he talked he deftly bent and cut, with large scissors, the sheet of aluminum he had brought upstairs.

"When I look back on my adolescence, I had a terrible fear of people. I was sickly shy. I couldn't face the rough and tumble of the world. That's why I decided so early for the priesthood, and I think that's why many men decide to be priests. I'd always been neurotically religious in school back in Australia, where I come from—always the altar boy, always the one to clean up the grotto, constantly lighting candles in my room. Prayer had always been easy for me. I often imagined myself in mystical ecstasies.

"The community I joined at the age of sixteen was the Congregation of the Blessed Sacrament. It's as unworldly an order as you can find. The chief discipline of its priests is to adore the exposed host. All over the world, Blessed Sacrament Fathers have set up 'thrones of exposition' to draw the largest possible crowds into their churches to adore the host. Our founder had the idea that in this contemplation you make 'a total gift of your personality.' We were told that we were to become nothing, *nada*, that we were nothing but a receptacle for Jesus. This meditation was based on a seventeenth-century belief that one should empty oneself of passion and ambition and be passive before divine will. Prayer came easily in my early years.

"From my early teens, I had been interested in poetry and in painting. When I was sixteen, I came across some reproductions of Jackson Pollock's in an art magazine, and

I started doing Abstract Expressionist pictures in my spare time. I threw gold dust on pieces of Masonite, poured paint over them—always very freely. I never have had a need to find objective representation in art. I think there's some relationship between my love for abstract art and the meditative discipline of my order: all that contemplation of that abstract white host—and the notion that God cannot be conceived in words, only apprehended by the spirit. These influences all cooperated, and by the time I was seventeen I was well on my way as an Abstract Expressionist painter. And I wrote poetry prolifically.

"That's when they started stepping on me. The novice master said to me, 'Blessed Sacrament Fathers don't write books or paint pictures. They just contemplate the exposed host.' Later, in the seminary, I was forbidden to paint or write for a year. It was a test. I was docile then and I obeyed. Men in seminaries live in the constant terror of not being ordained.

"I began to get impatient in my late teens, but I was delighted when they told me that I was 'Rome material.' That's what they say, anywhere in the world, to their prize students. It had been my ambition, since I was six, to go to Italy. Australia is such a dismal country, with this enormous and dreary middle class—I'd always wanted to get away from it. Sure enough, a week after I'd been ordained, I was sent to Rome to study liturgy. I was very excited, because I had always been more interested in liturgy than anything else. But when I got to Rome I was told that I had to study theology for two years before I could even think about liturgy. And I was sent to the Gregorian University."

Richard Mann rose. "I didn't want to do theology and Latin! I only wanted to do liturgy." He stood by the window looking down into 116th Street. "So by my second year in theology I went into a very depressed state. I couldn't study. Nothing seemed to matter . . ."

He sat by the window looking out.

"I can't tell you the horror of life in those Roman seminaries. Back then, we were given only enough money on Thursday afternoon, when we were off, to take the very cheapest bus to St. Peter's and back. We were not even given extra lire for a cup of coffee. I was sent some money by my parents, so I bought a bicycle and zoomed all around town. I painted a lot in my room. I even had an exhibition in Rome. I skipped classes. I refused to do that theology. One day, the superior came into my room and said, 'You have to pass the theology exam, or else you go back home.' Well, that really scared me. When I left for Rome, I'd sworn I would never go home. That would have been the worst blow to my pride . . .

"But it dawned on me that in the priesthood if you say no they can't put you in jail or in irons—they have to face up to you as a human being and dialogue with you. So I faced my superior and said, 'No. I refuse to go home.' I've never recovered from the power of that moment. What could they do to me? They had to compromise. He compromised. He said, 'All right, you'll go to a parish in the United States, and that'll give you a sense of responsibility.'

"So they sent me to New York, and posted me temporarily at the Church of St. Jean Baptiste at 76th Street and Lexington Avenue. I had the usual priestly routine— 5:30 a.m. Mass, adoration at midday, confessions at night. I painted in my room. I spent a lot of time during those months at St. Jean's stewing over how my Order might be updated. But I decided that the Order couldn't be reformed for another twenty years, and I wasn't going to dedicate my life to that task. I'd seen too many priests in my Order crushed, too many sour men who spent their time complaining about how the meat wasn't cooked properly. I decided that I simply refused to become like one of them. I felt lost. I didn't know what to do with myself. And then I found Emmaus House."

Richard suddenly looked like a serene, candid child. "I found Emmaus, and life became bearable for the first time since my boyhood. I met David Kirk in a bookstore; the owner introduced us because she said we were the only two priests she'd ever seen wearing peace buttons. I started to come to Emmaus regularly to help paint the house. It was the first community that appealed to me in years. I'd been so lonely all my life as a priest. Priests as a caste are lonely, scared men. When a letter came from my superior in Rome saying, 'Father Mann has to live full time in the St. Jean's monastery,' I again said no. I've learned to say no. I moved my things up to Emmaus and applied for permission to work here full time.

"I think that the only role for the priest nowadays is to be a prophet, an intellectual gadfly, a celebrator. All the other functions the priest used to have—the counseling, the social work, the administering of justice—are done now by specialized laymen. And the cultic, magic notion of the priesthood is equally defunct. In progressive theology, every man is a priest—the Spirit works exclusively through the people. It would be sad if there were nothing left for priests to do but dole out the sacraments. My definition of the priesthood is close to my definition of the artist. Priests must be catalysts, irritants. They must have the most acute conscience in society. Their function is to make people question, as St. Francis and Pope John did. Like artists, they must develop their intellect, their individualism, their receptivity to a more refined state than anyone else. Their liturgy must remain hypersensitive to the community's changing needs. If we worked with a community that liked vestments, incense, the old-fashioned wafer-thin host we'd be delighted to do it that way for them. But the fact is that the community here prefers a more informal, familiar service, and we've had to adjust to them. What a splendid Agape we had the other day! We had Molly Bloom's soliloquy from the last chapter of *Ulysses*—the 'Yes I Will' part. It is such a beautiful way of saying yes to reality. It's really the people who offer the liturgy nowadays. What the priest can do is to create the best kind of atmosphere for celebration—turn the audience on, in other words. It's more and more of a part-time job to be a priest, more and more of a full-time job to be a Christian."

One weekday evening at Emmaus House we sat in David's study sipping highballs. Jim Forest was also there, another close friend of David Kirk's. Forest, an amiable man in his late twenties, with a bristling reddish mustache, was a co-chairman of the Catholic Peace Fellowship, a pacifist organization whose founders included Thomas Merton and Dorothy Day. I had visited Forest a few weeks earlier at the headquarters of the Peace Fellowship on Beekman Street. The photographic array of radical Catholic heroes in Forest's office was even more abundant than that in David Kirk's. Forest had seemed particularly eager to introduce me to his picture gallery. Many of the photographs showed his friends either taking Communion or about to go to jail. "Here's Jacques Maritain taking Communion from Tom Merton," he said. "Here are Dorothy Day and David Kirk refusing to cooperate with an air-raid drill. Here are Philip Berrigan and I at a conference at Thomas Merton's hermitage in Kentucky. Here's Philip Berrigan, again, going to jail after he poured blood on the Selective Service files in Baltimore. That was an important gesture: it was a political, a liturgical, and an educational act. Here's a photograph of my son Benedict—I had wanted to become a Benedictine when I was younger."

The evening I saw Forest at Emmaus House he talked to me about his relationship to the Emmaus family. "It's the religious community that is most relevant to me, the one that mirrors most closely my concerns and my hopes. So many of us have become fed up with the impersonal, old-fashioned liturgy, the formalized blasphemy we have to sit through every Sunday for the sake of the Church. At Emmaus, we are free to speak out about the everyday problems that have concerned us most during the week. We see salvation in terms of trying to create a better world here and now, through social and political action concretely inspired by the Gospel."

Forest went on talking while slicing bread. "Have you noticed the revivalist, turned-on atmosphere of new liturgy in the past couple of years? Awfully interesting. The theologians say that it's because we've gotten away from the concept of the Mass as sacrifice. We're stressing the joyful element of the Mass, the celebration. But I think it goes beyond that. The new love elements in hippiedom and in liturgical renewal have a common source—the surge toward community. Also, the clergy's aspiration toward marriage—that might help to humanize the liturgy."

We sat down for dinner. The food was simple but abundant: a ham, large loaves of dark bread, a bottle of wine. Forest edged up to David Kirk, saying playfully, "Can I sit next to you, Father? Will you give me an indulgence, Father?" David Kirk smiled impassively. Lyle Young tapped on his glass, and everyone was quiet as he read a psalm:

> *Send out your light and truth.*
> *Let these be my guide*
> *To lead me to your holy mountain*
> *And to the place where you live.*

"I got a call today from those priests working in the factory in Brooklyn," David Kirk said. "There might be a real new worker-priest movement starting there."

"What a good dinner!" Forest said. "The Catholic Worker was never like this."

"Yes, at the Worker we were very arrogant about being the poor men of the Church," David said softly. "That was probably our chief sin. We said the rosary, we went to daily Mass. I miss that discipline. There is nothing that can quite take its place. There's a real danger in the secularism that Emmaus House represents. By secularizing the Church as we have done, you can throw the baby out with the bath. I mean by that, if you go too far with the Harvey Cox idea that picketing for better housing is a form of prayer, then you may end up with no meditative discipline whatever. The balance between meditative discipline and social action —that's the most important balance we have to strive for."

Later that evening, as I was leaving, David Kirk took me to the door of Emmaus House. Summing up our conversation of the previous weeks, he said, "All through the movement, we have moved on from ecumenism to parallel structure. We frequently bypass the old institution. We believe that we must share Communion with other faiths before any dogmatic definition of the Presence has been reached. We say, 'On the road to Emmaus we'll heal our division.' You know the story of Emmaus: Some disciples met a stranger on the road, but they didn't recognize him as Jesus resurrected until they had broken bread together. In the early Church, the differences of opinion about the nature of the Eucharist were infinitely more violent than they are now between Protestants and Catholics, and yet *they* were sharing Communion."

David Kirk looked thoughtful, and he added:

"Let's be reasonable. What I really mean is that you need both an institutional ecumenism and a grass-roots ecumenism such as ours. Just as you need both a liberal Democratic Party doing its official work *and* a strong grass-roots Left working outside the parties, so you need the liberal bishops doing the good, progressive things *and* the grass-roots insurrection to change the institution, to push the bishops on. The Church is inevitably heading toward pluralism. There will be a multiple-track Church, with a great diversity in ways of worship within its ranks. It's the only way to avoid schism. The Episcopalians, after all, have their Low, Middle, and High Church, and I think the Catholics must and will evolve toward that kind of pluralism to stay united. However, to work toward that unity many of us have to drop out of the self-worshipping institution, outside the Roman Complex, and that's what I've done."

"I thought you were against dropping out," I said.

"I do not in the least consider myself a dropout of the Church," he said severely. "I only said I've dropped out of the self-worshipping Roman complex. I consider myself at the very core of the Church, attempting to recapture its original meaning."

And he added gaily, with confidence: "A lot of bishops and cardinals are on the fringes of the Church. We're in dead center."

March 1968

The Berrigans

I/CATONSVILLE

II/THE TRIAL OF
THE CATONSVILLE NINE

I / CATONSVILLE

*Every Church is a stone rolled onto
the tomb of the man-God;
it prevents the resurrection, by force.*
—Nietzsche

The Catonsville Nine

Shortly after the hour of noon on May 17, 1968, seven
men and two women walked into the Knights of Columbus
Hall of Catonsville, Maryland, a suburb of Baltimore. They
climbed the stairs to the second-floor room which houses
the town's Selective Service office and proceeded to empty
the contents of several filing cabinets into large wire trash
baskets. The head clerk screamed. "My draft files! You
get away from my draft files!" After a brief scuffle the
clerk and her two aides stood still, helpless and astonished.
It was startling, as were many other details of that afternoon, that several of the raiders wore Roman Catholic
clerical attire. They stuffed the draft records into their wire
baskets, exhorting each other with terse, teamlike exclama-
tions. "You're doing great, kid . . ." "Don't pack them

too tightly or they won't burn . . ." "Okay, we've got enough, let's go." Toward the end of the raid, which lasted ninety seconds, the youngest of the three clerks, with a desperation accentuated by her extreme surprise, threw a telephone clear through a closed window to attract the attention of passersby in the street below. The raiders walked swiftly down the stairway and into the parking lot outside. They emptied their haul of papers into a single pile, doused it with home-made napalm, and ignited it with matches. As the fire blazed savagely, devouring the draft records of 378 young Catonsville residents, the nine men and women awaited arrest by joining hands and saying the Lord's Prayer.

A small crowd of onlookers had gathered at the scene. "They're burning draft records!" exclaimed a young woman who had wheeled a baby carriage into the parking lot. "No, they're praying," someone else said. "They're burning draft records, they should be shot," another spectator said. Meanwhile the nine Catholics, their heads still bowed, began to talk gravely among themselves, as worshippers talk before the Eucharist in one of the spontaneous liturgies of the modern Church. "We burn these draft records," said a tall, massive man in clerical garb, "in the name of that God whose name is decency, humanity and love." "We do this because everything else has failed," another man in black softly spoke. "May this make clear that napalm is immorally and illegally destroying human lives in Vietnam." "Our Church has been silent," said a jowly man in a business suit, "we speak out in the name of Catholicism and Christianity."

Cameras clicked and whirred as they prayed; a bevy of newsmen had appeared as the nine emerged from the Selective Service office. The press had been summoned to the scene by a statement, carefully released the preceding hour, which read, in part:

Today, May 17th, we enter Local Board No. 33 at Catonsville, Maryland, to seize Selective Service records and burn them with napalm manufactured by ourselves from a recipe in the Special Forces Handbook, published by the U.S. Government. We, American citizens, have worked with the poor in the ghetto and abroad. We destroy these draft records not only because they exploit our young men, but because they represent misplaced power concentrated in the ruling class of America . . . We confront the Catholic Church, other Christian bodies and the synagogues of America with their silence and cowardice in face of our country's crimes. We are convinced that the religious bureaucracy in this country is racist, is an accomplice in war and is hostile to the poor . . . Now this injustice must be faced, and this we intend to do, with whatever strength of mind, body and grace that God will give us. May God have mercy on our nation.

Five policemen ran into the parking lot, and a brief interrogation ensued.

"Did you burn these draft records?"

"Yes, I wanted to make it more difficult for men to kill each other."

"Your name, please?"

"David Darst, Christian Brother."

"Did you burn these draft records?"

"Yes, I wanted to say 'yes' to the possibility of a human future."

"Your name, please?"

"Father Daniel Berrigan, S.J."

"Thank you, Father . . ."

The policemen, shaken and courteous, awed by the sight of Roman collars, as are most members of the law-and-order professions, questioned and identified the other seven offenders: Thomas Melville, a former priest of the Maryknoll order; his wife Marjorie Melville, a former Maryknoll nun; George Mische, a former State Department employee; Mary Moylan, a registered nurse; John Hogan, a former Maryknoll brother; Thomas Lewis, a Catholic civil rights activist, artist and art teacher; and Reverend Philip Berrigan of the Society of Saint Joseph, curate of Baltimore's largest Negro parish. The last two men needed little identification to residents of the Baltimore area. The preceding fall, in an equally extravagant and notorious protest against the Vietnam war, they had poured blood on several hundred draft records in a Selective Service office in downtown Baltimore.

As the files still smoldered at Catonsville's Draft Board, the doors of the white paddy wagon opened. The Nine entered—cheerfully smiling, embracing, and congratulating each other, extending their fingers in the V of protest. It was a handsome, photogenic group. But a photograph of the Catonsville Nine, as they were henceforth called, remains a collector's item. For the cameramen had focused their lenses throughout on Fathers Philip and Daniel Berrigan, long-publicized shock troops of the Peace Movement, idols of the Catholic New Left, the Church's most militant and prolific writers on pacifism and on civil rights. And so the Catonsville incident was publicized, on the front page of the evening's newspapers, by a picture of the Berrigan brothers praying over the burning remains of government property. At left, Philip Berrigan, tall and silver-haired, stands with hands folded and head bowed, his massive body coiled in prayer like a paratrooper curled for the shock of space. By his side is Daniel Berrigan, a mysterious smile on his delicate and puckish face, his arm spread out before him as if he were casting a libation into the flames.

That afternoon the Catonsville Nine were arraigned on charges of conspiracy and of destroying government property. They were taken to the Baltimore County Jail in the western outskirts of the city. The two women were placed in the women's detention wing. The seven men were housed in a large cell block, with four cubicles at one end, an open area and a large table at the other. Their only request upon arrest was that flowers and an apologetic note be sent, through the intermediary of the prison warden, to the head clerk of the Catonsville Draft Board.

The scholarly prison schedule of the Catonsville raiders reflected the composure of men who had deliberately chosen jail as a new way of life. The mornings were dedicated to reading, the afternoons to writing, the evenings to seminars: Catholic Conscience and the Vietnam War; American Imperialism in Guatemala; How to Move the Catholic Bishops on the War Issue. Every hour, on the strike of the clock, a few minutes of deep breathing and calisthenics were in order. A ten-foot collage on the theme of peace, assembled from pages of various periodicals, soon decorated a wall of the room. In the evening, between the writing period and the seminar, the prisoners read their articles and letters to each other. Daniel Berrigan, poet laureate of the Jesuit order, had been awarded a cell of his own so as to concentrate better on his writing. And before the week was over, a variety of anti-war publications were already putting into print the articles that were written in the Baltimore County Jail and smuggled out via the vast underground of contemporary Catholicism.

The prisoners had begun a voluntary fast the evening they entered jail. Six of the men fasted on liquids: coffee, tea, milk, fruit juices. Brother David Darst, the youngest of the group, insisted on the purer Gandhian practice of fasting on water. Their fast was broken once, the Sunday after the Catonsville raid, with Communion bread and wine. The jail warden, a Roman Catholic who was particularly fond of Philip Berrigan, brought bread and wine into the cell block and shared with his wife and his five children in Father Berrigan's Mass. Later in the week the Catonsville Nine were visited by a group of Jesuits from Loyola University who presented them with a package of books. The visit was brief. The Jesuits were choked with tears. "We're embarrassed," one of them said. "We feel we should be right in there with you . . ." He turned away, sobbing, and led the group out. The package was opened. It contained the latest volumes of Che Guevara, Herbert Marcuse, Régis Debray: all books on revolution.

Precisely a week after the Catonsville incident, on May 24, the Nine were arraigned again, this time in a Federal District Court. Daniel Berrigan, George Mische, Mary Moylan, Thomas Melville, Marjorie Melville, John Hogan, and David Darst were released on bail. But Philip Berrigan and Thomas Lewis were held captive, because two hours earlier, in another chamber of the same courthouse, they had been sentenced to six years' imprisonment for their attack on the Baltimore Draft Board the previous fall. They were denied bail pending appeal. It was an unusually severe legal move, but they had broken the self-recognizance bond placed upon them for their first protest. Thomas Lewis and Philip Berrigan were returned that same day to Baltimore County Jail. And Father Philip Berrigan, the Catholic Church's first Freedom Rider, its earliest anti-war militant, became the first Catholic priest in the history of the United States known to serve sentence as a political prisoner.

A few weeks after he was freed on bail, Philip Berrigan's older brother, Daniel, was asked by Dorothy Day to celebrate Mass at the new headquarters of the Catholic Worker. The Worker had recently moved a few blocks north of the humble building on New York City's Chrystie

Street which had served for many years as the center of Christian pacifism in the United States. The Mass had two intentions: to bless the Worker's new home on East First Street; and to celebrate the departure for jail, the preceding day, of Thomas Cornell, one of the Worker's most dedicated disciples.

The liturgy was scheduled for ten o'clock. At nine-thirty Dorothy Day came in and sat down at a desk by the entrance of the bare, freshly painted ground-floor room on East 1st Street. Imperious, silver-haired, statuesque, looking at seventy-four like the retired head of a very blue-stocking women's university, she opened mail, crisply greeted incoming visitors, and made a few impatient phone calls to be sure that Father Dan was on his way.

It was, as always, a small and motley company at the Worker: a handful of those mumbling, grizzly Bowery men who had been living on the Worker's charity since the Depression; a trio of Mexicans from Cesar Chavez's Farm Workers' Union; a scattering of the admiring young students and priests who inevitably turn up at any of Daniel Berrigan's public appearances; and a group of the gentle, quiet young men who live at the Worker in Franciscan poverty, engaged in works of mercy and relentless dissent against secular power.

At a quarter of ten, three young women with a galaxy of small children came into the room. Dorothy Day rose hastily from her desk. "Ah, here are my draft resisters' families!" she exclaimed. Her aloof manner thawed. She gave a motherly embrace to the three women, and she proceeded to introduce them, with great pride, to the congregation. Their three husbands had all been, at some time, her right-hand men at the Worker. Here was Raona Wilson, whose husband Jim was serving a three-year sentence at the Allenwood Federal Penitentiary in Pennsylvania. Here was

Monica Cornell, the wife of Tom Cornell, who had just the day before begun a six-month sentence in Danbury, Connecticut. Tom had a conscientious objector status, but he had burned his deferment card as a gesture of sympathy for those who had not been able to avoid the draft, was reclassified 1-A, and had refused induction. Finally, here was Cathy Miller, married to David Miller, who was also in a Federal Penitentiary. "David Miller was the very first American," Dorothy Day said with pride, "the very first American to be prosecuted for burning his draft card in protest against the Vietnam war. Way back in 1965. A three-year sentence! Ah this war, this most insane of all wars, and these gallant young men . . ."

"Here comes Father Dan," one of the young wives said. Daniel Berrigan entered the room with an entourage of students. After a warm embrace for Dorothy Day he hugged the three young wives with special solicitude, caressed and dandled their children, exchanged news of the prisoners. The other members of the congregation stood in a reverent circle, waiting to shake his hand. He held court for a while, greeting everyone in the casual, hip manner of the avant-garde college chaplain. "Hey, how goes . . ." "How you doing, kid?" "Shalom, man . . ." He was dressed in a black turtleneck, an old ski jacket, a beret, in that elegant emulation of the French worker-priests which had been his style for some years. His face had a grim, gaunt handsomeness which recalled some medieval or Renaissance heroes: the knights in Ingmar Bergman's allegories, the medallioned profile of a Medici. His eyes were kind, ingenuous, and mocking. They had the jaded, guarded warmth of a matinée idol who knows the power of his seduction, who is both pleased and unnerved by the fervor of his admirers.

At the back of the stark room, which overlooked a

stunted tree that Dorothy Day furtively nourished with holy water, a table had been set with a clean white table-cloth, a bottle of red wine, and a loaf of bread. A few minutes after he arrived, Daniel Berrigan walked toward the table and said in his boyish, friendly voice, "Well, good morning . . . welcome to the new Worker home . . . shall we begin?" It was a stark, skeletal Mass. The guests slid onto the five wooden benches that faced the makeshift altar. Daniel Berrigan, standing by the side of the table, made the sign of the Cross. And after a short confessional sentence he launched into the traditional Gloria: "Glory to God in the highest and on earth peace to men of good will. We praise you, we bless You, we worship You, we give You thanks for Your great glory . . ." He said the litany calmly, softly, with a deadpan air that verged on boredom. His entourage exchanged amused looks, for a Berrigan liturgy, these days, would more likely consist of long readings from Pablo Neruda, Auden, T. S. Eliot . . . but today he had conceded, with delicacy, to Dorothy Day's traditional tastes. And she followed the service rever-ently, wearing on her head a black mantilla similar to the one she had worn to receive Communion, a few years earlier, from the hands of the Pope. It was her total reverence to the Holy See which had allowed the Worker to survive in all its radical fervor.

Daniel Berrigan read a passage from Saint Mark, and then, in lieu of a homily, asked one of Caesar Chavez's men to speak. A short, wizened man with the face of a Mayan statue, a Mexican shawl draped over his shoulder, came to the front of the room and softly urged the congregation not to buy grapes, not to let any of their friends buy grapes, until the Delano strikes were settled. "That Delano V..lley's a bad scene," Daniel Berrigan said with his dead-pan smile. "I haven't eaten a grape in years . . ." The Mexi-

can sat down, serene as an idol. Daniel Berrigan patted the
heads of two of the draft resisters' children, who had been
wandering around the table since the beginning of the
service trying to reach for the Communion bread. He said
the Creed, prayers for the farm workers, for the new
Catholic Worker house, for the draft resisters. And then,
one hand stretched over the bread and wine, he improvised
a Canon. The children were getting restless, their voices
rose like sirens over the priest's flat litany. One of the
prison widows walked her two-year-old up and down the
room. Another kept snatching at her three-year-old, who
was intent upon climbing onto the altar. After the Lord's
Prayer and the *Agnus Dei*, Daniel Berrigan gravely broke
the loaf of bread into several dozen pieces. "Kumbaya My
Lord, Kumbaya" a feeble voice struck up. The worshippers joined in the song, and, headed by Dorothy Day, filed
up to the front of the room to receive the bread and wine.

The voice of the Miller child had grown louder. The
tension between mother and child grew apace, rising to an
uninterrupted dialogue of screamed protest and sharp
words of warning. "God be with you," Daniel Berrigan
said shortly after the Communion. "And with Your Spirit,"
the congregation answered. Upon those words the child
screamed stridently; the mother shook her sternly and the
little girl, freeing herself from her mother, vomited. She
threw up violently, explosively, repeatedly, until the area
between the front bench and the altar was covered with
curdled milk, and an acrid smell filled the room like a heavy
fog. "Thank you," Daniel said imperturbably. "Welcome
to the new Worker home, bless you all." The child quieted
quickly and slumped over her thumb. Her mother went
cheerfully to work on her hands and knees, wiping the floor.
Dorothy Day, equally impassive, had taken a seat next to
Daniel Berrigan on the front bench. "Children can be dis-

ruptive," she said with the smiling aplomb of an Eleanor
Roosevelt. "Does anyone have questions for Father?"

A flurry of hands were raised by the students scattered
throughout the room. Where had Father been all year?
What was he up to this summer?

Daniel Berrigan sat relaxed, leaning against the wall of
the room, looking at his audience with a knowing smile.
Well, as some already knew, he'd been at Cornell University all year. He was a co-director of Cornell United
Religious Work, an interesting mixed bag, a very bizzazz
outfit. He'd been running the show with two Protestant
ministers, heading a team of fourteen chaplains of all faiths.
It had been the happiest winter of his life . . . two other
members of his staff were in trouble with the government
too. The Catholic chaplain and the United Church of
Christ minister had turned in their draft cards, had been
reclassified, had refused induction. That made three out of
seventeen Cornell clerics in hot water . . . a great scene!
This summer he was in Yonkers, working with a team of
students, tackling problems of racism in white suburbia.
They were all staying with an Episcopal priest whom he
had met years ago, picketing somewhere for peace. That
was the Episcopal scene these days. The Episcopalians
were providing the real estate for the Catholics' revolution.
They loaned the offices, the beds, the typewriters, the
phones, the carbon paper, for the Catholics' radical work,
very generous . . . And by the way, what did everybody
think of the Catonsville action? Wasn't the Catholic scene
something? Some beautiful polarization! The majority of
American Catholics were still the worst flag-waving hawks
in the country, but look at this glorious minority! Miller,
Cornell, Wilson, Lewis, Phil Berrigan, the Melvilles, what
a beautiful bunch of people! And since their Catonsville
caper the Catholics were leading the radical fringe of the
peace movement. It gave you hope for the Church, no?

The Berrigan smile shot out, impish, irresistibly luminous.

But why had *he* joined the Catonsville Nine, one of the students asked.

Ah well, how different was that from Christ overthrowing the tables of the moneychangers? There were times in history when men had to destroy false idols to jolt people into justice. Four years ago when he and Phil had started marching, picketing, writing, lecturing against this war there had been fifteen thousand men in Vietnam; now there were half a million. For years they had gone easy, they had nursed the peace movement in a gentle, liberal way. Then they'd realized that men don't grow by this gentle escalation . . . For months now the peace movement had been on a plateau, draft-card burning had become establishment. Something majestic and symbolic and new had to jolt the nation. How long could the Berrigans remain wet nurses to the Movement? They were threatened with becoming the golden boys of the anti-war protest . . . well, the Berrigans weren't ever going to be the golden boys of any establishment!

He shook his head and thrust it back in a very proud and arrogant way. Dorothy Day, stony-faced, fiercely nodded her approval. The resisters' wives, soothing the sleepy children on their laps, looked at him with adulation.

But how practical a gesture had it been, someone asked timorously from the back of the room? Hadn't it turned too many people off?

Daniel Berrigan stared at the questioner with cynical, hard eyes. And his delicate hand lashed at the air with unexpected anger.

Well, that was a really square question. Of course it had not been a useful act, a political act. Too many people were hung up on usefulness these days. If you're useful, you know, you become disposable. Who wants to end up in the trash can with Godot? How useful were the acts of the Martyrs? How many martyrs ever had any practical programs for reforming society? Since politics weren't working anyway, one had to find an act beyond politics: a religious act, a liturgical act, an act of witness. If only a small number of men could offer this kind of witness, it would purify the world. Wasn't there a time in England when every Quaker was in jail? What a great scene that must have been! Perhaps that's where all Christians should be today . . .

One of the resisters' wives asked softly how he felt about going to jail.

He smiled, again serene.

Ah well, jail was the most beautiful experience in the world. He'd been in twice now, for a week at a time, once after the march on the Pentagon last October, then for a week after Catonsville. The nine of them had been so united . . . in these days when it was so difficult to find community, risk was the greatest basis for friendship. And the most important thing about jail was that it might give you the only complete vision of the world. For the fate of most mankind, after all, life is like jail: what Pope John called the common fate of man, the violence of under-development. It's only in prison that you can place yourself at the edge of mankind's suffering, that your conscience can be absolutely free . . . why, Phil Berrigan was the freest man in the world, just listen to this letter . . .

Daniel Berrigan pulled out of his pocket a crumpled envelope which was postmarked from Baltimore County Jail.

"Tom Lewis and I feel that we have the world by the tail," he read very quietly. "The Cardinal's secretary has just called to restore my faculties of saying Mass and hearing confession in prison. We are surrounded by much friendship, comfort, and support from all our friends. I ask you, ain't this the millennium?"

An expression came over Daniel Berrigan's face which only appeared when he spoke about his brother. The elfishness, the Zen cool disappeared and gave way to a reverent gentleness. He shook his head. "Incredible man that Phil Berrigan," he muttered. "The equipment that guy has, I've never known anything like it . . ."

Dorothy Day put an end to the meeting. Speaking slowly and loudly, she towered majestically in the tiny room, as if addressing a multitude.

"I would like everyone of you to meditate on the acts of witness given by Fathers Daniel and Philip Berrigan and the rest of the Catonsville Nine . . . on the witness offered by Jim Wilson, Tom Cornell, David Miller, and many other of our Catholic Workers . . . there is only one way to end this insane war. Pack the jails with our men!"

"Pack the jails!" she repeated imperiously.

A Fable by Daniel Berrigan, S.J.

There was once a man who carried a tempter on his back. The Thing was the size of a black squirrel with a nearly human face. He used his forked tail for a third hand; he spoke six languages in a voice like a drama coach.

One day the two were walking companionably in Central Park. The Thing as usual was badgering the man. "Look at yourself," he said in English, "you'll be forty-six years old on May 9th, and what have you to show for it?"

The man did what he was told. He closed his eyes and looked. He saw nothing new; a pleasant slob with an unpressed look, a life that was now pleasant, now hellish, but mostly gray. But he said nothing, being resigned to the sight.

The two turned north at the edge of the lagoon. The man suddenly had an idea. "Get behind my eyes," he said softly, "and you'll see what I have to show for it." He stretched out his arms, scooped up the pool in his hands, held the waters a moment like a libation, and then tossed them over his left shoulder. The Thing, taken unawares, was drenched. A minute before, he had undeniably been black, but when he shook and blinked and looked at himself, he had turned white.

"All right, joker," he snarled, "so you won that round."

The man turned about with a new look on his face. Central Park South towered serenely in the air. "Let's play for it," the man said. "Tallest building wins." "Agreed," said the Thing. He was shivering in spite of himself. The man stretched out his arms from Fifth to Central Park West, and brought them slowly together. The buildings came in softly like a pack of cards. He held the deck and the Thing drew. The man drew. The Thing showed: the Plaza. The man showed, and laughed: the Huntington Hartford Museum.

Of late a Thing lurches through the Park, harmless and errant as a disincarnate shadow. It walks only at night, when it feels safe from marauders—children, nurses, sunlight, Good Humor men. It has something on its back: a pleasant homunculus with an unpressed look. The man likes to badger the Thing. "Just look at yourself," he says. "All hell, all history, and you can't win. You can't even pull a right card."

"All right, get off it," whines the Thing.

"Not yet," the man smiles. "Once more around the towpath. I need exercise. Let's go."

They get going.

Childhood and Rebellion

A biographical questionnaire returned by Daniel Berrigan to the Macmillan Company, which has published eight volumes of his verse and prose in the past twelve years, contains the following exchanges:

1. *Birthplace? Date?*

   Virginia, Minnesota, May 9th, 1921.

2. *Immediate family: Parents, brothers, sisters?*

   Mother and father; five brothers. A fairly heterogeneous double troika moving at present in several directions with interesting stress and balance.

3. *Education? Degrees?*

   Two equivalent M.A.'s, one in theology, one in philosophy. Continuing education, courtesy of the American Correction System. According to the first, I might be considered incorrigible; to the second, perhaps, educable.

4. *List of awards and honors?*

   Lamont Poetry Award, 1957.
   Indictment, 4 felonies, U.S. Government, May 1968: Conspiracy, Entering Government property, etc. etc.

5. *Why did you become a Jesuit?*

   They had a revolutionary history. I only suspected it at the time; now I am more certain, and more proud.

The Berrigan brothers' rebelliousness has myriad sources; each Berrigan picks a different one. Jerome, fourth of the six sons, oldest member of the younger "troika" of brothers, attributes it to the spirit of the Irish Revolution. Daniel, at the center of the triad, blames it on a wicked, witchlike aunt who tortured him during a year of his childhood. Philip, the youngest, says he was made a rebel by his father, Tom Berrigan, "a tyrannical, brutal man who made me bristle against authority."

Tom Berrigan was born in Syracuse, New York, a few years after his own parents—poor Tipperary farmers— had fled the Irish potato famine. The suffering of the Irish at the hands of the English overlords had obsessed centuries of Berrigans. Tom's generation conquered hard times by unusual brilliance. Many of his brothers and cousins, by 1900, were college-educated: they were teachers, nuns, priests, labor leaders, founders of hospitals and of interracial councils. The Berrigans never remained in the conservative mainstream of Irish immigrants. They were that maverick brand of Irish progressives which continues to produce, in our day, a Eugene McCarthy and a Paul O'Dwyer. "Dado was a Walt Whitman type, a final model of nineteenth-century man," Daniel says about his father, "well-versed in classics, poetry, theology, knowledgeable in all realms . . . and if he wasn't, he thought he was, which comes to the same thing."

Labor movements and poetry were the loves of Tom Berrigan's life. He had drifted away from the Catholic Church in his teens because of its failure to support trade unionism. Impatient, enamored of physical exertion, he also left college after two years to go to work as a railroad engineer, and immediately rose in the ranks of labor boards. "At the age of thirty-three," he says, "I puffed through Minnesota, and met my bride." Frieda Fromhart was a devout, infinitely gentle German girl, whom Daniel describes as "a woman of marmoreal patience." She swiftly brought Tom back to the Church, and bore him six sons. To live with Tom Berrigan, as Philip says, was rough. A tall, powerful, belligerent man given to terrible tantrums, he made huge demands upon his family. He lost his job in Minnesota because of his militant participation in the Socialist party. When he moved his family back to Syracuse, at the start of the Depression, to a brick house by Onondaga Lake, Tom decided to live off his land and save. With his sons' help, he farmed the reluctant clay earth on evenings and weekends off from his new job at the Niagara-Mohawk electric plant. The farm work was laid out on a daily basis. Tom cuffed and buffeted his boys when the assigned tasks were not done. The three oldest children, Tom Jr., John, and Jim, frequently and angrily fought back. Brawls seemed to soothe Tom Berrigan. Philip recalls seeing his father strangely becalmed some mornings at the breakfast table, his face full of cuts and bruises. "One of your brothers and I had a good, good fight," Tom would say with satisfaction.

Tom Berrigan's intellectual demands were equally exacting. His memory for poetry was gigantic, and he requested a docile audience. Every few weeks, a pint of homemade cider under his belt, he'd drag his six sons into a corner of the parlor. "Now listen to this," he'd roar, "and mind you listen well!" And he'd spout by the hour, belting out the Yeats, the Shakespeare, the florid stanzas of the Catholic poet Francis Thompson whose verses, at the age of ninety, he still declaimed in a feeble voice:

> *Across the margents of the world I fled*
> *And troubled the gold gateways of the stars*
> *Smiting for shelter on their clanged bars . . .*

Tom Berrigan wrote poetry as voluminously and as floridly as he spoke it, and many of his fits of temper were triggered by editors' rejection notices. ("The old man's at it again," Philip wrote Daniel in 1965, when their father was well on in his eighties, "taking it out on the furniture because the diocesan paper turned down some more of his

crap . . .") It was a turbulent household. When Tom
Berrigan returned to the Church, it was in a bristling and
militant way. He never ceased to agitate for the under-
privileged and the underdog. He helped to found Syracuse's first Electrical Workers' Union and its first Catholic
Interracial Council. The Berrigan farm was like a Catholic
Worker house of hospitality, its barns and spare rooms
filled with the needy, its frugal table always ready to accommodate passers-by.

One more incident stands out in Daniel's childhood,
which he believes turned him into a maverick. It was the
time when his mother fell sick with tuberculosis and had
to be hospitalized for over a year. Daniel loves to dramatize
his life with Aunt Maggie, an arrogant spinster sister of
Tom Berrigan's who was called in to run the house. "She
was stingy and mean, like that bicycling witch in *The
Wizard of Oz*. She actually starved us; bread and butter
sandwiches, molasses cookies, meat once a week, that was
our diet. What a scene. I know that's what made revolutionaries out of us. We used to have underground committee meetings in closets behind her back, and then Tom
Jr., the oldest, would lead the delegation to ask for better
treatment—never to any avail. Dado was stingy and we
were very poor, and he was thrilled with her because she
saved so much of his paycheck. We grew terribly pale and
weak." Daniel pinches in his cheeks. "Every Sunday we'd
go to see Mom at the hospital and she'd lean out of bed
and look at those six pale, thin little faces" (he draws his
cheeks in still farther) "and she would cry out of sorrow,
and we'd cry too . . . The doctors had been very pessi-
mistic about my mother surviving, but she recovered out
of sheer willpower, in order to get the witch out of the
house. A lot of our kookiness and aggressiveness, especially Phil's and mine, came out of the unhappiness we
suffered that year . . ."

Daniel, at an early age, had singled himself out as the most sensitive and studious, the frailest and most devout of the six children. "From the age of six," his mother says, "Daniel was obsessed by the suffering in the world." He was the readiest for tears, the top of his class, the tender mother's helper who cleaned up the kitchen while his brothers struggled with the farmwork. He spent much time by the family bookshelf, which held the Bible, back issues of *Commonweal* and *The Catholic Worker*, a few books of poetry, a five-volume work by a Jesuit entitled *Pioneer Priests of North America*. Daniel had inherited his father's passion for writing poetry. His weak ankles required special shoes, and exempted him from farm work. He was indifferent to sports. Philip, two years younger, the sibling who has remained Daniel's closest friend from earliest childhood, was the mirror opposite: a brawny outgoing all-American boy, a baseball and basketball star, an enormously gifted athlete who was constantly anxious to test his physical prowess. But Daniel, the ephemeral poet and dreamer, would lead and inspire, as poets often do, the men of action. Of the three Berrigan boys destined for the seminary, Daniel led the way. He had felt the call of the priesthood since childhood. At the age of seventeen, he applied for the Jesuit order because, he says, "it ran such a cool scene."

"When I was sixteen a friend and I wrote in for literature from all the orders in the United States we could think of—Benedictines, Augustinians, Dominicans—about forty of them. What impressed us about the Jesuits was that they didn't seem to want us. All the other orders were trying to rope us in by showing us photographs of jazzy swimming pools in their prospectus. But the Jebbies just had a couple of tight little quotes from St. Ignatius in a very stark pamphlet. We thought that cool scene was revolutionary. We applied immediately." The Society of Jesus accepted the application, and in 1939, aged eighteen, Daniel left Syracuse for the Jesuit seminary near Pough-keepsie, New York, to begin the ardous thirteen-year train-ing which the order imposes on its men before ordination. The loving ties of the younger Berrigan brothers were severed for a long time.

One forgets, in our age of worldly, picketing priests, how strict seminarians' rules were in the past. Short of a death in the immediate family a Jesuit was not allowed to leave the house of his order for the first two years of his novitiate. He could only be visited by his family four times a year. Daniel Berrigan, shy, studious, obsessed by the suffering of the poor, a model seminarian, did not come home for seven years.

After graduating from high school, Philip had spent a year doing the grimiest work possible, scrubbing loco-motives in a railroad round, to earn money to go to college; he supplemented his income by playing first base on a semi-pro baseball team. Having saved a year's pay, he enrolled at St. Michael's College in Toronto. He only had time for a semester. In January 1943 he was drafted. And after a brief training period in the deep South, an experi-ence which moved him to dedicate his life to helping the black people, he was sent abroad to fight. "Philip Berrigan is like Saint Paul," a friend has said, "an exceptionally gifted warrior. Before his conversion, he could kill men more enthusiastically than most soldiers can." Philip fought in France and Germany with a field artillery battalion. He switched to the infantry and was commissioned in France as a second lieutenant. It is a period in his life which he dislikes to discuss.

When Philip returned to Syracuse in 1945, he found that his brother Jerry, after three years of the army, had

followed Daniel into the seminary. Philip was the third of
the triad to decide on the priesthood. In 1950, after
graduating, an English major, from Holy Cross College,
he joined Jerry at the Josephites' seminary. Officially called
the "Society of Saint Joseph" (Philip's initials, "S.S.J.,"
have led to much confusion with Daniel's "S.J."), the
Josephites are an American order founded a century ago
to help the black people. They had been, in their beginnings, revolutionary. They were later to prove a disappointment to Philip.

"Three sons in the priesthood, Mr. Berrigan, that's being a quality parent," an admiring neighbor said to Tom
Berrigan. And Tom's devoutness, stifled in his youth by
his loyalty to trade unionism, grew apace with his parental
pride. It even cost him his career in labor. In 1949, a
gravediggers' strike hit the New York Archdiocese. On
the second day of the strike, Daniel received an agitated
call from his father, asking him to meet him at the Syracuse
train the following afternoon. Pondering what the old
man was up to, David went to Grand Central Station,
where he saw Tom Berrigan step off the train with an
enormous homemade shovel under his arm. "I've come to
support the Cardinal!" Tom roared. "I've come to break
the strike for Cardinal Spellman!" Daniel, truer to the
Berrigans' labor heritage, pleaded with him not to break the
strike. But Tom, aged seventy that year, was determined to
help the Cardinal. He spent a week at the Chancery in his
overalls, offering support and being politely turned down
because of his age. Some time after he returned to Syracuse
he was deposed from his twenty-year tenure as business
agent of the Electrical Workers' Union local. Tom Berrigan's younger colleagues never forgave him for being a
strike-breaker; and it was a blow from which this father of
rebels never quite recovered.

Daniel Berrigan and the Worker-Priests

On June 21, 1952, Daniel Berrigan lay prostrate before the altar of a church near Boston, Massachusetts, and was ordained a priest.

> On a June morning, I lay in the chapel of Weston, while the voice of Cardinal Cushing shook the house like a great war horse. His hands lay on my head like a stone. I remember a kind of desolation, the cold of the floor on which I stretched like a corpse, while the invocation of the saints went over me like a tide, a death. Would these bones live? I arose to my feet and went out into the sunshine and gave my blessing to those who had borne with me, who had waited for me. A most unfinished man! What would it mean to be a Catholic? Who would be my teacher? It was, finally, the world. It was the world we breathe in, the only stage of redemption, the men and women who toil in it, sin in it, suffer and die in it. Apart from them, as I came to know, the priesthood was a pallid, vacuumatic enclosure, a sheepfold for sheep.

The paragraph comes from a long essay written by Daniel Berrigan in 1961. The Society of Jesus took a dim view of it because of its condemnation of the Catholic Church's lack of social consciousness. And it had become a favorite pamphlet of the Jesuit seminarians' underground. Five years later, after Pope John's liberalizing influence had opened the gates of the Catholic sheepfold, Daniel's essay became a Jesuit classic. It was printed by the thousands, distributed to numerous Catholic bookshops, assigned to novices' reading lists. The Berrigans have always been uncomfortably ahead of their time.

Docile seminarians though they were in their youth, Daniel and Philip were soon affected by the progressive theology that poured out of Europe after World War II.

The French, Belgian, and Dutch churches had been radicalized by Catholics' participation in the Resistance Movement, by priests' and laymen's militant political involvements under the Nazi occupation. Even liturgy had been renewed by the improvised Masses which were often said, during wartime, in private homes, factories, or open fields. The Berrigans' vocations were deeply affected by the ideology of the French Resistance. In the late 1940's, when Daniel Berrigan was studying at Weston and Philip was at Holy Cross College nearby, the French avant-garde was a favorite theme of their Sunday afternoon conversations. Their heroes were men like Cardinal Suhard, a guiding spirit of the Missions de France and of the worker-priest movement, whom Philip regards as the greatest single influence on his life; the Jesuit Father Henri Perrin, who became a factory worker after his return from German concentration camps; Abbé Pierre, the Resistance leader and MRP deputy who ministered to thousands of homeless families in the Paris suburbs, and needled the French government into starting a massive new housing program for the poor. These men had preached, in Cardinal Suhard's words, "a fearless involvement in the temporal and social spheres." The classical missionary tactic of Saint Paul ("With the Jews I live like a Jew, to win the Jews") had been put into reverse gear by the worker-priests. The Berrigans had learned from them that their task was not to convert the world to the Church, but, rather, the Church to the world.

So when the Jesuits sent Daniel to France for a year's study, shortly after his ordination, it was, as he says, "like throwing Br'er Rabbit into the briar patch." France was the country which he would always regard as his spiritual home. "Something says 'I was born here,'" he wrote. "Nothing like it on earth. The French for a steady diet are like Cognac before breakfast." Daniel was assigned to ministerial work and study in a little town near Lyons, and made friends with many of the worker-priests whose writings had already influenced him. Most of them had been active in the Resistance, and many of them had been deported. The emotions of the Occupation period were still violent. Daniel agonized, during this first stay in Europe, over the silence of the Catholic clergy in Hitler's Germany. The worker-priests' militance in the French underground, and their experience in German prisons, became models for his later theories of civil disobedience. The worker-priests' political philosophy, largely socialistic, anti-colonial, anti-imperialistic, also transformed his view of history. Daniel today looks sheepishly on the American innocent who came to France in 1953.

"Arriving in France was like landing on a fresh-air planet after being locked up all my life in a capsule. The American Church, at the time, was an Irish ghetto. I had never been politically aware before. I arrived so American, such an idiot . . . I remember heatedly defending the altruism of foreign aid programs, the execution of the Rosenbergs. I even went to Germany at Lent as a chaplain, traveling all through Bavaria giving retreats. What a scene for me! I didn't know my rear end from my elbow. Like Uriah Heep I'm very proud of my humility.

"The worker-priests radicalized me like nothing else had before. They gave me, for the first time, a practical vision of the Church as she should be. They also transformed me politically in a historic year. The French had just lost Dien Bien Phu and were forced out of Indo-China, and my French friends woke me up to the evils of colonialism. To make it all the more traumatic, I saw this worker-priest movement, which I so admired, squashed before my very eyes. In the winter of 1954, our icebox Pope, Pius

XII, had the movement dissolved in one swift stroke, ordering every single worker-priest in France to report to his bishop. Earlier, in 1950, Pius XII had issued that shameful document *Humani Generis*, which was directed against many of the great French theologians who had nourished me for years. Teilhard de Chardin, Henri de Lubac, Yves Congar were condemned for deviation from doctrine and for other errors. I saw at close hand intellectual excellence crushed in a wave of orthodoxy, like a big Stalinist purge. It hit me directly, it made me suffer deeply, it filled me with determination to carry on the work of the men who had been silenced."

The French worker-priests' vision of the Catholic Church had been too militant for the Vatican's comfort. When Daniel returned to New York City in the summer of 1954, he modeled his work on the movement whose suppression had so scandalized him.

At that time, the most progressive movements in the American Church, apart from the Catholic Worker, were such Catholic Action groups as the Christian Family Movement, the Young Christian Workers, the Walter Farrell Guild. During his three-year assignment to teach theology and French at the Jesuits' Brooklyn Preparatory School, Daniel also chaplained the local chapter of the Young Christian Workers. He led his students to the Lower East Side to work with Dorothy Day, to East Harlem to organize the black and Puerto Rican communities. Daniel likes to flaunt the avant-gardism of all his cadres. He looks back on his YCW chapter as "a religious precursor of SDS." He was also chaplain and director of the Walter Farrell Guild ("a unique pre-hippie precursor of Vatican II"), which aimed to give the laity more participation in the Church. Daniel's Farrell Guild jolted the diehards, in the fifties, by meeting in church basements over cocktails to discourse upon such secular literature as *The Brothers Karamazov*. But Daniel's unusual style was already gaining a large following of liberal laymen and seminarians. "From the time he was ordained," says John Grady, a Catholic educator who worked closely with him in those years, "Daniel was obsessed with two issues: Alleviating poverty, and breaking down the traditional structures of the priest-layman relationship. Most priests, then as now, keep a guarded, closed professionalism in their rapport with laymen. But Dan dared to enter the relationship to a point where he was absolutely exposed. He was always ready to run behind the layman and learn from him. In the fifties, he was revolutionizing the role of the layman in the Church faster than any other priest in the country."

In 1957, Daniel was promoted to a professorship at LeMoyne University in his hometown of Syracuse, where he was happily reunited with his parents and his brother Jerry, who had left the Josephites' seminary a year before he was due for ordination. Philip, two years ordained, was teaching in an all-black high school in New Orleans. The three older Berrigan brothers had scattered to different parts of the world. Now, the three younger Berrigans began to work in close cooperation. Philip, Jerry, and Jerry's wife, Carol, picketed the Niagara-Mohawk electric plant in protest against discriminatory hiring. Daniel sent Philip white students to work on CORE projects in the deep South. Philip found black scholarship students to go to LeMoyne. Daniel urged his friends to sell their houses, move into the ghetto, live in Christian poverty. His Syracuse acquaintances look back on those years with a delight mingled with terror. "One Berrigan needles away enough at your conscience. With two or three, there's no letting up."

Daniel was known at LeMoyne as a conscientious, affectionate, and demanding teacher. He was a heavy-handed assigner of book reports, a stickler for impeccable syntax, for terse and accurate expression. He also requested, from any student who wished to be close to him, frequent reception of the Sacraments and a total dedication to social work. He quickly became the most popular and controversial lecturer on campus. His style was intense and mesmerizing. His social content—militant on pacifism and on civil rights —was often too radical for the authorities' comfort. "Half of us thought that he was Christ returned," one of his students says. "The conservative half thought he was subversive. Very few of us could offer the absolute dedication and honesty he required of us." Daniel had the classical Jesuit zeal for shaping young souls, for forming spiritual cadres of perfect young Christians. And he had a Pied Piper's gift for making the students follow him. But his methods were unorthodox.

One of Daniel's more controversial actions, during his last years at LeMoyne, was to set up an off-campus house for his elite which he looks back upon as "a pre-Peace Corps scene to desegregate the Catholic ghetto." Daniel founded International House, as his project was named, to get closer to his students, to make them feel freer to talk, and to train them for social work in underdeveloped countries. The house, which had an austere little chapel with an altar built by Tom Berrigan, was particularly frowned upon by Jesuit superiors for being a center of liturgical modernism. Daniel's innovations—turning the altar around to face the congregation, saying parts of the Mass in English—seem routine today. But he was pioneering them two years before the Second Vatican Council gave them formal approval.

"In 1961, when I turned the altar around and said the Gloria in English, the older Jesuits were horrified—they thought I was working at the family jewels with a sledge hammer. But I went right ahead because I knew that we absolutely had to have something more bizzazz going for the young people. The kids and I felt that for the first time in a thousand years we were building community around the altar . . ."

The Berrigan bizzazz never pleases the hierarchy. And in 1963, Daniel Berrigan was sent to France for a sabbatical. There is fierce pride in the Berrigans and a reluctance to discuss past sorrows. Daniel today dismisses this crisis with a blithe smile, a few aphorisms; "The first generation of Jesuits worked in the streets; the second generation bought a house; the third air-conditioned it. I belong to the first generation, and the men inside don't like my *façon d'agir* . . ." But it is evident that there were more precise causes: his liturgies, his involvement in the ghetto, his unprofessional intimacy with the students. The rector of the college had a large empty table in his study which the young priests called the "think table," to which they were called for disciplining. The rector got Daniel over the "think table," and it was decided that he should spend a year in France.

The 1963 crisis is made explicit in a letter which Thomas Merton, the Trappist monk and poet, wrote to Daniel at the end of that school year. The two men had always had an affectionate but complex friendship. As the Church's two star poets, and its most distinguished pacifists, they observed each other in the manner of prima donnas whose mutual admiration is mixed with some criticism about how the other handles the art form. Daniel had accused Merton of "leading a whole generation into the cloister whom you'll never lead out." Merton always tried to curb the Berrigans' rash gestures. In each severe crisis of the Berrigans' lives, Merton sent the Berrigans a long paternal missive. Merton's tone, in this emergency, was more cautionary than usual:

"A violent break with the authorities would tend to

cast discredit on all the initiatives you have so far taken . . .
if you allow this to happen you may turn adrift those who
have begun to follow you and profit by your leadership . . ."

The 1963 crisis had been deepened by the fact that
Daniel had asked his Superiors for permission to go on a
Freedom Ride in the deep South with his brother. The
permission was not granted, and Daniel, with much grief,
obeyed. In his letter Merton enlarged, with much anger,
on the problems all priests faced when they spoke out on
peace and civil rights:

"Look, a lot of the monastic party line we are getting
ends up by being pure, unadulterated—crap. In the name
of lifeless letters on parchment we are told that our life
consists in the pious meditation on scriptures and withdrawal from the world. Try anything serious and immediately you get the line 'activist' thrown at you. I have
been told that I am destroying the image of the contemplative vocation when I write about peace. Even after
Pacem in Terris, when I reopened the question, I was told:
'That is for the bishops, my boy.' In a word, it is all
right for the monk to break his ass putting out packages
of cheese and making a pile of money for the old monastery, but as to doing anything that is really fruitful for the
Church, that is another matter altogether . . ."

And Merton advised Daniel to leave for Europe in good
spirit:

"Europe is obviously the next step, because over there
you may find out what's what. And you need to. When
you do, let me know."

Daniel took his friend's advice, and left for Paris in the
summer of 1963. Like his earlier trip to France, it went to

his head like brandy before breakfast. Another change took place in Daniel during his second stay in Europe. No one describes it better than Jim Forest, a young Catholic pacifist who was to become one of the Berrigans' closest friends.

"The Daniel Berrigan of 1962 was an earnest, chubby, well-fed man who looked just like a priest: terribly prosperous, all neat and clean, with very shiny shoes and an impeccably clean collar. I had met him one night when I accompanied Dorothy Day to a meeting of the Fellowship of Reconciliation. Dan's talk was full of what he now hates most, what he calls 'omnivorous pontifications' . . . he talked about encyclicals, his hopes for Vatican II and so on, so much the earnest liberal. I had been recently converted to Catholicism and meeting Dan was an unnerving experience for a new convert. It made me understand why so many people could be anti-clerical. Dorothy Day reacted just the same way. As we left that meeting she turned to me and said, 'Wasn't that Berrigan something? Just like a priest! Talk talk talk and doesn't give anyone a chance to open their mouth.'

"I didn't meet Dan again until the summer of 1964, when I flew to Prague for a Christian Peace Conference with some mutual friends of Dan's and mine. He'd spent the year in Paris, and he was at the airport to meet us. I almost passed him by. I did not recognize him at first. The man standing at the airport was dressed in a turtleneck and a green ski jacket and had a satchel-full of wine bottles strung over his shoulder. That chubby face of his had turned gaunt, yet incredibly serene . . . he had become ascetic, spiritual, un-priestly! It was a totally new vibration. He had finally become deparochialized."

Daniel had been deparochialized, that year, by suffering and loneliness. He is a gregarious person, terrified of solitude, needing friendship, family, warmth, attention more than he needs food or shelter. He found few such comforts among Parisians of the nineteen-sixties, whom he assessed as "selfish, bourgeois, ambitious, materialistic kids trying to make it in the de Gaulle regime . . . bad news compared to the idealists I'd met right after the war."

Daniel was also transformed that year by his trips to Marxist countries. He was one of the first American priests to be granted visas to Hungary, Russia, and Czechoslovakia, and these excursions shook him. He worked behind the Iron Curtain with Catholic families whose jobs, schooling, and income were constantly jeopardized by their religious practices. And he was very affected by the courage of Christians whose faith survived the duress of Marxist regimes. His trips behind the Iron Curtain confirmed him even more firmly in the philosophy of *kenosis*, the theology of poverty which had germinated in the French avantgarde of the forties. One could sum up the theology of poverty as such: The truest Christians are the ones who are poor and persecuted, who pay no obeisance to secular power, who live in a community of risk; the golden years of Christianity had been its first three centuries, when to be a Christian meant to live under the constant threat of martyrdom; Constantine's conversion had been the big sell-out; it had made Christians safe; it had forced that marriage of convenience between church and state which sullied the virginal martyrdom of the early Church. This is the extreme reformist view which began to seep into the Catholic Church in the last years of the Vatican Council. The philosophy of *kenosis*—the Greek word for "emptying out" used by Saint Paul when he asked the Philippians to strip themselves of worldly ambitions—asks the Church to strip itself of all material wealth and power. (One of its most famous exponents, a Dutch Augustinian, has coolly asked the Pope to sell the Vatican, give the money to the poor, dress in a black business suit, and live in a small flat in Rome.) *Kenosis* theology sees the Church as a dissenting and impoverished minority, a constant critic of the state and a guardian of Christian values, a kind of saving remnant which, like the Ten Just Men, could save the cities of the plain. This extreme reformist view demands a return to early styles of liturgy, early modes of Christian poverty, protest, and pacifism. As advocated by the Berrigans, it also asks a return to early styles of Christian martyrdom.

"Originally, as you recall," Daniel had written in the essay which criticized the docility of the Catholic sheepfold, "one was not brought to the baptismal font in his mother's arms. One came to baptism as Paul did: by a shattering change of heart, by many deliberate renunciations . . . to be baptized was in a sense to be marked for destruction. And this inner death to all that ordinary men live by was dramatized by the occurrence of martyrdom, which sealed publicly what one had already pledged to become in the sacred waters."

"The churches in the Marxist countries," he said when he returned from his stay in Europe in 1964, "are small but purified by persecution. It seems that God is cleaning up the old state-church arrangements. The Christians under Marxism have returned to their pre-Constantinian situation of being poor, pure, and persecuted, and they are leading the life which I believe God had decreed for the Church . . . what a great feeling, to be in a country where there's no head of state going to church every Sunday and corrupting it!"

Filled with zeal to reform "the old state-church arrangements," Daniel boarded ship for New York City in the autumn of 1964. His brother Philip, after a controversial career in New Orleans, had recently been assigned to a new teaching job in Newburgh, New York. The two brothers would live within an hour's reach of each other for the first time in a decade. "We wait to welcome you, and to drink with you, and to marvel at you," Philip wrote as he eagerly waited for Daniel's return. "I will never cease to trace whatever maturity or goodness I have to you, and to wait upon the next spur of growth from you. We'll muckle through for old Mother Church in absolute confidence."

It was the fall of 1964. Selma was just around the corner. The Vietnam war was about to be escalated. And with ample help from the Berrigans, the American Catholic Church began to stretch out of its long somnolence. From that year on, the Berrigans' lives read like the Book of Acts.

Philip Berrigan and the Unjust War

Philip Berrigan, S.S.J., a very tall, massive, handsome man with piercing blue eyes, has been described as "a compulsive leader of men," "a street-fighter with a paratrooper's daring," "a desperado obsessed by the Gospel," "the Gary Cooper of the Church." His teutonic, terribly respectable good looks conjure up the image of the affluent suburban in the Coca-Cola poster, the aspiring chairman of the board in the Wall Street Journal ads, the American Dream Man as depicted by the capitalist society which all Berrigans profoundly disdain. He exudes a terrifying energy, a terrifying impatience, and a maddening freedom. He is devoid of all the fears, the cautions, the proprieties that motivate normal men. His smile, like his brother's, is radiant and irresistible. The spell he casts over other humans is as great as Daniel's and more alarming. Daniel might be content to have his disciples rattle and needle at the world. Philip wants them to transform society as totally and as soon as possible. His revolutionary zeal is like the cold blue center of a flame. His eyes are merry, affectionate, and yet fiercely impatient. One recalls Camus' phrase: "The revolutionary loves a man who does not yet exist."

"The Berrigans are very traditional, conservative men," says Reverend William Sloane Coffin, the Yale chaplain who has also risked a jail sentence for defending the rights of draft resisters. "They are conserving the fire of the Holy Spirit, they are conserving the pure message of the Gospel. They are radical Christians, which is a redundancy. Radical means root; it doesn't mean being way out, but going deep down."

Although his semantics are personal, Coffin understands the Berrigans well. The Berrigans' radicalism did not grow out of any philosophical theorizing, but out of a disturbingly literal reading of the Gospels. "They remained faithful to the teaching of the apostles, to the brotherhood, to the breaking of bread and to the prayers . . . the faithful all lived together and shared out the proceeds among themselves according to what each one needed." There is a moral fundamentalism in the Berrigans which makes them follow this passage from the Book of Acts with total fidelity. It is a torment, for many Christians, to decide how literally to interpret the socialism of the Gospels. The Berrigans are untroubled. They are men sworn to poverty by their religious orders, and a conversion to poverty is perhaps the only conversion which they desire to impose on mankind. With a simplism that is sometimes maddening, they view the problems of racism, of war, and of most human suffering as created by a system of unequally distributed wealth, by human beings' greed for private property. "The next car," Philip says, "is every man's *Dolce Vita*." "Read the Gospel, get poor, get with it," Daniel blithely told a student who had asked him how to live the Christian life. "It's just that simple."

Philip Berrigan had dedicated the first ten years of his priesthood to the plight of the black man. He realized with sorrow, after joining the only Catholic order dedicated to that task, that his Society of Joseph was as much of an Uncle Tom as any timid white liberal. And Uncle Tomism goes harshly against Philip's grain. For in his view the blacks are not children to be guided by the whites. They are rather the race of superior wisdom, gentleness, and maturity, the prophetic people purified and matured by suffering who could bring adulthood to the white man. "The Negro stands in perplexity and chagrin," he wrote in his book *No More Strangers*, a formidably documented work on the psychological roots of racism, "at the inconsistency of the white man-child who rules his world . . . freedom for the Negro and maturity for us are reciprocal endowments." Philip dedicated his study "To my brother, Father Dan, S.J., without whom neither my priesthood nor this book would be possible."

Philip's profound reverence for the black race, his fierce anti-paternalism, made him capable of communicating—as few white priests can—with the most militant blacks in the United States. He inspired virility and confidence in black men, and in their women he inspired a blind and total trust. "He never made a fuss with us because we were black," one of his parishioners says. "He was just more at ease with us than any white man we'd ever met." "If Father Phil said to me 'Come on, I'll take you to the moon,'" said another of his parishioners, "and all I'd see there was a little contraption to get into, I'd get into that little contraption because I know with Father Phil I could get to the moon in any contraption . . ." Even Stokely Carmichael is reported to have made the ultimate compliment. "Phil Berrigan," he has said, "is the only white man who knows where it's at."

Philip had won the black's confidence with years of rash gestures which sometimes put the welfare of his order at stake. In 1963, he had boarded a plane for Jackson, Mississippi, to join in a mass sit-in protesting the segregation of bus terminals. Even then, Philip wished to be the first Catholic priest to be arrested in a civil rights demonstration. He wanted to make his point by going to jail. But his plans were snafued. A news leak occurred, causing one of the first civil rights crises that have agitated the American Church in our decade. A few hours after Philip had left New York, the Bishop of Jackson is said to have phoned the Josephite superior, and warned him that he would make a direct complaint to Rome if Father Berrigan arrived at his destination. Philip was paged to the phone as his plane stopped in Atlanta, and ordered by his superior to return to New York. He obeyed. But thanks to his talent for public relations, the incident hit the front pages. It was Philip's first confrontation, his first glory. For the greatest joy of this modest man's life is to flaunt his rigorous conscience, with as much publicity as possible, in the face of all institutions.

"Phil had been weaned in the Catholic Worker ideology," one of his friends says, "but there is a grimness about the Worker which he dislikes. He's a joyful man. Whether he's praying, eating, drinking, protesting or going to jail, he absolutely insists that everything be done with joy."

Gregarious and proverbially generous, Philip was known wherever he worked for his radiant good nature, his Falstaffian capacity for downing half a bottle of rye without showing it, his enormous tenderness. His lecture fees have helped to support several families through years of trouble. He was notorious, in every parish he worked, for being the first priest to arrive at any scene of accident and the first to empty his pockets for men in need. The power of his handshake, even upon a first meeting, is excruciating. He is devoid of Anglo-Saxon reserves. His greetings to friends, men and women alike, are accompanied by powerful, back-breaking embraces. "Thank God for womenkind he's not married," says the wife of one of his close friends. "He puts my spine out of joint each time he just kisses me." Everything about Philip Berrigan is magnanimous, obsessed, a little extreme. And his religious vocation dominates it all. "Christ's love, and this kid's," he signs his letters, "—Phil, S.S.J." "Carry on ole sport; Yours in Christ—Phil, S.S.J." "Great work buddy; God's love—Phil, S.S.J." "God's increase to you. Love ya, man—Phil, S.S.J." "Cool it man, we must all learn to live with Brother Ass. In Christ—Phil, S.S.J." The "S.S.J." always keeps its place, even in his letters to his family. The Berrigans long ago made a pact with each other that they would never leave the priesthood. Their attitude toward the Church is one of cynical but dogged loyalty. "The Church is a sinner," says Daniel, "But She's my mother." "The guys who leave," Philip says, "just don't have enough guts. It's our society that's evil, and the Church reflects the society. Staying in the Church gives you a chance to use the institution against itself."

It is a political attitude, for politics is to Philip's life what poetry is to his brother—a passionate second vocation. The brothers' reading tastes are explicit. Daniel reads *Partisan Review, Hudson Review,* and various obscure journals of theology and poetry. Philip subscribes to *The Nation, The New Republic, U.S. News and World Report, Dissent,* the *Progressive,* the *Guardian, Liberation,* the *Civil Liberties Quarterly, Ramparts.* He studies the

Wall Street Journal and *Business Week* to keep abreast of the American economy. He looks upon progressive news analysts as the prophets of a society which the Churches have failed to reform. *I. F. Stone's Weekly* is the periodical which he prizes most highly for its advanced opinions, and which he sometimes sends in gift subscriptions to the congressmen and friends whom he judges to be in need of enlightenment. ("Read your *I. F. Stone*," he signs off a letter to a friend. "Best love, and the Lord's keen peace.")

Armed with this formidable documentation, Philip Berrigan became a popular lecturer on progressive Catholic campuses in the early 1960's. The threat of nuclear war had converted him to a pacifist position. His expertise on the nuclear missiles race was as great as his knowledge of civil rights problems. But his lecturing style had less charm than his writing or his conversation. It simply suffered from an overabundance of facts. His lectures inevitably included massive barrages of figures and statistics with which he battered mercilessly at his audience, as in this talk of 1965:

> *Let us see some of the paradoxes and contradictions of our position, both moral and political. Forty to fifty million of our people are in poverty, with annual incomes ranging from the $3,000 level depicting poverty, to $1,000 and below. Our gold stock is just above the legal twelve billion required by law as the foundation of our currency—the main source of depletion being the heavy dollar spending of our military overseas. Over fifty per cent of our budget goes for the support of our military machine. Seventy per cent, and perhaps more, of our overseas aid is military- or defense-oriented, giving faint idea of what we have not done for societies which should be brought to levels of political and economic sufficiency. We have at the present time perhaps four thousand aircraft and missiles*

capable of delivering our nuclear arsenal. They can deliver warheads with explosive power equivalent to two billion tons of TNT, and this equals one ton of TNT for every person on our planet. In addition, we have stockpiles of nuclear warheads twice in number of those for which we have carriers—some thirty-four to fifty billion tons of TNT. If we were to attack the Sino-Soviet block, and lose in the process thirty per cent of our carrier vehicles, we could overkill both China and Russia five hundred times. If we attacked the Soviet Union alone, and suffered fifty per cent loss of delivery weapons, we could overkill it twelve hundred and fifty times . . .

It is a worldly expertise which Catholic diehards find unattractive in a priest. After six controversial years in New Orleans, Philip had been transferred to the Josephites' seminary in Newburgh, New York, where he was assigned to teach English. But like all moves aimed to keep the Berrigans out of public view, Philip's term in Newburgh created a greater stir than the poor Josephites could ever have dreamed of.

Newburgh, center of the Orange County Birch Society, a preponderantly Roman Catholic town dominated by small-business people and veterans' groups, was an ideal spot for a Berrigan to get into trouble. Newburgh had made headlines when its city manager, Joseph Mitchell, tried to restrict distribution of welfare funds. Sometime before Philip arrived, Mitchell's efforts had been blocked by the Rockefeller administration, and he had resigned with the announced intention of accepting a post with the John Birch Society. Newburgh was not much improved by Mitchell's departure.

It is hard to know how the Josephites' Newburgh seminary, a sprawling Catholic nightmare of red brick and glacial opulence, could train white men to help the Negro race. Philip had always compensated for his Uncle Toms by starting community centers modeled on the Catholic Worker wherever he was stationed. The social center on Newburgh's South Street, which he founded with great speed in the first month of his stay, offered food and shelter around the clock, used clothes, baby-sitting services, remedial reading. He went on to organize his seminarians with a militancy unheard of in his order, dividing them up ward by ward. They were ordered to visit every poor family in town to survey building violations. The authorities were unnerved: Father Berrigan was keeping some seminarians out all night surveying the wards. But he was the Josephites' most distinguished writer, and fulfilled his teaching duties punctiliously. They let him be until later that winter, when the problems of the Vietnam war began to divide the United States.

On January 4, 1965, President Lyndon B. Johnson warned, in his State of the Union Message, that "In Asia, communism wears a more aggressive face. We see that in Vietnam . . . Our own security is tied to the peace of Asia . . . To ignore aggression would only increase the danger of a large war."

On February 8, President Johnson ordered "retaliatory strikes" on North Vietnamese targets, and soon thereafter the round-the-clock bombardment of North Vietnam began.

A few days later, the first statement against the Vietnam war, a "declaration of conscience" pledging total non-cooperation with the government's Vietnam policy, was made public to the press. Daniel and Philip Berrigan were the only Catholic priests in the United States to sign it. They were in a company of hundreds, which included Bayard Rustin, Martin Luther King, Lewis

Mumford, Linus Pauling, Benjamin Spock. Within the following fortnight, the Berrigans attended the first major public demonstrations against the war. At an anti-war rally at New York's Community Church, Daniel joined David Dellinger, A. J. Muste, and Kay Boyle on the speakers' rostrum. His indictment of the United States' Vietnam policy had a Papal absoluteness about it: "To wage war in modern times as war is being waged in Vietnam is forbidden . . . in such war, man stands outside the blessing of God. He stands, in fact, under his curse." A week later, Philip Berrigan was prominently protesting the war at a sidewalk vigil on Times Square. The magazine *Commonweal*, in its editorial of March 5, remarked that the Berrigans were the first Catholic priests in the United States to publicly criticize their government's policy in Asia. It praised their courage, and predicted "plenty of fall-out."

Philip, always joyous in a controversy, commuted to the New York City protests from Newburgh, where he nursed a month-old peace group called the Emergency Citizens' Group Concerned About Vietnam. "I've formed a great peace clan here," he wrote to Jim Forest in March, "meeting every Sunday night, knowledgeable and gung-ho . . ." And blithely, two weeks later: "Just got a corker of a letter from the Superior, who threatened to move me if I would not curtail my activities in peace . . . I wrote him a corker of a letter back to explain my position. God's love and strength—please pray for an overinstitutionalized cleric."

And he stormed around the New York area, whenever he had a moment off from his teaching duties, to lecture against the war. His diatribes were, as usual, powerfully documented. Very few priests in the United States, in 1965, knew the chronology of the Vietnam conflict as well as Philip Berrigan:

Let this be said about the moral untenability of our position there. The only international agreement which could possibly justify our action in Southeast Asia was the Geneva Conference of 1954. Yet, in opposition to the wishes of Secretary Dulles, the Conference called for a United Vietnam in two years by national plebiscite; we refused to sign it, but promised to honor its terms. In seven months, we had broken our word, and had begun to organize and train the South Vietnamese Army. By 1956, we had again broken our word by refusing to hold the Geneva-ordered elections. Ho Chi Minh, with a patience that goes largely uncredited, waited until 1958 before calling for guerrilla action in the South, and from that time on our position has grown increasingly disastrous.

Philip frequently laced his lectures with bold criticism of his Church's silence on the Vietnam war:

The Christian Church has been one of the staunchest allies of nationalism and the natural armor of weaponry and militarism that nationalism demands; of the imperception and witch-hunting relative to communism; of the trivia and baubles of American bourgeois living . . . The American Church, in regard to Vietnam, has already reached the measure of default of the German Church under Hitler and a position far less defensible, since in speaking of the immorality of Hitler's aggressive wars the German Church had to confront a totalitarian regime, and we do not . . .

That was, and still is, a hard pill for most Americans to swallow, not to speak of the average Newburgh Catholic. And the predicted fall-out began.

In Newburgh on March 29, at the Catholic College of Mount Saint Mary, Philip's peace group sponsored a public discussion at which a panel of economists and historians from nearby universities denounced the Vietnam war. The community's reaction was violent. The speakers were shouted down by a group of vigilantes, and the meeting turned into a shambles. The Newburgh *Evening News* described the forum as "the long application of propaganda advanced by the Kremlin." Philip sent the clipping to Jim Forest with these comments: "This editorial from the local rag gives you an idea of the climate we're confronting here. The hate calls and the letters have been appalling. The rector was aroused at 2 a.m. the other morning by a poor sick guy who was wondering if I was the man who raped and killed a widow recently in New York. The rector has been magnificent throughout."

Not satisfied with complaining to Philip's rector, the citizens of Newburgh had also been directing their complaints to the Superior of the Josephite Order. In the first days of April, Philip was called to Baltimore to see his Superior. He was ordered to resign as chairman of his peace group, and to stop speaking about the Vietnam war. He complied—for about four days.

Philip Berrigan is obsessed and obstinate, a man impervious to any sanctions. Less than a week after being reprimanded by his Superior, he went to lecture at the Newburgh Community Affairs Council, a date he had made several months previously. The Council had asked him to lecture on civil rights, a traditional theme for Josephites. But in the middle of the talk Philip chose to launch again into a jeremiad against the Vietnam war, analyzing it as an evil inextricably related to the race problem.

> *Do you honestly expect that we could so abuse our black citizens for three hundred and forty years, so resist their moral and democratic rights, so mistreat, exploit, starve, terrorize, rape and murder them without all this showing itself in our foreign policy? Is it possible for us*

to be vicious, brutal, immoral, and violent at home and be fair, judicious, beneficent and idealistic abroad?

The association between the black problem and the Vietnam war, between American violence at home and abroad, drew great criticism the following year when Martin Luther King expounded it. A year earlier, in Newburgh, as stated by Philip Berrigan, it was a bombshell. The local paper reacted the very same day with an editorial entitled "Civil Rights and the Reds." It accused Philip Berrigan of alienating "those good and loyal Americans who dearly want to help the Negro, but who are reluctant to put themselves beside individuals actively serving communist objectives." During the next three days, the rector was swamped by phone calls. The calls threatened that unless Father Berrigan was immediately removed, the parents of each seminarian would receive a letter stating that their English instructor was a Communist.

The rector admitted that his college could not afford such animosity from the public. Two weeks after Philip had dared to associate American violence at home with American violence abroad, his removal was made public. He was to be transferred to Baltimore.

FR. PHILIP BERRIGAN OUSTED, SILENCED was the front page headline, that week, of the *National Catholic Reporter*. The ouster enraged every Catholic liberal in the country except Philip. To him, it was another glorious confrontation. He seemed overjoyed that the issue of the Vietnam war was finally being given public airing in the Church. "Don't worry about this," he wrote to Jim Forest the day after his transfer had been made public. "We have many things working for us. People have been magnificent and they are rallying to issues with uncommon vim and vigor. I feel that God will be very powerful in the lists.

Fraternally in our Lord, may Christ make us a leaven worthy of Him. In His Body—Phil, S.S.J." And he left Newburgh more confident and at peace than he'd been all his life.

He was, indeed, anything but alone. Hundreds of letters arrived praising his outspokenness on the Vietnam war. One of them was from Father Richard McSorley, S.J., professor of theology at Georgetown University, mentor and confessor of the Kennedy family, one of the most influential Jesuits in the United States. "I respect you, I salute you," wrote Father McSorley, "I thank God for the example you have given me by letting the light of your faith shine brightly before men . . . the light that comes from your faith encourages me to believe that the Church is not dead."

With Philip's first Vietnam confrontation, the Berrigans became the high priests of the Catholic peace movement, the commandoes of the new Guerrilla Christianity which, two years later, would invade the draft boards of Baltimore and Cantonsville. The Berrigans' belligerence, and the actions of the Catonsville Nine, are a strictly Catholic phenomenon. They are not only a protest against the Vietnam war; they are also a defiance of the heavy-handed authoritarianism, the blind nationalism that makes the American Catholic community the most war-mongering segment of the nation. Goaded by the silence of his Church's hierarchy and of its hawkish flocks, the Catholic radical can become a desperado.

"What do you think of our policy in Vietnam?" a reporter asked Cardinal Spellman during his trip to Saigon in 1965. "Right or wrong, my country," the Cardinal staunchly answered. Catholics have always tended to give to the commands of the state a sacred and unchallengeable character. Spellman's flag-waving was a holdover from the extremely ancient idea that the power of the state is God-given, a notion which the Reformation, in theory, tried to dispel. It has even deeper theological roots. The Catholic dogma that bishops speak with the voice of God, a distinction not offered to the Presbyterian or the Methodist hierarchy, has an intimidating effect upon independent political pronouncements. ("If I thought that God was likely to offer his views on the Vietnam war through me," says Lutheran Pastor Richard Neuhaus, one of the most militant peace organizers in the United States, "I too would be reluctant to speak.")

There are other causes. The moral absolutism of the Catholic Church tends to satanize Communism more readily than other religious traditions, and the American Catholic community has been steeped in a visceral fear of monolithic Communism, of which Joseph McCarthy was but an average exponent. It had as its spiritual leader, for three decades, a cardinal who was a patron of Diem, an architect of our intervention in Vietnam, and an enthusiastic supporter of the domino theory. There is also an immigrant nervousness in the American Church not evident in other countries. The Irish, Italian, and Polish who compose its rank and file resort to a simplistic flag-waving patriotism in their yearning for acceptance and quick assimilation. Finally, the enormous vested interests of the American Church makes it scandalously timid about dissenting from any aspect of government policy.

The Catholic pacifist, therefore, found himself infinitely more embattled and more controversial than the Protestant pacifist when the Vietnam protest began. The Protestant's hierarchy is more secularized and better geared to social action; his churches have smaller fortunes to protect; his religion is more steeped in a tradition of dissent against secular power. Among Northern Baptists, Unitarians, Presbyterians, and United Church of Christ members, there is nothing outrageous about being anti-militaristic or supporting conscientious objectors. The pacifists A. J. Muste and Norman Thomas remained in fairly good standing with their churches during their terms as Protestant ministers. Whereas the Catholic Peace Fellowship, when it was founded in 1964 by the Berrigans and James Forest as a Catholic offshoot of A. J. Muste's Fellowship of Reconciliation, was immediately attacked by a Catholic member of the Birchite press as being "subversive" and "red."

As the Vietnam issue began to polarize the nation, the Catholic Church remained either hawkish, or silent, on all its levels. A Gallup Poll taken at the beginning of 1966 showed that Catholic support of Johnson's Vietnam policy had a substantial lead over Protestant and Jewish support: fifty-four per cent of Catholics polled approved of it, as against forty-one per cent of Jews, and thirty-nine per cent of Protestants. When the Vietnam protest spread to the grass roots, the Jewish or Protestant clergymen chairing chapters of peace groups tended to be distinguished leaders of their religious communities. The Roman Catholic pastor was conspicuously absent. The Catholic priest participating in any local peace group was apt to be the fourth curate of Saint-Serapio-in-the-Slums, an embattled man radicalized by ghetto work and transferred to an obscure post for having sermoned on civil rights in the mid-sixties, before it was fashionable to attack racism from the pulpit.

The Catholic hierarchy has been even less committed. In 1967, when the moderate movement called "Negotiation Now" sent its petition to every religious leader in the country, the ratio of Episcopal and Methodist bishops to Roman Catholic bishops who signed it was about thirty to one. It was signed by only four Catholic dignitaries: the archbishops of Atlanta and of Oklahoma City–Tulsa, the auxiliary bishops of Saint Paul and of Newark. "The Pope is still fornicating with the Emperor," Dante wrote in his *Paradiso* seven hundred years ago. In the case of Vietnam, it would be fairer to accuse the American bishops, rather than the Pope, of illicit relations. Pope Paul started speaking out against our Vietnam intervention in 1965. The American bishops, notorious for their high level of materialism and their low level of theological finesse, did not take heed. This blind nationalism seems all the more ironic in a church which so venerates its martyrs—men who, without exception, placed the law of conscience above the laws of governments—and in a church which still heaps such high praise on its doctrine of the Just War.

The Just War theory is a long-rooted marriage of convenience between the pure pacifism of the Gospels and the demands of the secular state which emerged after the fourth century, when Christianity became the official religion of the war-loving Roman Empire. It crystallized from its original formulation by Saint Augustine into a doctrine that the Church still finds valid today. The theory specifies that a war can be considered just only if it meets all of the following conditions: (1) that it be declared by legitimate authority; (2) that it be a defensive war waged against an unjust aggressor; (3) that all peaceful remedies have been exhausted before resorting to war; (4) that the lives of innocents and non-combatants are protected; (5) that it follow the "principle of proportionality," a scholastic aphorism meaning that the war's methods are no more oppressive than the evils being remedied.

This doctrine has fallen into great disfavor in past decades because a nuclear war would make it patently impossible to discriminate between combatants and non-combatants and would totally negate the "principle of proportionality." However, the Just War theory is still pragmatically resuscitated, even by such sophisticated pacifists as the Berrigans, to jolt a conventional Catholic audience out of its apathy. With the air of pulling a rabbit out of a hat ("Look, it's still alive!"), the Berrigans have been heard to launch into a careful analysis of why the Vietnam war does not fulfill one condition of a beloved Catholic doctrine. It is a tactic which Philip often resorted to, in battering fashion:

> *Our support of the Saigon government, which is, in reality, no government; our indiscriminate attacks with bombs and napalm against innocent peasants in the hope of killing a few Vietcong; our bombing of industry and transportation in a nation against whom we have no cause for grievance, and against whom we have not declared war; our testing of inhumane weapons and the increasing troop commitment to a combat role; the whole rising ride of savagery and ruin which we have provoked and which we now sustain—these not only contradict the Gospel and make fidelity to it a mockery, they also reject, out of hand, the theory of the Just War . . .*

The Catholic Church can be compared to a zoo of wild beasts, held in captivity for over a millennium, whose bars Pope John removed. There are as many new pacifists among the rampaging animals as there are liturgical innovators and structural reformists. Before the Second Vatican Council, Catholic pacifists were a rare species. They have proliferated since the Council ended in 1965. Pope John's encyclical *Pacem in Terris* issued a clear call for total pacifism in a nuclear age. An important Council edict, "The Constitution of the Church in the Modern World," called for clearer government recognition of the rights of conscientious objectors. And by 1967, Jim Forest estimates that he was counseling some two hundred Catholic C.O.'s a month at the Catholic Peace Fellowship. But by that time, a schizophrenia had set into the American Catholic Church concerning the Vietnam war. The Pope had condemned it. Progressive theologians such as Notre Dame scripture scholar John McKenzie, Boston College Law School Dean Robert Drinan, and the Berrigans, as well as the progressive Catholic press—*Commonweal, Jubilee, Ave Maria,* the *Critic,* the *National Catholic Reporter*—had called it the most immoral war in our history. The lines were drawn: the pleading Pope versus the timid, property-loving American bishops; the lonely young curates radicalized by ghetto work versus their cautious, Bingo-mad pastors; the Catholic intellectuals versus the warmongering law-and-order Catholic masses; *Commonweal* versus the Brooklyn *Tablet;* the guerrillas versus the gorillas. It was getting to be, as Daniel Berrigan said, "some beautiful polarization."

Daniel Berrigan, Typical Jesuit

Within two years after his return to New York from France, Daniel Berrigan had become one of the most controversial and idolized Jesuits of his generation. The Society's *enfant terrible* was so feared by its older members, and so loved by its younger ones, that the middle-of-the-roaders were forced to tolerate him for the sake of their order. As one of them said, "If we ever got rid of Dan it would mean bye-bye Jack to a thousand seminarians. We could never afford it."

When Daniel returned to New York from his second trip to France he had begun a three-year term as associate editor of *Jesuit Missions,* a politely liberal monthly publication which had invited him to join its staff. The Jesuit Missions House where he lived was an elegant brownstone on East 78th Street which had once belonged to Emily Post. He received innumerable invitations to lecture on theology and on pacifism at universities, convents, and literary clubs. He was writing reams of poetry and essays, and had published four books since winning the Lamont Poetry Award in 1957. He participated in civil rights teach-ins and sit-ins, which soon became *de rigueur* for liberal clergymen. His popularity was unnerving to some of his old friends: "You can't ever be alone with Dan anymore. Wherever he goes there's this crowd of kids swarming around him."

Like all glamorous Jesuits, it was inevitable that Daniel would mingle with the powerful. He was invited to give the Benediction at the opening session of the United Nations' General Assembly. He fraternized with the Kennedys, whom he considered "excellent world servants." He celebrated liturgies in Sargent Shriver's living room which participants described as "fit to knock out your right eye." But there soon became something respectable about Daniel's unconventional style, his breezy manner, the informal garb—turtleneck, beret, ski jacket—which he had adopted during his last stay in France. And there is nothing that distresses a Berrigan more than the sense that he is becoming respectable.

So Daniel compensated for his growing popularity with spurts of whimsy unnerving to his order. He pasted a poster-size photograph of his friend Sister Mary Corita on the walls of his shower. It was a happy picture, showing Corita laughing heartily, and on her shoulder Daniel had pinned a button, bought in an East Village psychedelic shop, which said, SAVE WATER, SHOWER WITH A FRIEND. He also talked disconcertingly about the possibility of adopting a child. It was part of his agitation against compulsory celibacy. He loved children, he said, he had always wanted a son, why should he be robbed of a joy which priests would have ten years from now? He delighted in expounding on all the embarrassments which such an adoption would cause to the Church. Could they look it up in Canon Law? Were there any precedents? What would Spellman's Chancery say?

Another Berriganism which unnerved the 78th Street Mission House was Daniel's love for spontaneous, artistic liturgies. He had grown increasingly impatient with traditional parish services during his last stay in Europe. And when he returned to New York he shared a weekly liturgy with Jim Forest, who had become a close friend. The two men would meet at lunch time, in Daniel's room at Jesuit Missions, to discuss the running of their newly founded Catholic Peace Fellowship. After a brief business session Daniel would reach into his desk drawer, where he always kept a loaf of bread and a few bottles of wine, and arrange his drawing board into a little altar. Jim read the Epistle, Daniel read the Gospel, and they would talk at length about the implications of that day's Scriptures. Then Daniel improvised a Canon, which usually included long stretches of his favorite writers—Auden, Péguy, Pablo Neruda. And after a poetic consecration the two men shared Communion. Although neither Daniel nor Jim Forest ever resolved who the informer was, authorities grew very edgy about these services, and after a few months Daniel lowered his window shades in the middle of the day to thwart the spies.

One day Jim Forest walked in to find Daniel very despondent. A superior had scolded him harshly about their liturgies, Daniel said, and like each of his Society's chastisements, it had hurt him deeply. He would, today, change the format of their Eucharist . . . Daniel reached into his drawer, as usual, for the bread and wine. Forest read the Epistle, Daniel read the Gospel, they had their dialogue homily. And then Daniel made it understood to Jim that the rest of the service would consist of total silence. Daniel stood in front of his desk, holding the plate of bread in his hand in the traditional gesture of consecration, staring into space with his serene, ingenuous gaze. After twenty minutes of absolute silence, Daniel turned to Jim and said, with his most pixyish smile: "Let the Lord make of this what He will!" He broke the bread, and shared it with his friend.

The fall-out continued to descend upon Father Berrigan's poetic liturgies. Father Patrick Cotter, his immediate superior at Jesuit Missions, a bearish, kindly man who had been a loyal friend since LeMoyne days, kept urging him to cool it. "Cool it on the liturgy, cool it on the civil rights, cool it on peace, cool it man," Father Cotter moaned every week. And Daniel cooled it on the liturgy, because more important issues were arising in the year 1965. "If I am to be removed some day from the New York scene," he wrote to a friend that summer, "it should be on a real issue, something having to do with the man in the ditch, rather than on the issue of liturgy." The men in the ditch were being killed at an increasing rate in Vietnam during that year, and Daniel was soon speaking out so loudly against the war that his liturgies were all but forgotten.

On October 15, 1965, David Miller, aged 22, a Catholic Worker and a member of Daniel's spiritual elite at LeMoyne College, became the first American to violate the new federal law against burning draft cards. Like the numerous Catholic war protests that were to follow, the act was done with superb aplomb and a meticulous sense of public relations. Catholic war resisters like to come on respectable, looking like bankers. Miller, a six-foot-two, impeccably clean-cut former football star dressed in a Brooks Brothers business suit, put a Zippo lighter to his draft card in front of 500 war protesters and newsmen gathered at the Whitehall Street Induction Center in New

York. Within a few hours the press had converged on Dorothy Day as she sat on a battered suitcase at the New York pier, waiting for customs clearance. She had just returned from Rome, where she had lobbied and fasted for an endorsement of pacifism in the Vatican Council's Schema on the Church in the Modern World. "Our boys and our priests have been tearing up their draft cards for years," she said in a quiet, bored voice. "I can't imagine why people are so excited about David burning his." Miss Day's aide, Tom Cornell, had indeed burned nine draft cards since 1960 to protest the Selective Service System, once on NBC television, and had frequently expressed chagrin that no one had paid attention. But Cornell's burn-ins had not been illegal; the destruction of draft cards had become a federal offense only the previous August, some eight weeks before Miller's performance, when Congress passed a law specifically outlawing the destruction of Selective Service cards.

David Miller's close friendship with Daniel Berrigan at LeMoyne, and his close association with Philip Berrigan's civil rights work in the deep South, did not evade the press or the church authorities. Although Daniel had warned all his young disciples of the consequences of burning their draft cards, the Berrigans' names were immediately linked with Miller's protest. Later that week, Philip Berrigan nimbly poured fat on the fire in an interview with the Baltimore *Evening Sun*:

Q. Do you feel David Miller was disloyal when he burned his draft card?

A. On the contrary, I think this was the highest expression of loyalty. I believe this was an attempt on his part to illustrate the urgency of the situation and his own per-sonal refusal to collaborate with government policy.

His action expressed that at a certain point the Christian has to say "NO" to something so foreign to his own beliefs.

Q. Do you believe that the draft card burnings, teach-in's etc. are setting an unfavorable pattern of civil disobedience, albeit nonviolent?

A. No. We as a people came from a revolutionary heritage. Dissent is a cherished part of the democratic process, and today as alternatives to that process arise dissent becomes even more important.

Q. Father, have you participated in peace demonstrations and do you feel your position as a Roman Catholic priest in any way compromises this involvement?

A. I have participated in demonstrations. It would seem to me that in the present order of things the clerical voice is absolutely essential to promote the democratic process and to give guidance to those whose consciences are searching along those lines.

("How do you like *this* one?" Philip wrote to Jim Forest in a note accompanying the Baltimore *Sun* clipping. "I pulled it off right under the Superior's nose. The poor man merely phoned in fear and trembling.")

The "clerical voice" began to shout even more vigorously a few weeks later, at the founding of a new anti-war group called "Clergy Concerned About Vietnam." The co-chairmen of the new organization were Reverend Richard Neuhaus, a young Lutheran pastor from Brooklyn; Rabbi Abraham Heschel, the most prominent theologian of Conservative Judaism; and Daniel Berrigan. The national committee of "Clergy Concerned," which later changed its name to "Clergy *and Laymen* Concerned

About Vietnam" and became the largest single peace group in the United States, read like a Who's Who in the American Church: The President of Union Theological Seminary, Dr. John Bennett; the Methodist Bishop of Boston, James Matthews; the Secretary of the World Council of Churches, Eugene Carson Blake; the President of the Unitarian Congregations of America, Dana McLean Greeley; Reinhold Niebuhr, Martin Luther King, Robert McAfee Brown, Harvey Cox, William Sloane Coffin, Jr., and countless other clerics, bishops and theologians who were not only concerned, but very angry, about the Vietnam war. Clergy and Laymen began to program rallies, vigils, pickets, fasts, demonstrations in the nation's capital. The group's clerical composition made many Americans uneasy. From the time of the French Revolution the Church had lived in political exile, doling out medicine for the metaphysical blues and for individual salvation. What were all those clerics doing in front of the White House? Clergy Concerned was proposing the startling notion that the issue of war and peace was a valid concern of all churches. The United States has the highest rate of churchgoing citizens in the world; and it was unnerving, for the officials of this most clerical of nations, to be suddenly confronted with these distinguished churchmen protesting the illegality and the immorality of the Vietnam war. It was equally unnerving for Cardinal Spellman's Chancery to see the Jesuits' golden boy be their cheer leader. Catholic participation in the group was conspicuously small. The New York Archdiocese was the least auspicious place for a priestly dove. Following closely upon Miller's draftcard burning, Daniel's leadership of Clergy and Laymen was the second step that led to a new Berrigan confrontation.

There was a third step, a tragic one. On November 9th, a young Catholic Worker, Roger LaPorte, whom Daniel had met once in the company of Dorothy Day, doused himself with gasoline and immolated himself on the steps of the United Nations in protest against the Vietnam war. The Catholic Worker asked Daniel to deliver the sermon at a memorial service for Roger La-Porte. In order, as he said later, "to assuage the emotions of his very grieved friends," Daniel did not censure the youth's suicide. He ended his funeral sermon with the sentence "His death was offered so that others may live." Daniel's refusal to publicly decry LaPorte's immolation electrified the Chancery. Cardinal Spellman and much of his staff had been in Rome that fall, attending a session of the Second Vatican Council. When Spellman's second in command, Bishop John Maguire, flew back to New York in the third week of November, he is said to have returned for the express purpose of removing Daniel Berrigan from the United States.

Upon Bishop Maguire's return, intricate diplomatic negotiations opened between Chancery authorities and the superiors of the Jesuit order. The result was that on the night of November 16, a pale, shaken Father Cotter walked into Daniel's room at the Jesuit Missions House. And the following conversation, or something very similar to it, took place:

"The fat's in the fire," Father Cotter said.

"I haven't got much fat, and where's the fire?" Daniel said.

"You've got to go on a trip," Father Cotter said.

"I don't feel like traveling this winter," Daniel said.

"You have to go on a trip," Father Cotter repeated.

"What if I don't want to?" Daniel asked.

"Be sensible," Father Cotter pleaded. "I've fought for you. It's infinitely better than what they'd originally planned for you."

"What was that?" Daniel asked.

"I can't tell you," Father Cotter said darkly.

"The meat cleaver, huh?" Daniel quipped. He packed his bags, having been given orders to leave for Mexico within the week. A fortnight later, on November 28, Clergy Concerned About Vietnam held its first public meeting at New York's Christ Methodist Church. Some four hundred clerics present passed a resolution that "the conflict in Vietnam, according to our religious convictions, is not a just war." An empty chair stood on the platform, alongside that of Pastor Neuhaus's and Rabbi Heschel's, to mark Daniel Berrigan's absence. Philip Berrigan gave a ringing speech in his brother's place.

The spookiest thing about Daniel's exile, to Catholic observers, was the Jesuits' uncanny *esprit de corps*. The Church's shock troops immediately closed ranks around their man, phalanx-like, and refused to admit that Daniel was in any kind of trouble. His trip, the Society said, was "just a routine reporting assignment"; Father Berrigan's great literary gifts were being used to report on Latin America for *Jesuit Missions* magazine. The Chancery's interference was denied in the face of massive evidence: Bishop Maguire had flown home from Rome two days before Daniel's ouster became public; two other young Jesuits, Fathers Francis Keating and Daniel Kilfoyle of St. Peter's College in Jersey City, were ordered to take their names off the Clergy Concerned list the same day Daniel was ordered to leave. Yet Father Cotter sat in his office at Jesuit Missions impassively denying that any chancery could ever interfere with any Jesuit's peace activities. "The Jebbies made fifty lies a day to hide the facts," complained an exasperated reporter; "in any other order the boys would have leaked the news out." It is typical of the Jesuits, in their moments of crisis, to close ranks in military fashion and to save face for their Society—to defend it, if need be, against the rest of the Church.

The progressives launched a vast counterattack. On December 4, two weeks after Daniel's departure, fifty Fordham students picketed Cardinal Spellman's residence on Madison Avenue, demanding that the Chancery either define or deny its censure of the three Jesuits. "Saint Paul Was A Rebel Too," their pickets read; "End Power Politics In The Church"; "Exile And Constraint Are The Tools Of Totalitarianism"; "Merry Christmas Dan Berrigan Whereever You Are." In mid-December, a new group called the "Committee for Daniel Berrigan" took a full-page ad in the New York Times protesting its hero's exile and demanding his return. It was signed by some ten thousand priests, nuns, seminarians, and Catholic laymen. Facts began to seep through the Society's cool façade. The *National Catholic Reporter* printed an interview with a Jesuit who admitted that "Our provincial would have let Dan go on the peace issue, but Spellman wanted him out of the country . . ." The liberal wing of the Catholic press blew up. *Commonweal* called Daniel's exile "a shame and a scandal, a disgustingly blind totalitarian act, a travesty on Vatican II." Meanwhile Daniel sat in the sunshine of Cuernavaca, desperately missing his friends and the crescendo of the peace movement, writing home in that blithe tone with which he often shields his deepest griefs:

"I am going along from day to day here, marvelling at the strange ways of providence . . . what other moves are on the horizon? How are things leveling with Clergy Concerned? Are people in good spirits? Has anyone been arrested? Has Merton written? Someone wrote from Boston shortly before my demise that a group should start a fast in a Church, with prayers and talks for intermission. What do you think? I could fast here too! Mucho love to all . . ."

He had darker moods. "A strange levitated time," he wrote at Christmas to his family, "deprived of the faces of those I love, of their voices, of evening gatherings, of the Eucharist shared with those I love . . . the important thing is not that injustice has happened to me, but that injustice is still possible, an exile of this kind, the defeat of good works, the silencing of truth . . ." Old Tom Berrigan tried to cheer up his son. "Dear boy," he wrote, "I slept on thoughts of you and the true dimensions of your Greatness."

It is said that Jesuits always travel in pairs, to keep a watch on each other's actions. Two weeks after Daniel's arrival in Mexico, the Society sent a companion to join him in Cuernavaca. Father Alden Stevenson, who had distinguished himself as a photographer and Asian scholar, was assigned to accompany Daniel through ten Latin American countries. They flew around at a hectic pace, Daniel writing bitter essays on South American poverty, Father Stevenson taking bitter photographs. They met with young Peace Corps workers, Young Christian Workers, progressive bishops, militant members of Latin America's new worker-priest movement. Whatever exile is imposed upon the Berrigans to keep them out of public sight —Newburgh, Baltimore, Paris, Brazil—radicalizes them still further. Daniel, obsessed by poverty since his childhood, was more revolutionized by two months of Latin America than he could have been by ten years of the peace movement. "The scandal of this incessant misery of millions perpetuated by American investments which are to the tune of billions, the scandal of our missionary policy, which supports a reactionary church standing in the way of human progress . . ." News of the death of Camillo Torres, the Colombian guerrilla priest, reached them in Brazil. Could justice come to Latin America without guerrilla warfare and revolution? This was a frequent theme of conversation between Daniel and Father Stevenson, who soon began to look at the problems of racism, poverty and war through Daniel's eyes. While further radicalizing their *enfant terrible*, the Jesuits acquired a new progressive in the person of Father Stevenson.

They also acquired new radicals on their campuses. Hardly a week had gone by since Daniel's departure without a demonstration on some Jesuit campus. Throughout December and January pickets marched at Marquette, Fordham, Loyola, LeMoyne demanding his return. Several hundred young Jesuits threatened to leave the order if Daniel was not recalled. Although the New York Chancery is said to have asked for his permanent exile, he was allowed to return to the United States a bare ten weeks after he had left because of the sheer pressure of public opinion. Through a feat of top-level diplomacy, the Society was able to send for him in mid-February. He stayed in Latin America for an extra three weeks "to finish his writing assignments." He flew back to New York on March 8, his bags bulging, as they always do when he returns from trips, with souvenirs for friends and with a new manuscript of poetry and prose.

The day after his return, Daniel Berrigan held a news conference at the Biltmore Hotel, surrounded by a triumphant platoon of priests and seminarians, and announced that he planned to resume his peace activities more militantly than ever. Father Cotter was at his side, repeating that Father Berrigan had just returned from a most successful routine reporting assignment; that he had never, never been silenced for his protests against the Vietnam war; that he was free to resume them immediately.

"The reason you get into such hot water," a Jesuit once told Daniel Berrigan, "is that you're one of the few real Jesuits around."

"I can not abide," Bismarck wrote a century ago, *"these Jesuits' unpatriotic international spirit, their abjuration of all national bonds."*

"I do not like the reappearance of the Jesuits," ex-President John Adams wrote to Thomas Jefferson in 1816. *"Shall we not have regular swarms of them here, in as many disguises as only a king of the gypsies can assume, dressed as printers, publishers, writers and schoolmasters? If there was ever a body of men who merited eternal damnation on earth as in hell, it is this Society of Loyola's . . ."*

The Society of Jesus: Founded in 1540 by a controversial Spanish noble who begged in the streets, and demanded military obedience of his men. Charged with the task of securing compliance with the decisions of the Council of Trent. The only order required to make a special vow of obedience to the Pope. Disavowed ascetic medieval disciplines of fasting and scourging to make the body "in health for the service of the Lord." Jesuits attacked by Pascal for their stress on free will, by the Dominicans for their divergences from Thomist doctrine. Feared by some for their tolerance of local customs, their gift for making subtle compromises between contemporary thought and the creeds of the Church. Admired by others for their "receptive, elastic minds," their skill at literature and the sciences, their talent for converting the heathen and educating the young. Teachers of Racine, Corneille, Molière, Descartes, Diderot, Voltaire, Lamartine.

Jesuits, sought and feared for their gift for high diplomacy, quickly became the spiritual directors of kings and princes and suffered the consequences. Banished by Queen Elizabeth for charges of conspiring against the Church of

England; Father Edmund Campion condemned for high treason, hanged and quartered. Expelled from Portugal in 1759. Banned from France in 1762 by the machinations of Madame de Pompadour, whose position was compromised by the Jesuits' refusal to give her the Sacraments. Banished from Spain and the Bourbon States of Naples and Parma in 1767. In 1773, Pope Clement XIV ordered their expulsion from the Papal States and their suppression in every nation of the world: "The light cavalry shall have to be disbanded. . . . It appears quite impossible to maintain a true and lasting peace within the Church as long as this order exists." Jesuits sought refuge for over thirty years in Russia at the invitation of Catherine the Great, the only ruler who would tolerate them.

Jesuits in Asia: Arrived in the sixteenth century, impressed the Manchu rulers with their expertise at cartography, astronomy, painting, and clockmaking. Affected Chinese dress and manners, said Mass in the Chinese vernacular at the great discomfort of the Holy See. Concealed the crucifixion of Jesus Christ from the natives in order to secure as many conversions as possible. Brought back from the East the first translation of the Vedas, the making of Chinese porcelain, the use of the umbrella.

Jesuits in North America: First Catholic Bishop of the United States was Jesuit John Carroll, native of Maryland and friend of Benjamin Franklin. Excelled at converting Indians: Father LeMoyne among the Iroquois. Excelled at exploration: Fathers Marquette, Joliet, Dolbeau, Albanel. "Not a cape was rounded, not a river discovered," wrote George Bancroft in his *History of the United States*, "without a Jesuit's having shown the way." Excelled at martyrdom: Fathers Brébeuf, Lalemant, Bressani and Daniel scalped and burned at the stake. The Society of Jesus was reinstated in North America in 1812 to Jefferson's discomfort.

Jesuits in South America: Established a fully armed and independent communist republic in Paraguay to guard natives from the corruptions of the European settlers. Common ownership of property and equal distribution of wealth lasted in the area for over one hundred years. Jesuits' Paraguayan experiment was vastly popular with Enlightenment philosophers. Voltaire: "A triumph of humanity." Montesquieu: "The Society of Jesus . . . was the first to prove to the world that religion and humanity are compatible." Goethe: "Unlike members of other spiritual orders, who persist in an old, outworn devotion, the Jesuits reinvigorate all things with pomp and splendor in the spirit of the times."

Daniel Berrigan: "I became a Jesuit because they had a revolutionary history. I only suspected it at the time; now I am more certain, and more proud."

The Baltimore Draft Party

Philip Berrigan, upon his transfer to Baltimore from Newburgh in the spring of 1965, had again been given strict orders to remain silent on the subject of the Vietnam war. He complied for about three months.

He had been assigned to the Church of Saint Peter Claver, a Josephite parish serving some 6,000 black people in the heart of the inner city. He spent his first months in Baltimore trying to rehabilitate the district. He organized the neighborhood into block clubs to petition and picket the landlords, started a community center, founded the inner city's first chapter of Alcoholics Anonymous. He enlisted young black men to draw up weekly reports on the delinquency, drug addiction and alcoholic cases in their precincts. The Berrigan method created tensions within the Society of Saint Joseph. Philip had growing reservations about the extent to which his order, or any whites, could help blacks in the era of Black Power. He was militant on the subject of the blacks handling their own problems. Any pacification seemed to him "a white liberal hand-out" which obscured the tragic reality of racism, and which must be stopped. He particularly criticized his order's practice of handing out food to the blacks and to the National Guard during riots. "I suppose you just want us to feed the blacks?" a fellow Josephite once asked. "You're wrong," Philip answered. "I particularly don't want you to feed the blacks. You can keep right on feeding the Guardsmen, but I want the blacks to know what's keeping them hungry."

The traditional parish Mass was a center of Philip's life, his way of reaching the black people. Unlike Daniel, Philip was never interested in reforming liturgy. "If liturgical renewal doesn't change people's hearts about war and racism, to hell with it." And it was a source of deep frustration to Philip, during his Baltimore ministry, that he could not reach black men on the subject of the Vietnam war. He hammered away, in his sermons, on the theme that it was a rich man's war; that blacks were being sent on higher-risk missions than the whites to fight other colored people; that black casualties were out of proportion to white casualties. The women were easily persuaded, as women are, but the men were difficult to convince. "Phil baby, I know what you mean," a young black militant said to him after a sermon, "but I can't bother, I don't know where the next meal is coming from." The reluctance of Philip's black friends to join the peace movement, and their militant impatience with their own plight, played a role in radicalizing his means of protest.

"Given the critical nature of the world," Philip wrote to a friend a few months after he arrived in Baltimore, "I feel less and less obligated to help the institution continue its navel-gazing. I feel in conscience that I can not remain quiet." And in the fall of 1965 Philip organized a new anti-war group, with a number of Protestant and Catholic clergy and laymen who had been active in SANE, CORE and other civil rights and pacifist organizations. Philip's cadre, which met in the basement of his church, was called the Baltimore Interfaith Peace Mission. It grew to become one of the most militant peace organizations in the country. It ultimately earned Baltimore a new name: "The Christian Guerrilla Capital of the United States."

The Baltimore peace group spent its first year, as was the fashion in 1966, thrusting its views upon various congressmen. Philip met with Senators Brewster and Tydings of Maryland in their Washington offices. He debated Maryland Representative Clarence Long at Johns Hopkins University; with the help of Congressman John Dow of New York's Rockland County, one of the most outspoken doves in Congress, he tried to appear before the Senate Foreign Relations Committee with a group of anti-war clergymen to discuss the morality of the Vietnam policy. Senator Fulbright promised a meeting after the senatorial elections, but he never came through with his pledge. And the Baltimore peace group decided to make its protest more visible.

On December 29, 1966, twenty of the Baltimore war protesters, most of them clergymen, drove to Washington to picket the homes of Secretaries Rusk and McNamara. The requests painted on their placards followed on U Thant's recent pleas: "Stop the bombing to make negotiations possible"; "Include the NLF in negotiations"; "Reconvene the Geneva Conference." The Baltimore *Sun* carried their photograph on its front page: twenty respectable, middle-aged men in white collars standing in the snow in the Secretary of State's driveway; in the doorway of the house, two of the Rusk children staring uncomfortably at the group. After an hour, the pickets moved on to Mc-Namara's home, and knelt in silent prayer on his snowy lawn. The protest did not go unnoticed. Dean Rusk phoned Saint Peter Claver's the next morning and invited Philip to meet with him the following day to explain his views. Philip brought along two members of his peace group. The interview lasted almost two hours. Philip's friends were jubilant over the fact that they had been given an audience, but Philip, always wary, was not impressed. He complained that "that guy couldn't once look at me straight in the eye." He fulminated over one particular phrase of Rusk's: "I leave all morality up to you clergymen." And a few weeks later the Baltimorians escalated their protest with a series of increasingly tumultuous demonstrations at Fort Myer, Virginia.

The first invasion, fifty strong, was led by Philip Berrigan and Father McSorley. The group parked by the gates of Fort Myer and picketed the homes of the Chiefs of Staff. They had drafted a letter protesting the United States' support of an undemocratic South Vietnamese government. A marshal came out and Father McSorley stepped forward with Philip to hand him the letter. The marshal, made nervous by this first clerical invasion of his grounds, stammered terribly as he ordered the demonstrators to disband. "What if we don't?" Philip asked. "You'll be sorry," the Provost muttered. Philip was elated by the threat. His second raid in Washington, a few weeks later, was more dramatic. The police had been alerted by a CBS newsman and guards were stationed at the entrance of Fort Myer, checking all out-of-state cars. One of the protesters' cars, driven by an agile young Jesuit, flew past the guards. Philip, known for his speedy, cabby-like driving, whizzed through a gate of Arlington Cemetery. The protesters met at the parade grounds and knelt in prayer around the flagpole on the lawn facing the Chiefs of Staffs' homes. The marshal was less gentle this time. "The next time you return," he yelled at Philip, "you'll get three years!" It was a short demonstration. Philip had made his point. A man sitting in Philip's car said that "he looked illuminated, like Moses receiving the commandments," when he drove away from Fort Myer that day. Philip turned to his friends and said, with an expressive gesture, "Kids, we've got them by the balls. If they don't arrest us next time, we give a mandate for all peace groups to enter government property. If they jail us, that'll be just the kind of witness I want to offer ..."

It was the first time that Philip had stated, with such directness, his desire to go to jail in protest against the Vietnam war.

The Provost's threat had spread. The third raid on Fort Myer, in June, was limited to twelve men, the militant nucleus of the Baltimore peace group. Eight of them were clerics. Four of them were the men who would bring the war protest into Baltimore's Draft Board the following October: Philip Berrigan; twenty-eight-year-old artist Thomas Lewis, the cherubic and cheerful son of a Nabisco executive, a devout Roman Catholic; poet and teacher David Eberhardt, twenty-six years old, graduate of Oberlin College, the agnostic son of a Presbyterian clergyman; and James Mengel, thirty-eight, former army chaplain in Korea, a frail and pixyish minister of the United Church of Christ whose sallies in court gave comic relief to the Baltimore Four's trial the following spring. ("Who told you to pour blood on these files?" "God told me, and that's peanuts compared to what He's going to tell me next.")

This third and last raid took a more violent turn. The

twelve knelt again in prayer around Fort Myer's central flagpole. Reverend Mengel, who carried a Bible on all his forays, began to read passages from the Book of Acts which he found fitting for the occasion: "Peter and the Apostles said: Obedience to God comes before obedience to men. This so infuriated the Sanhedrin that they wanted to put them to death . . ." "Stephen, filled with the Holy Spirit, gazed into heaven and saw the glory of God . . . at this the members of the council sent him out of the city and stoned him."

The Provost Marshal, Lieutenant Colonel Gebhardt, appeared with an intelligence officer loaded down with cameras. "Get *this* son of a bitch," he barked at his officer, pointing at Philip. Philip smiled radiantly, as he does for all photographers. He took great pride in the file which the F.B.I. started on him in Newburgh. The demonstrators ignored the Provost's orders to disband. All veterans of Selma and trained in the tactics of non-violence, they went limp and were carried by M.P.'s into buses which drove them off the Fort Myer grounds. A seminar proceeded to take place on the bus, with the Provost lecturing the group on civil disobedience, the protesters lecturing the Provost on the evils of the Vietnam war, and Philip acting as moderator. "Don't you worry about nuclear war?" one of the clergymen asked. "There are some big bombs around." "Well, nuclear war doesn't bother me at all," the Provost said. "Let the Provost speak," Philip commanded when one of his group got out of hand, "It's his turn, don't interrupt him." "Don't you have feelings about the Vietnam war?" the clergyman persisted. "I don't worry about things I don't understand," Gebhardt said, "I just take orders . . ."

The bus drove the demonstrators to an area near Arlington Cemetery, where their cars had been towed by Army trucks. The peace squad piled into their cars after shaking hands cordially with the Provost. Lieutenant Colonel Gebhardt thought he had settled the matter. But some ten minutes later, led by a forewarned CBS television man on a motorcycle, the protesters' cars screamed again through a gate at Fort Myer and headed for Generals' Row. They ran out, knelt in front of the Generals' homes, and prayed again.

This time the Provost lost his cool. "You son of a bitch!" he screamed at Philip, who was reciting the twenty-third Psalm in a loud, clear voice. The group was carried once more into a bus and driven, this time, to the base's M.P. headquarters. They were told to wait in the bus, and they waited an hour. It was apparent that the marshal was on the phone to the Pentagon, trying to decide what to do with them. It was also evident that the government was not yet ready to confront eight clergymen in court. After an hour Gebhardt, looking dark, returned into the bus. The bus drove out of Fort Myer and the passengers were unceremoniously dumped onto a small triangle of grass outside the Fort. Both M.P.'s and protesters had overlooked the fact that Reverend Mengel had not been dumped with the rest of his party. As the bus drove off Mengel jumped up from a canny hiding spot behind the vehicle's back seat, put his head out of the rear window and lustily sang the first phrases of "We Shall Overcome." A few seconds later, his friends saw a large, rumpled heap thrown out of the bus in front of a gasoline station. The heap did not move. Philip ran up to Mengel to see if he was still alive. Like a jack-in-the-box Mengel jumped up, threw his arms around Philip and bellowed again "We Shall Overcome!" It was the only lighthearted moment of the day. The protesters were sullen and bitter, as they drove home, about their failure to obtain a confrontation in court. Philip fulminated over the fact that he had not had his stay in jail. That night, back in Baltimore, the peace group held an eight-hour meeting—a "gut session," as Philip called them —to decide whether to return to Fort Myer a fourth time, or whether to escalate the war protest in some novel way. They opted for a radical escalation—for a non-violent destruction of government property.

During the next two months, Philip's group met as often as three times a week to define the form of the destruction. The idea of destroying an uninhabited part of the Green Berets' training facilities at Fort Howard, Maryland, was discussed and rejected in favor of destroying draft files. A lawyer in the peace group, whose advice was precious because only he could assess the possible jail sentences, favored escalation but did not approve of any burning. "How about *pouring* something on draft records?" the lawyer suggested at one of the meetings. "Defacing them instead of burning . . . like pouring molasses, ink, paint, blood . . ." The group approved. The idea stuck.

Philip's rage at the war, at the futility of the peace movement, grew to a terrible climax during the summer months of 1967. In August the Baltimore Peace Mission had arranged a long-delayed panel discussion with a local congressman, John Friedell. The congressman had been dogmatic in his backing of the Johnson policy. There was a general consensus among the group that the process of electoral politics was futile in bringing about peace. Philip frequently stayed up until the small hours of the morning to talk out his frustrations. One night the wife of one of his friends was awakened at four a.m. by a violent sound of knocking. She lived on the fringe of the black ghetto, as do many members of the Baltimore Peace Mission, and feared that a riot had started. She came downstairs to find Philip pounding his clenched fists into the walls and the furniture of her living room, with all the power of his enormous body, as he declaimed against the illegality of the Vietnam war.

The liturgical aspects of pouring blood on draft files pleased Philip. It was the form of protest that he decided on, after consulting Daniel and one or two of his closest friends. Daniel, whose ideas had so influenced Philip's life, was often taken aback by the radical conclusions which his younger brother drew them to. Daniel was violently opposed to the idea of burning any property. But he approved the blood-pouring ritual, as did Thomas Merton. Others of Philip's friends, such as Father McSorley, tried in vain to talk him out of it.

"I told Phil that I was not sure to what degree he could be effective in jail," Father McSorley says. "Phil, after all, is one of the four or five most valuable priests in the country. I pleaded with him for hours at a time to use a more Gandhian tactic, to pick out an action which a larger segment of society would appreciate. But then, I am less brave a man than he, and if we have a nuclear war within a few years, which we may have, he's the one who will end up being the prophet of our time . . ."

Such pleas as Father McSorley's had no impact on Philip. The Berrigans, like all revolutionaries and most martyrs, have little faith in the redeeming power of time. Their theology is Apocalyptic. It sees the day of judgment as thrusting itself continually into the present. Like the Old Testament prophets who wrote in moments of historical crisis, the Berrigans feel that purification is immediate and necessary. Like the early Christians on whom they model their vocations, the Berrigans see the Second Coming—either man's perfectibility or his destruction—as imminent in their own lifetimes. It is a view in which there is no time to atone, to reform, to do penance. "Redeem the times," Daniel was to write the night before Catonsville, "the times are inexpressibly evil . . ." Throughout the summer of 1967, the meetings of the Baltimore Peace Mission lasted as long as twelve hours, perfecting the details of a protest that would send four men to jail for several years.

The United States Customs House, an elephantine turn-of-the-century building two blocks away from Patapsco River that houses Baltimore's Selective Service Offices, was chosen as the target. The Customs House is replete with symbols of Federal Authority: the United States Coast Guard, the Federal Communications Commission, the Treasury Department, the Recruiting Office. The Selective Service Office was an easy mark for the protesters' raid: ground floor, plunk in the middle of the building, reached from the street through a foyer and one glass door. An artist's loft straight across from the Customs House, belonging to a member of the peace group, would serve as a site for final briefings. The sortie was scheduled for October 27, six days after the large anti-war demonstration at the Pentagon. Members of the Baltimore Peace Mission attended the Pentagon show halfheartedly, as did both Berrigans. Daniel, who had just started a new job at Cornell University, thought, like Philip, that such mass demonstrations had become establishment, "just another liberal bag."

Nine men had originally volunteered to pour blood on Baltimore's draft records. Five dropped out of the project in the last weeks, pleading family responsibility or pending ordinations into the Church. Of the Baltimore Four, Berrigan and Lewis were celibates; Eberhardt was engaged to be married; Mengel was married, with two children. Philip had a magnetic hold on these three men. During the hectic June demonstration at Fort Myer, Mengel had turned to a fellow protester, an atheist, and said, "I don't see how you can do this without religion." He thought for a moment, and added "Oh well, of course you can do it because of Phil . . . with all the faith I have I couldn't do any of these things without Phil Berrigan."

The details of the action were perfected in the four days which followed the Pentagon march. Philip and Jim Mengel drafted the press statement. Tom Lewis arranged for a doctor to draw a pint of blood from each of the participants the day before the foray. David Eberhardt had been asked to obtain the receptacles from which the blood was to be poured: he settled on four empty plastic bottles of Mr. Clean detergent. The drawing of the blood proved to be the greatest difficulty of the week. The doctor who had volunteered his services changed his mind a few days before the raid. It was against the medical code, and after agonizing over his decision he decided against it. The night before the protest a member of the peace mission who had had some hospital training was asked to draw the blood. The group thought they had all the proper equipment— needles, syringes, gauze, disinfectant, tubing. But when the volunteer started to work the blood was found to be going in much too slowly. The tubing was too narrow and was not offering enough suction power. There was talk about going to the drugstore to buy some wider tubing, but the group felt pressed for time. The volunteer stuck the needle repeatedly into the arms of the four men, getting less than an ounce at each stab. After four or five stabs Jim Mengel fainted. Eberhardt and Lewis went pale and asked the volunteer to stop. There was the lethal possibility, in this dilettante enterprise, of air bubbles entering the men's veins. Much of the human blood used in the protest came from Philip, who was vastly amused by his friends' discomfort. "Stick it into me again!" he kept saying with his booming, good-natured laugh. "Stick it in further!" And after a dozen stabs his friends had to force him to stop. The total amount of blood drawn from the four men only amounted to a single pint, one quarter of the quantity needed. A member of the peace mission rushed to a delicatessen to supplement it with animal blood. A small quantity of duck's blood was added, and supplemented further by a resourceful housewife who squeezed blood from several pounds of calf's liver. The medium of protest was mixed and poured into the Mr. Clean bottles. Everything was ready. Before the group disbanded that night, Philip Berrigan performed the ceremony of marriage between David Eberhardt and his fiancée, Louise Yolton, neither of whom were Roman Catholics.

> *On Friday, October 27th, 1968, we are entering the Customs House in Baltimore, Maryland, to deface the draft records there with our blood. We shed our blood willingly and gratefully in what we hope is a sacrificial and constructive act. We pour it upon these draft files to illustrate that with them and with these offices begins the pitiful waste of American and Vietnamese blood- ten thousand miles away. We implore our countrymen to judge our action against this nation's Judeo-Christian tradition, against the horror in Vietnam and the impending threat of nuclear destruction. We invite our friends in the peace and freedom movements to continue moving with us from dissent to resistance . . . We ask God to be merciful and patient with all men.*

This statement, in a lengthier form, was handed in sealed envelopes to newsmen who had been called to meet at Saint Peter Claver Church on the morning of October 27 to witness "an unusual act of protest against the Vietnam war." The problem of protecting themselves from charges of complicity in the Christian Guerrillas' splendidly publicized raids was growing into a dilemma for the press. It became a jest, in this radical fringe of the peace movement, that reporters were much more nervous at any scene of protest than the participants. Eight tight-lipped and ashen-faced newsmen were taken to the loft on Gay Street across from the Customs House. They were ordered, for their protection, not to open the sealed envelopes until the action was over.

Tom Lewis went alone into the Customs House to check on the guard being off-duty. It was ten past noon, and some of the personnel were out to lunch. He reappeared at the entrance of the Customs House and bent down to tie his shoelace—the go-ahead signal. David Eberhardt and Philip Berrigan, blood-filled bottles in their pockets, joined him at the entrance. The three men crossed the foyer and entered the Selective Service Office. Reverend Mengel followed shortly afterward and hovered at the doorway, a package of Bibles under each arm, planning to feign a heart attack in case a guard appeared. His teammates went to the head clerk, and each gave a different reason for his visit. Philip said that he wanted to consult the draft record of one of his parishioners. Tom Lewis said he had lost his draft card. David Eberhardt said that he had recently changed his address. The clerk rose from her chair and went upstairs to comply with the requests. The three men swiftly advanced to the filing cabinets. By this time members of the peace group had ushered the newsmen into the Selective Service Office, and the cameras began to click and whirr. They focused, as usual, on Philip Berrigan, as he poured his bottle of blood, "quite methodically, back and forth," as one of the clerks described it, on two drawers-full of files. The clerks began to scream. Reverend Mengel started to pass out copies of the New Testament to the assortment of astonished guards, hysterical clerks, and pale newsmen who flooded to the entrance of the Selective Service Office. The Mr. Clean bottles were emptied in some thirty seconds. Berrigan, Lewis and

Eberhardt placed them on top of the filing cabinets and calmly sat down on the benches at the edge of the room to await arrest. By the glass door a newsman, on the verge of fainting, was held up by members of the peace mission. Reverend Mengel offered a New Testament to one of the clerks. "He's one of those bastards!" she screamed.

The offenders sat quietly for half an hour, occasionally attempting to hand out anti-war literature to guards and policemen. The police, who had arrived five minutes after the incident, hovered silently above them. The Customs House is government property and only the F.B.I. could make an arrest. The F.B.I. arrived shortly after the police. They spent a half hour studying the scene before taking the Baltimore Four, as they were henceforth called, to their headquarters a few blocks away. The Four were arraigned on charges of mutilating government property and interfering with the working of the Selective Service System. They were offered freedom in their own recognisance after signing a promissory note. Mengel and Eberhardt signed and were freed, but Berrigan and Lewis refused to be freed at that time. They announced their intention to fast in prison for a week, and were taken to Baltimore City Jail. In the Berrigans' home town of Syracuse, Jerry Berrigan, a burly, impassive man approaching fifty, heard about his brother's arrest on the four-o'clock news, sat down on his living-room couch, and wept for hours.

As of that Friday, October 27, both youngest Berrigan brothers were in jail. The previous weekend Daniel Berrigan had been arrested at the Pentagon march, with a group of his Cornell students and fellow chaplains, when their permits to demonstrate expired. Daniel, like his brother, had declined to post bail and had preferred to go to prison. Like his brother, he had begun a week of total fast in protest against the Vietnam war.

"For the first time," Daniel Berrigan wrote in his diary at the start of his stay in jail, "I put on the prison blue jeans and denim shirt; a clerical attire I highly recommend for a new church . . ."

"This is the day of Phil's action in Baltimore," he wrote on Friday, October 27. "*Oremus pro fratribus in periculo.* 'Give honor to the Lord of Hosts, to Him only. Let Him be your only fear, let Him be your only dread' (Isaiah 8:13)."

Guerrilla Liturgy

Philip Berrigan suffered terrible loneliness during the next few months. His blood-pouring ritual was not only beyond the comprehension of the Catholic community. It was beyond the grasp of most of the peace movement and most of the radicals. It turned people off, as Father McSorley had predicted it would. The blunt theatrical literalness of his protest, its use of the sacrificial medium of both liturgy and war, its destruction of actual government property instead of its symbols, made people cringe. Like all avant-garde aesthetics and politics, the Baltimore protest had savagely attacked middle-class sensibility. Draft card burnings, in comparison, were polite and illusionist acts. Philip's cohort, Tom Lewis, and his brothers Daniel and Jerry gave him most of the comfort he received. Daniel saw the action as a logical continuation of Philip's life, a natural Berriganism. "He was carrying on an old tradition in our family, of making noise, of being congenitally unhappy with phony peace . . . The poor had conferred on him that wisdom which sees and sees through the big talk of little minds . . . he is free, lucid and fearless—a man."

But Daniel suffered even more than Philip. At least Philip's conscience was, as always, rigorously clear. Daniel suffered from the guilt of not sharing his brother's loneliness, of not having taken any risks equivalent to his beloved Phil's. A great many of Daniel's friends at Cornell were taking such risks. Students and young instructors were turning in their draft cards by the dozens. Two of the seventeen clergymen on Daniel's staff at Cornell had been punitively reclassified I-A, had refused induction, and were facing jail terms. Daniel was forty-six, too old to turn in any draft card. His sense of solidarity with the young was broken. It had been central to his vocation. The Berrigans grew arrogant during the winter of 1967–8 and made some of their closest friends very uncomfortable. They criticized any anti-war protest that stopped short of Philip's. "One becomes convinced," Daniel wrote to the hard-working, devoted Jim Forest, after a sermon on the "softness and bureaucracy" of the Catholic Peace Fellowship that created a crisis in their friendship, "that equivalent risk is going to be the only source of community worth talking about; and that the expressive acts such as Phil's, once they are thoughtful and proceed from a sacrificing heart, must be multiplied. You sound as though we were keeping house in normal times. Ha. Give us a bit of anguish, or why talk about hope?"

In the same week, Philip was writing Forest to tell him he wished to resign from his co-chairmanship of the CPF. "I don't support CPF policy, so why say I do on the letterhead? You say that the movement must be orchestrated. Perhaps. But the term reminds me of white liberal jargon, jargon used by people who will still be building their broad base as the Bombs come in . . . I refuse to indict anyone's conscience, but I don't have to cheer their world, which seems to me safe, unimaginative, and devoid of risk and suffering. Both Dan and I have been dealing with clergymen and laymen, professional and family people who have come to the point of civil disobedience and the prospect of jail . . . as Johnson continues his war, we will either witness from jail, or we will go ahead with social disruptions including non-violent attacks against the machinery of this war. In a word, I believe in revolution, and I hope to make a non-violent contribution to it. In my view, we are not going to save this country and mankind without it . . ."

February came, and three thousand Clergy and Laymen Concerned About Vietnam converged on Washington, D.C., for their yearly rally. "We live in a nation which is the greatest purveyor of violence in the world today," said Martin Luther King in one of his last speeches. Father Robert Drinan, dean of the Jesuits' Boston College Law School, thundered about "the pattern of lawlessness adapted by our government." "Fighting Communism, we are the Communists' most formidable allies in that unhappy country," said Rabbi Maurice Eisendrath, president of the Union of American Hebrew Congregations. Every religious leader in the peace movement was there—except Philip and Daniel Berrigan. Clergy and Laymen Concerned had become splendidly establishment. Therefore, for the Berrigans, it had turned into "another liberal bag." As soon as it had become fashionable for progressive clergymen to march, picket, and lecture against the war, the Berrigans had bowed out of the movement which they had pioneered. They had created a new fringe of radical dissent, a new community of risk. Once again, they had refused to be respectable. The arrogance of their commitment estranged many of their friends. "You can't criticize the Berrigans this year. They look down on anyone who hasn't risked as much as they have. They'll barely break bread with you if you haven't burned your draft card. Talk about ghettos! That ghetto of martyrs is the most exclusive club of all."

Philip, during that winter, was also estranged from two

of his fellow martyrs, Jim Mengel and David Eberhardt. He was annoyed by their frequent bouts of self-pity. They complained about the suffering which their pending jail sentences would bring to their families. Philip's reply to them was tough: "You've got another family—mankind." Up to then Philip had championed, like most liberal priests, a reform of the Church's laws on celibacy. The emotional consequences of the Baltimore protest made him change his mind. He suddenly realized that celibacy was an essential tool for revolution. If priests were to take their proper role as non-violent revolutionaries, they had better remain celibates. Acts such as his were still prophetic and unique, to be undertaken by men of great austerity who had nothing to lose, no property or emotions at stake . . . Determined to make a second prophetic act before being jailed for the first, Philip spent the winter in search of such men. He found the nucleus of his new cadre in two Roman Catholics: Tom Lewis, who had emerged from the October event as unscathed and austerely dedicated as Philip; and George Mische, a thirty-two-year-old professional peace organizer who, like Philip and Tom Lewis, was quite devoid of any fear of prison life.

George Mische, burly, quickwitted, voluble, with a blond mustache and a luminous, demonic smile, comes from a background strikingly similar to the Berrigans'. His parents were Minnesota labor organizers dedicated to the cause of the poor and the blacks. He was brought up in a Catholic Worker atmosphere of strict piety and little respect for property. Mische had known the Berrigans since the early 1960's. An honor graduate of parochial school and a Catholic college, he had spent some years working for the Alliance for Progress and for AID (the Association for International Development.) AID had been founded at a progressive Catholic college, Seton Hall, to train laymen for community work in Latin America.

("We wrested money from Latin American governments to rebuild the slums," Mische says, "with the poor themselves calling the shots. None of that American colonialist crap.") A Conrad-type adventurer in reverse gear, Mische belongs to that novel brand of American radicals who dedicate their lives to stopping the United States' intervention in the Third World. The new isolationism! Mische believes in creating such a state of confusion at home that the United States becomes incapable of meddling in the fate of other nations. Ask George Mische what kind of political system he believes in, and he will give you one of his luminous smiles, full of charity and deviousness, and say: "Democracy of course. A multi-party Socialist democracy, with a redistribution of wealth according to Gospel principles. Do you know the Book of Acts? 'They sold their goods and shared out the proceeds among themselves, each according to his need . . .'"

Mische, although he was married, father of one child, had a revolutionary asceticism that had been lacking in the two married members of the Baltimore Four. "I don't believe in the nuclear family. We have plenty of relatives and friends around who can take care of the kids. I don't want my sons identifying with me. The lack of homosexuality in Latin families comes from the fact that the kids identify themselves with a variety of males. The child should belong to the community." Armed with these platonic values, Mische would have been happy if his wife had participated in the next action and shared his jail sentence, which, he boasted, could be as long as fifteen years.

As the winter wore on, Philip and George Mische traveled around the country looking for men to join them in the next assault. They aimed to get more clergymen involved, more draft boards hit. Their ideal would have been to have two or three draft boards raided on the same day or in the same week, in different parts of the nation, to make a strong point of it. It was a difficult recruiting mission. Time was running out for Philip, for his trial had been set for April 1. A hearing had been held for the Baltimore Four in March on a motion for continuance. Their lawyers had argued that the defendants could not be heard by an impartial jury because of the strong feelings generated by the Vietnam war. They had urged the court to delay the trial until after the war was ended. A distinguished group of scholars came to Baltimore to plead with the court to delay the trial: Seymour Melman of Columbia; Howard Zinn of Boston University; Father McSorley of Georgetown; Gordon Zahn of Loyola. But the motion of continuance was dismissed by the judge, and the trial was held on April 1. The four were convicted, as was expected, and freed on bail in their own recognisance. Their sentencing was scheduled for May 27. In the first weeks of April Philip's recruiting mission grew even harder. The peace movement became apathetic after Lyndon Johnson's withdrawal from the presidential race and the prospect of peace talks.

"What in hell can create his kind of mettle," a friend of Philip Berrigan's muttered during his trial, "the mettle of a man who can repeatedly defy the highest authorities in the land?" During the following eight weeks, feeling no strain from the fact that he was facing a maximum sentence of eighteen years in jail, Philip went buoyantly about the task of planning a massive new sortie against the machinery of war.

Philip's mobilization drive picked up when Thomas and Marjorie Melville, Maryknoll missionaries who were expelled from Guatemala for their sympathies with Guatemalan guerrilla fighters, returned to the United States. Mische wrote them immediately. The Melvilles, who had married each other and left their order shortly after their expulsion, were even angrier about United States intervention in Central America than they were about Vietnam. They were naturals for the action. The Melvilles moved in with Mische, who had just rented a house in Washington, D.C.—"an action-directed house of Christian radicals." Other volunteers began to dribble in. Next to join the group were John Hogan, another Maryknoller who had been recalled from Guatemala for his guerrilla sympathies; Mary Moylan, a Baltimore nurse who had spent years as a militant civil rights activist; and David Darst, a remarkably brilliant Christian Brother who was teaching school in Saint Louis's inner city. Darst, a summa cum laude graduate of Saint Mary's College who had just been offered a full scholarship at the Harvard Divinity School, had written to Philip the previous fall expressing admiration for the October protest. They had had a correspondence. Darst seemed so clean-cut, so enthusiastic when he came to Baltimore in April to meet his confrères, that he was suspected of being a plant. But he turned out to be as pure, as dedicated, and as angry as every other member of the party. Philip's new cadre was much more ambitious than the Baltimore Four, who had simply condemned the Vietnam war. The new group also set out to protest racism, militarism, capitalism, imperialism, colonialism, and the apathy of the Catholic Church on all those issues. They were rebellious members of a Church in Reformation, scandalized veterans of ghetto work; they were filled with that mixture of militancy and strident moral absolutism which turns the contemporary Catholic radical into the nation's fiercest security risk.

Participation in the forthcoming raid, to the surprise and delight of the protesters, restricted itself to Catholics. "We were inviting Protestants and Jews all over the place," Mische says, "but it only seemed to attract the Catholics.

A few Episcopal clergymen promised to go along but at the last minute they copped out because of their big hang-ups with their families. But this was healthy because the Catholic community had been the most silent on the war. Jews and Protestants had been the backbone of the religious peace movement on all levels. Since you can't talk to the Catholic bishops, we wanted to force a stand from the Church, we wanted to make it either support or condemn us, but take a stand . . ."

The site of the protest had to be decided upon. The month of May was spent scanning the Baltimore area for the right draft board. The little town of Catonsville, eight miles west of downtown Baltimore, was chosen because it was a sitting duck, and highly symbolic. Catonsville was a lily-white, middle-class suburban town of smug brick houses and pleasant oak-lined streets, a Maryland version of Larchmont or Purchase. "We loved the idea of hitting that kind of conservative, racist community," Mische says. "We loved to hit them with an action not performed by hippies but by college graduates, three of them clerics, all nicely dressed in white collars or in suits and ties . . ."

Tom Lewis checked out the Knights of Columbus Hall very carefully by visiting it several times under the pretense that he was searching for a place in which to get married. He executed, after each visit, delicate and elaborately detailed drawings of the building and its grounds that served as master plans for the Catonsville mission.

A decision had to be made next on the medium of protest: Should it be blood again, or ink, paint, fire? The October protest had been criticized for the obtuseness of its medium. The blood symbolism had been too liturgical, too special. Its message had been unclear, it had not seemed to reach enough people. The group was attracted again to the idea of burning draft files. Philip suggested napalm, and the idea was unanimously approved. It burned thousands of innocent people a month in Vietnam. Why not use it to burn some pieces of government property? A recipe for napalm was found in an issue of *Ramparts* magazine (a radical Catholic publication, as the group liked to stress), which quoted an Army handbook on its manufacture. The recipe specified gasoline and pure soap, heated into a solution. Dozens of boxes of Ivory Soap flakes were purchased, since Ivory had always been touted as the purest soap. "Ninety-nine and forty-four hundredths percent pure" became a motto of the protesters. A test batch was mixed in a basement. It burned beautifully.

But a most important ingredient of the new action was still lacking, and that was Daniel Berrigan. During the winter, he had been absent on a mission to Hanoi, sponsored by pacifist groups, to receive three American prisoners of war from the North Vietnamese government. After his return he was repeatedly invited, by persons other than his brother, to participate in the next raid. He acted mysterious, guarded, unhappy, unsure. A week before the scheduled foray Daniel and Philip Berrigan sat up alone, over a bottle, until four o'clock in the morning. A few hours later Philip telephoned Mische: "Dan's in." And that very day, according to his friends, Daniel came out of the gloom which he had been in ever since October. He seemed relieved of an enormous burden of guilt. He was his luminous and joyous self again. ("I was threatened with being the golden boy of the Movement," he wrote, "I was too old to burn a draft card. Suddenly I saw that my sweet skin was hiding out behind others.")

The night before Catonsville, after the definitive batch of napalm had been made and tested, the Nine met for a last briefing, each holding a copy of Lewis's exquisitely detailed plan of the Knights of Columbus Hall. Daniel, noted for his poetic vagueness, his inability to read any maps, train or plane schedules, studied the plan silently, with a quizzical expression, during the three-hour session. At one a.m., as the group was about to disband, Daniel looked up to his brother and said "I didn't understand anything, Philly . . . never could read a map. I'll follow you, Philly, okay? I'll just follow you."

The Catonsville Nine slept at a friend's house in the suburbs of Baltimore. They waited for one of their aides, who had assembled the press at a nearby motel, to phone the go-ahead signal. A Washington reporter was a half hour late. Philip was beside himself with impatience. When the phone call finally came he shouted "Let's go, let's go," threw himself into the nearest car and almost drove off alone. His friends spent a few minutes reorganizing him.

The Nine went to Catonsville in three cars, each driven by a non-participating member of the peace group. On the way to Catonsville, Daniel, smiling, jesting, was more joyous than his friends had seen him in years. "This is like going on a picnic," he exclaimed. "What a beautiful day for a picnic, what a beautiful day . . ." He turned to the man at the wheel and said: "After the long yawn of history, I've finally found something good."

The reporters, guided to Catonsville's Selective Service Office by members of the Baltimore peace group, had parked at the edge of the oak-lined street. It was a very hot, sunny May day. Three cars passed them and parked across the street. Seven men and two women got out—three of them dressed in clerical attire, two of them carrying large wire trash baskets. The group walked quietly into the Knights of Columbus Hall. The Nine's helpmates, drivers of cars, soothers of nerves, distributors of press statements, brewers of newsmen's coffee, quickly dispersed from the scene. Several of them had studied for the Catholic priesthood. After a minute and a half had elapsed the Nine ran out of the building, baskets filled with papers.

The reporters, as instructed, tore open the sealed envelopes that they had been handed earlier that morning, and read:

> *Today, May 17th, we enter Local Board No. 33 at Catonsville, Maryland, to seize Selective Service records ... We, American citizens, have worked with the poor in the ghetto and abroad ... All of us identify with the victims of American oppression all over the world ... We submit voluntarily to their involuntary fate ...*

II/THE TRIAL OF
THE CATONSVILLE NINE

*The ceremony of expelling demons,
diseases and sins . . . can be practised under
the form of the ritual sending away of
an animal or a man regarded as the material vehicle
through which the faults of the entire community
are transported beyond the limits
of the territory it inhabits.*
—Mircea Eliade, *The Myth of the Eternal Return*

*Society can never think things out;
It has to see them acted out by actors.
Devoted actors at a sacrifice—
The ablest actors I can lay my hands on.*
—Robert Frost, "A Masque of Reason"

Daniel Berrigan Free

July 1968. Father Daniel Berrigan, S.J., sat in his office at
Cornell University, pecking swiftly at his typewriter, sending out invitations to his trial. He was perched on a swivel
seat, his feet upon the bar of the chair, hunched up like a
leprechaun on a rock. Wafted by the gentle summer breeze,
a six-foot-high plastic Superman painted in brilliant reds
and blues floated above his desk. The small, tidy office was
dominated by a large photograph of Pope John XXIII; a
poster-sized quote from e.e. cummings: "Damn Everything
But the Circus"; another gigantic quote from Camus: "I
wish I could love my country as much as I love justice."
Relieved at last of guilt, facing a maximum sentence of

fourteen years in Federal prison for destroying Selective
Service records, free to share in the fate of his brother and
of thousands of young Americans awaiting jail terms for
protesting the Vietnam war, Daniel Berrigan was finally at
peace.

He has said that there have been three major influences
on his life: his family; the Society of Jesus; Cornell University. At progressive, 150-year-old Cornell, which prides
itself on its liberalism, Daniel Berrigan swam like a fish in
water. The outstanding fact which the college administration knew about Daniel Berrigan when it appointed him was
that he had been the *bête noire* of Cardinal Spellman's Chancery. With these impeccable credentials, the controversial
Jesuit poet and pacifist became the first Catholic priest
ever hired by Cornell. He was appointed co-chairman of
Cornell United Religious Work, a campus organization
which typifies that heady new blend of religion and progressive politics synthesized by the black liberation movement and the Vietnam protest. Daniel Berrigan was in good
company. One of his closest friends, Cornell's Catholic
chaplain David Connor, believed that the job of the modern clergyman was "to give funeral rites to the existing
Church and give it over to the people for rebirth." He had
been the second Catholic priest in the United States to risk
prosecution by turning in his ministerial deferment card
in protest against the Vietnam war. Cornell's militant New
Left described Cornell's religious men, with pragmatic affection, as "great radicals with white collars on—the best
fronts for our radical activity."

While sitting at his desk, Daniel Berrigan talked with
the students and visitors continually swarming in and out
of his office. It had become proverbial, along with the Berrigan seminar on nonviolence, as the most crowded place

on campus. Two men, this day, had his particular attention. One of them, a Jesuit seminarian who had just spent a week fasting in jail to protest the race scene in Wisconsin, was coiffed and dressed, like hundreds of Jesuits across the nation, in a meticulous emulation of the Berrigan style: Black turtleneck, peace medallion on chest, a medieval Joan of Arc haircut which scraggled in jagged peaks across the forehead. The other visitor was a bearded, gentle-eyed Cornell student pondering over the problems of the war. ("Dear Sister Corita," Daniel was writing, "Will you design an invitation to my trial? Four delicious colors . . . something very gay, very joyful . . . we could put 'R.S.V.P. to Fourth District Court' at the left bottom corner . . .")

Between dabs at the typewriter the Berrigan charm, a blend of solicitous warmth and sly teasing, wafted subtly towards his disciples. "How are you kid? How's the family? Give them a big hug for me. Are you hungry? Cold? Thirsty? Enough air for you? Is that chair comfortable? You SDSers are always so clean . . . you know Christ accused the Pharisees of washing too much. Are you religious? You're not radical if you're not religious. How about staging a mass baptism at the Pentagon? Why don't you start a new order, I mean a new disorder . . . you could destruct instead of instruct. Wild, man, wild . . ." The Pied Piper pecked away between jests. The graduate student talked about his family, his studies. "Aha, aha," Daniel murmured in his professional confessor's voice. The student spoke about his term in the army. It was so dehumanizing . . . "Oh, I can imagine!" Daniel said. He stopped typing, assumed a more interested air. The army experience, the student said, had driven him to a position of absolute pacifism. "No kidding!" Daniel exclaimed. And with a thrust of his foot, the swivel chair he sat on whizzed half way across the room towards the student. "Tell me more!" Father Berrigan commanded. The Jesuit at his side, one of hundreds of seminarians converted to pacifism by the Pied Piper of Syracuse, gave a knowing smile.

In neighboring offices, breezy Protestant ministers in Bermuda shorts talked with fearful affection about the leprechaun-prophet next door. Progressive campus ministers always want to be in the avant-garde. If they didn't back Berrigan then, it might become the fashion to back him next year. But Berrigan was tougher than ever to support. He'd set the fashion for nothing less than martyrdom. The Protestants hovered over approval. "We love everything Dan does," they said, "we don't always approve of the *way* he does it . . ." They peeked into the Berrigan office with friendly waves of hands. What was that elegant prophet, that dapper saint going to do next?

"Well Catonsville, okay, it was admirable, but maybe it turned a few too many people off . . . maybe not. It's a very Catholic kind of action of course, very liturgical. This Berrigan is unbelievable, right in the great old prophetic-apocalyptic tradition. He's a great Christian in the sense of the absurd man . . . he's Christian in the Bonhoeffer sense of the incarnational man . . . he's immanental rather than transcendental, don't you think? He is a true convictional model. He incarnates the theology of crisis. These Catholics are something. A volcanic release of pressures built up for years . . . wow, they're reforming the reforms of *our* Reformation, these Catholics today are way ahead of anybody else!"

Some chaplains, more defensive, caught up on their own records: "You talk of the Catholic New Left, let me tell you we've got a Protestant New Left here that would blow your mind! Why we were one of the first college ministries to organize a bus load of kids to Selma. We've had a summer project in Harlem since the early sixties. We've had kids in social action projects in Brazil, Honduras, Guatemala, Nova Scotia for the past eight years."

Still another chaplain, with the enthusiasm of a gourmet lauding a four-star restaurant, described Cornell's thriving underground church. It was the most exciting thing that's ever happened in his ministry, the guitars strumming, the folk songs, the readings clipped out of *The New York Times*! The intercommunion with California wine in paper cups and hearty pieces of rye bread! The saying hell to Canon Law! The people talking and laughing during the service, like the July 14 liturgy when they sang the *Marseillaise* in lieu of hymn, followed by loud clapping and cheering! All this talk about the new Church dying from lack of structure is nonsense, campus attendance has doubled since the liturgy has gone experimental . . . and our kiss of peace! Wow, man, that ain't no mere handshake! The chaplain's arms affected a lusty embrace with the air, and then they dropped, and he looked sad, like all the Protestants who couldn't get Daniel Berrigan to join in the underground hoopla. Curious, curious, he said, that such a liberal man as Dan doesn't get a kick out of our underground church. He came once, and looked uncomfortable. Nobody feels they really know him, except the kids and the young instructors who have taken risks with the government. It's said that he shares Communion only with them.

("The underground Church is a mess," Daniel says. "The underground Church is all talk and no action. Just another liberal white ghetto. What a country club.")

An estimated thirty men at Cornell, including several instructors and two clergymen, were facing government prosecution for defying the Selective Service System. Two of its student members, Joe Gilchrist and Bruce Dancis, were handed sentences, respectively, of five and six years for refusing induction, among the two stiffest terms given in 1968 for this offense. Daniel Berrigan, as expected, had become the spiritual director of Cornell's peace movement. He accompanied war objectors to their draft boards, induction refusals, and court hearings, attended their press conferences, appeared as character witness, raised money for their defense, comforted them in time of anguish, suffered that he was above draft age, too old to share in their action.

Meanwhile, with a Jesuit's suave infiltrational tactics, he charmed agnostic draft resisters and SDSers into reading the Bible at ecumenical services. For Daniel had also become the house guru of the university's thriving SDS chapter, which had discovered the pragmatic values of religious men. ("We're still anti-Church, but we're pro-clerical. Those guys are *useful!*")

Cornell SDS, three hundred strong at that time, complained that its university was as much a slum landlord as Columbia; that is was a middle-class profiteer subsidized by black people and the poor; that fifty-eight per cent of its budget was government-funded; that Cornell did nothing to break down racial discrimination; that the notoriously progressive Cornell administration played ball too gently with them. ("We can never have any radical confrontation with *this* administration. The Columbia kids were damn lucky to be clubbed. It demonstrated the establishment's *real* attitude towards students.")

With Daniel's blessings, Cornell SDS was busy forcing the administration's hand in building low-income housing; getting black participation in Ithaca's housing commission; inciting boycotts of Delano grapes in support of Cesar Chavez's Farm Workers; protesting the university's support, via its holdings in the Chase Manhattan Bank, of South Africa's apartheid government. Daniel frequently criticized the SDSers' rash, dictatorial tactics. He was about the only man over 25 at Cornell they listened to. Two thousand students came to a rally held in honor of his trial to show him their support. Yet many SDSers did not approve of Catonsville. "It wasn't efficient enough," they said. "We don't get all that symbolic crap of being a sacrificial victim, waiting around for arrest. We'd prefer a hit-and-run method of raiding draft boards. Catonsville was not politically serious, it was *machismo*, romantic. You can't afford to go to jail at this time. You've got to spend as much time as possible subverting the system by staying above ground."

("The New Left suffers from American pragmatism," Daniel says. "It fights violence with the tools of violence, I fight it with the Gandhian and Christian dimensions of non-violence. They measure effectiveness by pragmatic results, I see it as immeasurable, as the impact of symbolic action. The New Left only stresses political activity, I would like to be more classical and Greek, I am like Socrates choosing jail, choosing the *ideal*.")

The vice-president of Cornell university, Mark Barlow, found that it was a great luxury to have a mystic and prophet in residence. "Dan's strength is not as an administrator," Mr. Barlow said. "He's totally hung up on this war. However, Dan has done one important thing for us, he's made the radical kids less aggressive. Before Dan came to Cornell, each time I went to the coffee house I'd get the hate load: vituperation, cynicism, hostility, angry arguments. Now I go there at least twice a week and I never leave without having a darn good, peaceful discussion with the kids. No more bitterness. Dan has infused charity into our SDS. That's quite a feat. Dan has this magic of non-violence, he practices what he preaches, that's why he's in trouble, that's also why he's so influential."

Christianizing the SDS, as Dean Barlow said, was quite a feat. But so powerful was our Jesuit's magnetism for the young that he was even leading some SDSers into the seminary! They were choosing the ministry as a vocation without even knowing what denomination they were going to end up in. When asked what Church he would choose, twenty-four-year-old SDSer Carl Takamura, with an impassive smile, simply spread his arms out in the symbol of the Cross —any Christian Church would do. At Cornell, Takamura attended Catholic services because he found that Daniel Berrigan's and David Connor's faith was "more translated into action" than that of the other chaplains. Takamura, who had a B.A. in government and a Master's degree in education, believed that SDS and seminary were the perfect complements to a modern man's training. "I was led to the ministry, in great part, by the feeling that so many of the kids in my SDS chapter lack charity. They discard the whole 'middle-class liberal' segment of society with a violence that is often shocking. They try so hard to identify themselves with the underdogs, the blacks, the have-nots, that they simply exclude anyone else. Well, you know, SDS and true Christian ministry such as Dan's really have the same goals—alleviating the suffering of minority groups, demilitarizing the world, building a more just society. But SDS is divisive, I've learned from Dan that I want to unite. I chose the ministry when men like Dan and David Connor showed me how to be both radical and charitable."

("This is where I come in," Daniel says. "This is where religion comes in for the college kids: to give them an exposure to discipline and to sacrifice. These SDSers have the right social goals but some of them trample people too much, some of them are so messed up on their sex life, their friendships . . . I say to them: 'Have some charity in your relationships, don't be so pragmatic, don't use others as steps in your own self-exploration . . .'")

. . .

Daniel Berrigan was proud of showing off the Cornell University chapel, which was gutted by fire in the spring of 1968. The police concluded it was arson. The walls of the chapel were charred and singed. A seared cross lay askew across the gutted altar. The priest gently caressed the blackened wall, saying: "Isn't it beautiful this way? It shouldn't be repaired, it should be left just the way it is." Daniel Berrigan stood in the destroyed chapel, his gaunt and boyish face outlined against the blackened wall, looking like one of the grim knights of a medieval morality play. There was a forbidding, condemning gaze in the Jesuit's eyes as he continued to talk. "I don't often say Mass in a church building anymore, but I'd like to say one in this chapel, with all the symbols of death and warmongering left intact. This is an honest scene, this shows the Church as She really is. I am convinced that our Church has helped to write our modern liturgies of death because what with all its talks of sacraments of peace its faith has lain in war, in the continuation of original sin. How different from our early Church, in which the liturgy of baptism was an induction into a community of nonviolence! In their rite of baptism, the early Christians laid aside the imperialist state and all its social demands . . . Oh I don't care if it was only that way for two hundred years. There, in that early Church, is that pure model of nonviolence we must return to.

"Let me tell you how I talk about original sin when I teach scripture. I see original sin as war, beginning with the fratricide of Abel by Cain. I've always been turned on by the early chapters of Genesis, and I try to awaken my students' imaginations to the real meaning of the Fall. I discuss the parents inside the garden and the sons outside the garden. These two parents are challenged by God in their immaturity, their euphoria, their childhood. Their innocence has no real meaning, because it has no real price. It is a given, like mother's milk, like Freud's unconscious.

God now introduces a crisis as a way of bringing the parents into consciousness, into a relationship of love with Him, and they flunk the exam. Tough! God's will is always to bring us to adulthood, to offer us a choice, but we're always too young. Oh, the genius with which the consciousness of the tribe understood that sin is the neglect of love and the beginning of war! That the parents' rupture with God was also the rupture which led to fratricide, the killing of your brother! Yet we must not make this doctrine of original sin the measure of man. We are only as corrupt as we believe ourselves to be. Most men, most intellectuals, have a static idea of evil, they just want to wield the sword in such a way that they don't get stuck on it. But that's living in a zoo. You live in a zoo if you do not have the hope of human perfectibility. Hope is the radium capsule, Christ's release of energy which we must insert into the diseased body of society . . . this is the act of faith in life itself. And of course we must have faith in the life hereafter . . . I have no definition of it because to be good Christians we have to be in part agnostic, we have to confess our ignorance. I don't think that we're meant to understand much more than this: That we'll be personally immortal, that we'll see the Father and those we love.

"History is a fever chart between hope in the ideal of Christ and despair in the corruptible nature of man. At times men despair of Christ's ideal of perfectibility, they make it weightless, unhistorical. Then the fever chart changes and there's strengthening in our will to bring Christ's vision to pass, in our sense of closeness to the kingdom. In the community I live and go to jail with, we feel that the kingdom is very near. The world of corrupt power, the state as well as the corrupt Church, says 'Utopia!' to our kingdom. But we must refuse their definitions. We must refuse such liturgies of death as the ceremony of being inducted into armies, into the duplicity of original sin. These structures which try to define us, which corrupt us by depriving us of hope, they are forms of paganism and despair, what Saint Paul calls 'Powers and Dominations," what Christ calls 'Satan.' "

("I realized at Cornell," Daniel Berrigan testified a few weeks later at his trial, "that I could not preach the Gospel from a pedestal . . . I was placing on young shoulders the filthy burden of the original sin of war . . . I was too old to carry a draft card . . . I realized that there were other ways I must take to get into trouble with a state totally intent on war.")

Philip Berrigan Free

Father Philip Berrigan, the first Catholic priest in the history of the United States to serve sentence as a political prisoner, spent most of the summer of 1968 at the Allenwood Federal Penitentiary, near Lewisburg, Pennsylvania, a minimum security jail which houses many of the government's political internees. His letters to his family, throughout those first months of the six-year sentence he received for defiling draft files in Baltimore the preceding autumn, were of an unfluctuating cheerfulness. He enjoyed the fresh air, exercise and hearty farmwork which Allenwood offers to its convicts. The only things he missed were his beloved periodicals, particularly his *I. F. Stone's Weekly*. "Once my magazines start coming again I'll be in clover hay," he wrote in July to his brother Jerry. "I sit here composedly and even smugly while people outside suffer far more . . . there should be more of an equation." August 1: "A note to you between loads of manure. We are cleaning out a barn here that hasn't been touched in years. Pop would go wild with delight at a load of this! It is full of all the good ingredients that manure should have." August 15: "You see the Spirit is not chained! My friend George McGovern has declared himself for the Presidency. I only hope that his move will help McCarthy take the scene." On August 29, right after he had received the notice of his trial, scheduled for October 7 in Baltimore, he wrote: "We'll face up to our hallowed courts clear-eyed and bushy-tailed, and do our best to peel a few scales from the eyes of the electorate." A few days later, he was returned to the Baltimore County Jail to attend the various legal hearings that preceded the trial of the Catonsville Nine.

To visit Philip Berrigan at the Baltimore County Jail, one entered through a side door of the prison into a dark, impeccably scrubbed little hall whose far wall was pierced by five large screened windows. Visitors stood at four of the apertures, whispering to the prisoners behind the screen. At one of the windows a very tall man with pale and merry eyes waved his greeting. One could see Philip Berrigan clearly from the visitors' entrance, but as one walked towards him the outlines of his face grew uncannily and increasingly blurred. For the metal screen behind which he stood, which at first looked no thicker than a mosquito netting, was made of a diabolical alloy which totally clouded the features of the prisoner when one stood near him, fogging all colors and delineations. Behind the screen there was the blurred, hulking image of a man in a spectral gray shirt, with a prisoner's unaired gray skin, with graying close-cropped hair, who fingered a little Mexican silver cross. Only Philip Berrigan's fierce, fearless, impatient blue eyes pierced, like headlights, the mist of the screen. The massive, handsome prisoner stood there in his titanic isolation, talking softly, the silver crucifix flickering in his powerful hands. And his hushed and confidential voice, the darkness of the hall, the whispering at the neighboring grilles, that vision-obscuring screen in front of his face, the silver cross gleaming behind it, something awesome in his presence, carried one back into the confessional booths of childhood, into the terrors of sin and guilt which we commenced to wash away, as children, with the muttered words: "Bless me Father for I have sinned, Bless me Father for I have sinned . . ." One felt in greater need for absolution, in Philip Berrigan's presence, than one had ever felt, for his eyes carried the inhuman liberation of a man whose conscience was wholly cleansed, radically and absolutely purified.

Yet with all his awesomeness Philip Berrigan was gallant, relaxed, smiling frequently as he leaned, arms folded, spectrally gray, against the wall of his visiting cell. He had his brother Daniel's smile, wide, theatrical, irresistibly luminous. He had his brother's sorcerous delicacy; the Berrigans could tame, exorcise, hypnotize anyone who dared to hazard the consequences.

In a cool, modulated voice, but with the eagerness of a man who had been very lonely, he talked about his priesthood, his Church, and Catonsville. He had been made desperate by the outdated structures of the Catholic Church, he said, by its silence on racism, on war, on most matters relevant to human progress. That, after all, was in good part what Catonsville was about: the Church's total misunderstanding of the Gospel. And what was the Gospel about? Oh well, the Gospel was about revolution, and if you didn't understand that, forget Christianity, for the Gospel was the greatest revolutionary document of all times. The Gospel sought to subvert the domination of men by men, it asked for the triumph of the dispossessed over the wealthy, for the equality of all men in Christ. The sacraments of the Church were the signs of that revolution, of the upsetting of temporal power, of all men gathered in Christ in love and peace. Christianity preached a redemptive community of the poor, as Marx did, but it took Marx many steps further. Christianity, one could say, was the revolution within the revolution . . . and the priest of course must be the revolutionary leader. The sign of this leadership is his struggle against the material values of the secular world. And when shall we recover fully the Christianity that we have lost since Christ? The only true sign of its recovery will be the hostility of the world, the reduction of the Christian community into a small, persecuted enclave of men. He quoted Saint John: "I passed Your word on to Your Apostles, and the world hated them." All his ideas came straight from the Gospel, Philip Berrigan said, he hadn't read theology in years. He only read Scripture, and everything he could find about politics, history, economics. He smiled, a sly look in his kind impatient eyes, and added: "It's an explosive mixture . . ."

Towards the end of the visit, which was only allowed to last twenty minutes, the prison guard left his table at the entrance of the jail and started pacing up and down the visitors' area, staring at the clock. The prisoner leaned back against the wall of the visiting block, talking about why there had been only Catholics at Catonsville. He hadn't quite figured it out, but it must mean that the Holy Spirit was saying something about revelation, that some Catholics were being led to a greater understanding of the Gospel. It made him very proud. When a war as demonic as this comes along, when all other means of protesting it have failed, you have to resort to desperate gestures to make yourself heard. For electoral politics had failed, and the Marxist hope for radicalizing the proletariat had failed too. We were living in an advanced, decaying stage of capitalism which offers just enough prosperity to the masses to make them apathetic, to tame the forces of opposition.

Perhaps only a Wallace victory could expose American society for what it really was, its militarism, its racism . . . it would polarize the nation, lead people to the proper confrontations. For when a system fails as ours has failed you've got to polarize society by dramatic, provocative action, jolt the apathetic middle ground, radicalize the liberals, inspire them to new commitments. There would have to be many more reckless acts of sacrifice such as those of the Baltimore Four, the Catonsville Nine. The jails would soon be packed in this country. Only such acts of sacrifice could redeem our society . . .

When the visiting time had drawn to a definitive close the guard tapped gently on his table and pointed to the clock. The prisoner's hand waved in a gesture of parting. "It'll be easier talking at the trial," Philip Berrigan said. "That trial will be quite an event, I look forward to it."

From the entrance of the prison, away from the screen's distorting optics, Philip Berrigan's features were again as clear as if there were no barrier between him and his visitors. And as seen from that distance, his face had the arrogant serenity of a man who firmly believed that his actions were redeeming the sins of his society. Whatever good or evil he had brought to others, he had totally redeemed himself. Philip Berrigan's conscience was, as ever, severely cleansed, rigorously clear.

He waved a last time. "Remember," he said gaily, "I'm here because of my sanity!"

Saint Paul's Epistle to the Corinthians, chapter IV, verses 10–13: *"Here we are, fools for the sake of Christ . . . we are treated as the offal of the world, still to this day, the scum of the earth."*

"The problem for us Protestants in all these radical

actions," said William Sloane Coffin as he mused over the Berrigans' jail sentences and his own protests, "is that we worry about whether we're being fools for Christ's sake, or just plain damn fools. The great thing about the Berrigans is that they don't care to know the difference."

From Catonsville to Milwaukee

Shortly after 6 p.m. on September 24, 1968, two weeks before the trial of the Catonsville Nine, fourteen men broke into the Selective Service Offices in Milwaukee, Wisconsin, seized some 20,000 draft records, carried them to a small park across the street, and burned them with homemade napalm at the foot of a steel flagpole dedicated to the veterans of World War I. Copying style and substance from the Catonsville Nine, the raiders prayed, read from the Gospel of Saint Luke, and sang religious hymns as they awaited arrest. Twelve of the Milwaukee Fourteen —as the group was henceforth called—were Catholics. Six of them were priests. One of the Milwaukee Fourteen was the Berrigans' friend James Forest, co-chairman of the Catholic Peace Fellowship. As of that evening, the three chairmen of the nation's most active Catholic pacifist organization—Philip Berrigan, James Forest, Tom Cornell— were all in jail for their protests against the Vietnam war.

A few weeks later, after he had been released on bail pending his trial, James Forest talked about how he came to participate in this third raid of the Catholic Resistance.

"When I first heard about Philip's blood-pouring action in Baltimore last October, I was cowardly and numb. My reaction was one of total emotional paralysis. I felt as if someone I loved had died and I wasn't brave enough to react to it with so much as pain or sorrow. I instantly thought of Camus' stranger who lights up a cigarette while standing in the funeral parlor next to his dead mother's body, who is devoid of all emotion, who is a scandal to his community because he's so devoid of emotion. I accepted the information very dumbly, blankly. It was a shock of course . . . Phil was my co-chairman at the Catholic Peace Fellowship and one morning I pick up *The New York Times* and there he is on the front page, pouring blood on draft files. Like everyone else at that time I must have been an astonishing disappointment to Phil. I must stress that my lack of response was typical of the reaction Phil got from everybody. He was totally alone, totally deprived of any support from any of his friends. None of us could say at the time, even in the radical fringe of the Resistance Movement, 'I would do likewise.' It was too extreme, too alienating. Phil's action was a truly prophetic one, it was the only truly prophetic action I have witnessed in my life-time. It was the beginning of a whole new era of Resistance in this country. It changed the whole character of the Peace Movement. How much those four people in Balti-more gave to us on that October day! How long it took us to accept this gift!

"When you get a whiff of such an action as Phil's, you know, instantly and instinctively, that it's dangerous stuff. I can only compare it to the emotions I had, while I was in the Navy, about the possibility of converting to Catholi-cism. I dimly sensed that it would lead me into trouble. I had an apprehension about it, I kept putting it off for months, I knew that if I committed myself to Christianity trouble would be imminent. I didn't yet know what form the trouble would take—the anguish of being a C.O., or of having all my ideas about life and property revolution-ized. I only felt a kind of dumb fear. That's the emotion I had when Phil poured that blood in Baltimore. It was this subconscious fear which kept me from embracing his action, even symbolically. I barely even wrote to Phil. Oh, I dashed off a half-hearted little note. But it was a hollow, polite, unreal support, the kind that couldn't comfort a man for a minute. The whole thing continued to be in outer space for me throughout the winter and most of the spring. I lived in dumb fear of Phil's action.

"I learned about the Catonsville incident while I was in California last May. I had been feeling depressed about the peace movement. There wasn't enough peace or brotherhood in it, it had acquired a dehumanizing, bureaucratic atmosphere. And all our means of protesting this insane war, over four years, had failed. One day I picked up the Los Angeles paper and I stared, with enormous emotion and elation this time, at the picture of the nine men and women on the front page: There was Dan Berrigan, who'd been closer to me than any other man in my life, and Phil Berrigan, putting his life on the line for the second time in a row! The burning was a much more efficient symbol for me than the blood-pouring. Blood has never been as clear a symbol to Americans as it is to other societies. Blood had just defiled draft records in Phil's first protest. But one thing that Americans do understand is the *destruction* of property! Think of how much more upset the average parent is when his kid smashes the family car into a tree than when he receives an induction notice. The Catonsville protest led me again to re-examine all my notions of property, as I had some years ago when I had been converted to Catholicism and had accepted voluntary poverty at the Catholic Worker. And even though I still did not feel capable of equivalent action, it filled me with extraordinary elation.

"In June, a few weeks after Catonsville, I went up to spend a day with Dan. When I drove off after our visit I told myself all the reasons why I couldn't go into a

Catonsville-type action. I told myself that I was scared; that I like to see my family, travel, read, eat well, go to the movies. Then, later that summer, when I went on the road things began to fall into place, ideas crystallized. It dawned on me that the kind of support I was giving the Catonsville Nine—designing the folder to raise money for them et cetera—was not enough. I realized that it was not enough to be the leader of the cheering section. That what they were really hoping for was that others would follow suit. Well, you know, these decisions have a funny way of growing. In August I visited in Washington with some of the Nine. Still later I went to Milwaukee and stayed at the new Catholic Worker house there. The people at the Milwaukee Worker really knew where it was at. It was while staying there that I decided that an action of the Catonsville sort was next in line. After all, what are we taught by the Worker movement? To let human need control property. To work for a radical change in the social order. To create our own lifestyles. To extend works of mercy into works of peace. When I told my wife about my decision to join the protest she was too shocked to do anything but stare. I was the one who was doing all the crying. I felt, as I was telling her about my decision, that I was telling her about a new man. A new man had come out of all this, for as soon as I'd made my decision I felt purified, cleansed, free of guilt, transformed. All those days in September when I was preparing for the Milwaukee protest, a phrase kept running through my mind, a quote from Saint Justin Martyr: 'The Church is a field of wheat which is nourished by the blood of those who give witness.'"

A group of newsmen had been summoned to the scene of the Milwaukee Fourteen's raid by their statement to the press:

> *Generation after generation, religious values have sum-*
> *moned men to undertake the works of poverty and peace.*
> *In times of crisis these values have further required men*
> *to cry out in protest against institutions destructive of*
> *man and his immense potential . . . We wish to offer our*
> *lives and future to absorb, blockade and transform the*
> *violence which our society has come to personify . . .*
> *We who burn these records of our society's war machine*
> *are participants in a movement of resistance to slavery . . .*

During their stay in jail, the Milwaukee Fourteen fasted, held seminars on peace, and sent flowers to the cleaning lady whose keys they had seized to enter the Selective Service Office in downtown Milwaukee. "Who organized you?" one of the raiders was asked at the Fourteen's arraignment. "The war organized us," he answered. "What was your intent?" another man, a priest, was asked. "We seek a lifestyle to match the Church's rhetoric," he answered.

Holy Week in Baltimore

"Come to Baltimore," Daniel Berrigan wrote to thousands in his invitation to the Catonsville Nine's trial, "for an event that will blow your minds and open your hearts. Come in joy, as a sign of life. We promise a defense proceeding that defends you, a prosecution that prosecutes you. What more could one ask, after Chicago, before November 5th?"

In the grandiose tradition of Jesuit didactics, Daniel Berrigan wanted the trial of the Catonsville Nine to be a morality play, a celebration, a massive teach-in. The Baltimore peace movement, wishing to dramatize the second trial of its high priest Philip Berrigan, had the same intent. It had sent its own set of invitations, in a more political tone, to protest groups throughout the United States. "A

National Call," the invitation read. "Come to Agnew Country! Free the Catonsville Nine! Confront the Slavemakers!" The Baltimorians promised more than just a trial. They offered daily marches and demonstrations, nightly forums with four consecutive shifts of distinguished speakers, free lodging and suppers for out-of-towners, "continual action" to keep attention on the trial, and a few surprises. The response was handsome. Some two thousand war protesters from all over the United States appeared in Baltimore for the trial of the Catonsville Nine. Two hundred additional Federal marshals were shipped into the city, from as far away as California, to fortify Baltimore's Federal Courthouse. Governor Agnew's police force was doubled to round-the-clock shifts. The Nine's trial spread to the streets like a Mardi Gras festival. It was a triumph of confrontation politics.

The peace movement had learned from some recent disappointments. The closest legal precedent to the Catonsville Nine's trial had been the trial in Boston, the preceding May, of Benjamin Spock, William Sloane Coffin, and three other men accused of conspiracy against the United States government in abetting young men to resist the draft. The more militant half of the peace movement had accused the Boston Five, with varying degrees of malice, of sabotaging the anti-war protest by not making their trial into a notorious political event. Activists had hoped that the Boston trial would bring a far-reaching indictment of government action in Vietnam and would publicize these indictments by massive demonstrations. But the Boston Five's defense lawyers prevented the movement from staging any substantial protests. The Boston defendants' statements against the illegality of the Vietnam war were barely reported to the press. The radical fringe of the peace movement was bitter about the lack of confrontation and of publicity. And the

Catonsville Catholics, obsessed by the silence of their Church upon the Vietnam war, were determined to take their case to the people with infinitely more drama and turmoil than had the Boston Five.

"Why has your Church been so silent about the war?" a reporter asked Dorothy Day in Baltimore. "What do you think this trial is all about?" she answered. Although the Catholic hierarchy, to the Nine's chagrin, remained as mute as ever on the war issue, the ecumenical "lowerarchy" responded vociferously. The night before the court proceedings began, a thousand supporters of the Nine had already gathered in the vast basement of Saint Ignatius, the largest Jesuit church in Baltimore, which was to serve throughout the four-day trial as headquarters, forum hall and sleeping-place for the protesters. The hall overflowed, for quite suddenly, the secular, Protestant and Jewish left —after years of disdain— had become fervent supporters of the new radical Catholicism. Rabbi Heschel, Bishop Pike, Harvey Cox, Rennie Davis, Howard Zinn, Noam Chomsky, I. F. Stone mingled in the basement of Saint Ignatius with hundreds of Jesuits, with parish curates and seminarians from twenty states, with nuns in habit, nuns in high heels and teased hair, nuns writing their Master's theses on the development of Daniel Berrigan's theology. They were joined by Protestant ministers, three hundred Cornell students, hundreds of college teachers and college-age war protesters from all over, and a large contingent of priests from Milwaukee, which, since the September Draft Board raid, vied for Baltimore's place as "the Christian Guerrilla Capital of the United States." The black-suited priests, vociferous and militant, swarmed and chattered around the church like flocks of migrating starlings. They came from schools and parishes called Saint Peter's, Saint Barnaby's, Saint Jude's, Saint John's, Saint Anthony's, Saint

Joseph's, their name-places sounding like a calendar of saints. They were constantly being embraced by delegations of student radicals from various campuses who had suddenly decided, since Milwaukee, that Catholics were hitting straighter on target than anybody else. "Twenty thousand draft records in Milwaukee!" yelled one midwestern SDS leader as he stomped into the basement of Saint Ignatius. "Hey, you guys are *effective*! I'm joining the Church!"

This motley crew of the Catonsville Nine's supporters had evolved their own liturgical symbols for the four-day Saturnalia. They wore black bands on their right arms as signs of mourning for the American war dead, white bands around their foreheads to honor the Vietnamese dead, red bands on their left arms in support of the Milwaukee Fourteen. Around their necks, the supporters wore the familiar peace amulet—an upside-down Y enclosed in a circle—which had come into fashion a decade ago as a symbol for nuclear disarmament. The symbol was present in a staggering array of materials—leather, bronze, silver, terracotta, glued cardboard, stained glass. It hung from leather thongs, metal chains, shoe strings, tatters of linen, on the black breasts of the priests and seminarians, on the students' rumpled shirts. This savage, angry army, bandaged, right and left, like soldiers too long in the field, had a fervid and decimated look. They had the frazzled fervor of men who had been in the peace movement from its beginnings, who were ravaged from fasting on university steps and at induction centers, weary from marching on manufacturers of chemicals and weapons, haggard from nights in jail and in church sanctuaries. Catonsville was the protesters' protest, supported by no newcomers to the movement, but by its *conoscenti*, by the long-initiated who shared the Nine's rage at the futility of marching, picketing, writing, voting against the Vietnam war. There was wrath and brotherhood in the air. The veterans harangued in corners like

Jacobins, they cheered each other, they embraced each other with the effusive tenderness of the peace movement which had recently overwhelmed the Anglo-Saxon diffidence of American males. ("I revolt," Camus wrote, "therefore we exist.") And as every new influx of supporters arrived from campuses, churches and seminaries, they started stomping: "We want Dan! We want Dan!" Daniel Berrigan appeared, made his V sign, smiled as for the press, clutched and embraced his disciples, signed copies of his latest book, and held out for everyone to see the large silver amulet which gleamed on his black turtleneck. The amulet was in the shape of an abstract, dismembered fish. "That," Daniel explained repeatedly, coolly, "is Jesus Christ after the institutional Church got through with Him."

The hall of Saint Ignatius was rife with rumors. There were rumors that the Catholic guerrillas were going to strike again, very soon, probably in the West, to jolt a new part of the nation. There were rumors that there would be nineteen of them next time, that the Catholics, for some arcane liturgical reason, would continue to escalate in fives. It had been Baltimore Four, Catonsville Nine, Milwaukee Fourteen. Would it next be Santa Fe Nineteen, San Francisco Nineteen, Anchorage Nineteen? It could be nineteen anywhere, for the Catonsville Nine's admirers, their potential emulators, had come to Baltimore from enormous distances to support them. As the rally started in Saint Ignatius' basement the Sunday night before the trial—it was an efficient place with a stage, a fine sound system—a scholarly-looking young man grabbed the microphone and cried out, to thunderous applause, "I bring greetings from Hawaii Resistance!" This was James Douglas, professor of Catholic theology at the University of Hawaii and a distinguished author on pacifism, who had recently spent a month in jail for refusing induction. Douglas opened a large cardboard box which he carried under his arm, and triumphantly took out nine flowered leis which he had brought by plane from Hawaii, that very morning, to offer to each of the Catonsville defendants. He was joined on the speakers' podium by a fellow Catholic, a short, merry seminarian who announced, to more thunderous applause, that he would burn his draft card the next day in front of Baltimore's Federal Courthouse to "adequately represent the anti-war feelings of the fiftieth state." It was gauged that one third of the states of the Union would be represented at the protest; for as the trial and its attendant demonstrations started the next morning, on Monday, October 7, another contingent of a thousand priests and students arrived in Baltimore to honor the Catonsville Nine.

As the court proceedings began, uneventfully concerned, that first day, with the selection of a jury, two thousand protesters rallied at Baltimore's Wyman Park for a mile-long march to the Federal Courthouse. It was a curiously archaic procession. For into a peace movement starved for new symbols, its music confined to the worn strains of Martin Luther King's liberation song, its placards repeating the three-year-old pleas to end the war and the draft and the Utopian local request to "Free the Nine," the Baltimorians had chosen to inject the emblems of pre-Revolutionary America. The parade proceeded under the banner of two pre-Revolutionary flags studiously copied from encyclopedias. One of them was the Gladston flag used in Virginia's Culcuppen County in 1775, on which a black snake on a green field is surrounded by the motto "Thou Shalt Not Tread on Me." The other was the Continental flag of a pine tree on a field of red and white. Thus playing at American revolution, the marchers, accompanied by a platoon of medics, teams of volunteer doctors, and hundreds of riot-helmeted, mace-carrying police, wound through the streets of Baltimore. It was a peaceful demonstration, praised by city authorities for its "militant orderliness," with no mace or medics needed; it was run, after all, by one of the most virtuoso peace groups in the country. Later, in another part of town, in another act of protest-liturgy-drama, in another desperate search for symbols, a contingent of the Nine's supporters carried a black coffin to the Customs House where the Baltimore Four had performed the previous autumn. They futilely tried to engage the guards in conversation about the evils of the war, were coolly handed a receipt for the coffin, carried letters of protest to every member of the Baltimore draft boards asking them to resign. Following upon Robert Kennedy's death, McCarthy's defeat, and the Chicago debacle—six weeks after the young had begun a new cycle of alienation and cynicism—there was a terrible yearning, in this particular march as throughout the peace movement, for new leaders, new tactics, new emblems, new theatrics. The most novel script for the living theater of protest had been brazenly written by the nine Catholics being tried inside Baltimore's Federal Courthouse; and the most poignant symbol in the demonstrations that dramatized their trial was the presence of several hundred Catholic priests.

The priests were young, beautiful, and terrifying. The black rigor of their dress, the strictness of their posture, the austerity of their freshly shaven faces, gave them an air of military stamina, military endurance, military fanaticism more threatening than that of the most incendiary SDS leaders in the country. One felt that the stringencies of their monastic life, of their matins and their disciplines had steeled them to walking farther, fasting longer, fighting harder than any laymen at their side; that they were capable of more inflammatory anger, of greater sacrifice; that their wrath against the war and their ire against their Church's silence fed upon each other like ogres. Covered with talismans of peace, bandaged with the black-and-white symbols of mourning, they marched more crisply, sang more vociferously, looked angrier than any of the Nine's supporters. The priests walked in platoon formation, and carried a placard which read "To speak of God and remain silent on Vietnam is blasphemy, blasphemy, blasphemy." The rage of the peace movement was given a new fanaticism by these religious men. They had come not only to protest the war, but also to participate in an archaic festival of absolution, to celebrate and mourn the incarceration of the young Church's two greatest idols. Their passion made it plain that the sacrificial theatrics of the Catonsville Nine could only have been enacted by members of the religion which still retains, as the matrix of its faith, the immolation of a victim to absolve the sins and ease the conscience of the tribe. "*Agnus Dei qui tollis peccata mundi, dona nobis pacem . . .*" And so the young priests marched throughout those four penitential days, with that grim ambivalence of sorrow and of joy which rituals of sacrifice have always brought to men. How many more Catonsvilles and Milwaukees would be ignited by the continuing war and by the explosive cycle of expiation begun by Philip Berrigan?

It was a former Catholic, Episcopal Bishop James Pike, an early and outspoken opponent of the Vietnam war, who was the first of the week's star speakers to voice his support of the Catholics' guerrilla liturgies. Flamboyant as a peacock, a huge peace amulet from Haight-Ashbury swinging on his brilliant magenta-colored shirt, decorated with numerous buttons urging protest and resistance, Bishop Pike brought down the house with his praise of the Catonsville Nine.

"They accuse you of burning some paper with napalm when they're using napalm in an unconstitutional war to

burn innocent women and children . . . well I say burn on,
men, burn on! You Catholics are getting greater and
greater! I'm an American, and Americans love success!
Four hundred in Catonsville, fifteen thousand in Milwaukee,
burn me 250,000 next time and I'll be a happy man!"

The crowd roared with delight. "Sock it to 'em Jim
baby!" someone shouted.

"The morality," the Bishop bellowed, "is often to
resist the law!"

"Sock it to 'em Bish!" someone else yelled.

The Bishop loved that. "The government is chicken,"
he roared, pointing his finger towards the back of the
room, where a few F.B.I. men stood throughout the week,
one of them awkwardly disguised as a black militant
"Chicken! You're chicken not to indict me for inciting and
abetting young men to resist the war!"

The protesters rose to their feet and whooped. The
Bishop held up his fingers in a V sign and left the microphone to hold court with a bevy of resisters, priests,
cameramen, and members of the Catonsville Nine, who
were enthroned upon the speakers' podium, throughout
the nightly rallies, like college trustees at graduation exercises. There was an intermission during which a vast
variety of pamphlets were passed around, manifesting, as
would the Nine's testimonies at their trial, the peace movement's growing obsession with United States interference
in Latin America. There was a pamphlet from an organization called AVILA (Avoid Vietnams in Latin America);
a call to boycott all products of the United Fruit Company
(bananas, Revere Sugar, S and W Root Beer); a petition
protesting the government's strike-breaking against Cesar
Chavez's Mexican farm workers. Meanwhile, seminarians
distributed petitions demanding amnesty for war resisters.
They also handed out statements of support for Daniel
Berrigan from the Jesuits' Maryland province; statements

of support for David Darst from the Christian Brothers; and brochures which said "WANTED: JESUS CHRIST: This man is threatening the American way of life." Telegrams of sympathy for the Catonsville Nine were read, over the loudspeaker, from Coretta Scott King, Ralph Abernathy, Benjamin Spock, Tom Hayden, David Dellinger, William Sloane Coffin. A plea for contributions to the Catonsville Nine's Defense Fund was passed around by a former Benedictine monk who had gotten married the previous week and was honeymooning at the trial with his pretty young wife. A contingent of sandaled students arrived from California, laden down with sleeping bags, tape recorders, guitars, amulets of peace, and calmly went to sleep on the floor. It was announced over the microphone that the next speaker would be Dorothy Day. As she walked to the podium, statuesque, austere, a little lame, the harangues quieted, the applause was as reverential as it was tumultuous.

"I came here to express my sympathy for this act of non-violent revolution," she said, "for this act of peaceful sabotage which is not only a revolution against the state but against the alliance of Church and state, an alliance which has gone on much too long . . . only actions such as these will force the Church to speak out when the state has become a murderer. The act of the Catonsville Nine is another desperate offer of life and freedom. But my friends, we must restrict our violence to property . . ."

She paused and looked sternly at the hundreds of faces turned devoutly towards her. "I've been in jail for civil disobedience more often than any of you," she said arrogantly, "and I know more clearly than any of you the courage it entails . . . and I know that we must hang on to our pacifism in the face of all violence. We must retain our pacifism the way Gandhi, Martin Luther King, and

Cesar Chavez retained it, it's the most difficult thing in the world, and the one that requires most faith."

The men in black rose in one body to lead the ovation. The applause continued to welcome the appearance of Noam Chomsky, the M.I.T. linguistics expert who had coined the phrase "From Dissent to Resistance" the previous fall. Chomsky's lecture, a calm and meticulous dissection of American imperialism in the Philippines, was like a Bartok quartet amidst the rock 'n roll of the angry clergymen. Religious passion returned to the podium in a talk by Baptist minister Harvey Cox, the militant Harvard theologian who had started the fashion, the previous year, of accepting draft cards on collection plates at his war-protest services. Cox, who had recently volunteered to be co-chairman, along with Father James Groppi, of the Milwaukee Fourteen's National Defense Committee, compared the act of the Nine to Jeremiah destroying the clay pots on the steps of the Temple; to William Lloyd Garrison's public burnings of the Constitution in protest against slavery; to Martin Luther's burning of Canon Law, ("the bad side of the good news") in front of the University of Wittenberg. "Catholic priests," Cox exclaimed to more thunderous applause, "have a special task of carrying out sacrificial acts which lead to redemption!" Guitars strummed in between speeches, more angry clerics came to the podium to condemn the war. One of them was Lutheran Pastor Richard Neuhaus, a co-founder, with Daniel Berrigan, of Clergy and Laymen Concerned About Vietnam. Thirty-four-year-old Neuhaus, pastor of a black parish in Brooklyn's Bedford-Stuyvesant district, had been an elected delegate, pledged to McCarthy, at the Chicago Democratic Convention, and had been jailed for leading a protest march with Dick Gregory after the defeat of the peace plank. Neuhaus accused the government of murder, accused Johnson of betrayal, accused Johnson of "selling out the American dream of liberty for the mailed fist of repression." The indictment brought more clamor from the audience. Neuhaus's passionate diatribe, and its tumultuous reception, carried the demonic side of the sacred. The rage of this austere young man in a pearl-gray pastoral suit, the terrifying fervor of the young face surmounting the starched white collar, recalled the Parliamentary Fast Sermons of the pre-Cromwellian decade, those jeremiads against the "wasteful and corrupt" monarchy, preached by youthful country parsons, which precipitated the beheading of Charles the First in 1648. Seldom had the *vox populi* which deposed Lyndon Johnson sounded more enraged.

And there came to be a climate of unease, of latent violence, in the hall of Saint Ignatius on that first night of the Catonsville Nine's trial. There were rumors that some of the younger peace agitators, against the advice of their elders, had gotten into trouble at a Wallace rally that was being held downtown that night. There was confusion about whether or not to join them. There was general dissent in the air. Suddenly everyone started accusing each other of imperialism—Noam Chomsky had ended his talk with a ringing condemnation of American imperialism in all parts of the world. Daniel Berrigan stalked the hall like an angry panther, complaining that some older Jesuits had refused to support him, but had promised to pray for him. "That," he grumbled, "is a form of spiritual imperialism." Blaise Bonpane, a Maryknoll priest who had been recalled from Guatemala, along with the Melvilles, for helping insurgents to arm, went to the podium to accuse pacifists of imperialism. "Non-violence is an imperialist solution!" he clamored with a pointed look at Dorothy Day. "Only guerrilla warfare will alleviate the misery of the masses in the underdeveloped countries . . . the peasants do not start violence . . . it is inflicted upon them and they have the Christian right to retaliate!" Even the SDS militants were taken aback by that. "Is he really a priest?" one asked. Father Bonpane finished clamoring and stepped down, a sirupy smile on his face, looking, off the speaker's stand, like the servile sextons who sell holy water, phosphorescent rosaries, candied skulls in the basements of Mexican churches. Soon after the end of his tirade two young men ran into the hall, bringing news of violence at the Wallace rally downtown, of peace movement kids being jailed. One of them grabbed the microphone: "Our brothers are being bitten by dogs and trampled by horses! It is our duty to go downtown and give them our support!"

Rage, pandemonium, and indecision spread among the young protesters until members of the Catonsville Nine took control. After a brief consultation the defendants fanned out into the hall, persuading their disciples to boycott the Wallace rally. George Mische grabbed the microphone and ordered the kids to cool it. "We must abstain from violence at all times!" he shouted in a commanding voice. "If you go out and call Wallace and the cops a bunch of pigs you're playing their game!" And then he added, threatening, magnificent, "You'll go to that rally over the bodies of the Catonsville Nine!" The activists quickly calmed down. The Wallace rally was boycotted. Instead, a group of priests and students marched to the Baltimore jail, where, at one a.m., they negotiated for the release of the peace demonstrators. Then they returned to their sleeping bags on the floors of Baltimore churches, to rest for the next day's dramatics.

The Trial

Every morning between nine and ten o'clock, as a core of the Nine's supporters began their theater of protest on the streets of Baltimore, the defendants were brought into the courtroom, in two separate shifts, to thunderous applause. It was a partisan audience, packed daily to capacity with those students, priests, nuns, and friends who had had the stamina to line up on the steps of the Federal Courthouse in the pre-dawn darkness, leaving several hundred disappointed latecomers excluded from the trial. Tom Lewis and Philip Berrigan, accompanied every morning, handcuffed, from the County Jail by Federal marshals, came in through a door by the side of the Judge's bench. As the applause started Tom Lewis, cheerful and cherubic, gestured a V at his supporters. Philip Berrigan, looking worn and tired, wearing a brown civilian suit provided by the Federal Government, acknowledged the greeting with sweeping gestures, in the manner of a weary political candidate riding through crowds in a limousine. The applause began again with equal fervor, a few minutes later, as the seven free defendants came into the other side of the courtroom through the front door. Daniel Berrigan made a spectacular stage entrance, prancing, gazelle-like, towards the bar, frequently stopping to autograph copies of his latest book, *Flight to Hanoi*, for his fans. He took a ballet position, one foot pointed behind the other, to sign each volume with a comical flourish of his pen. Pirouetting, relishing the laughter (he had been, according to his mother, a stage actor of phenomenal talent in his adolescence), he took deep and cynical stage bows as he stood at the brass bar of the courtroom. Then, with a wide grin, he exhibited his talisman of the week for everyone to see. It was a color photograph of his brother Philip which he had mounted into a medallion, and which he wore around his neck throughout the trial, just as, in the Church of long ago, Christians wore images of their patron saints in times of crisis. The seven free defendants then crossed the bar, and, under the impatient gaze of the burly, bristling Federal marshals who lined the courtroom, each of them embraced the two prisoners. And it was evident, as soon as Federal Judge Roszel Thomsen took the bench, that he would not dispel the powerful atmosphere of tenderness that the Catonsville Nine's "community of risk"—as Daniel Berrigan put it—infused into his courtroom.

Roszel Thomsen, sixty-six years old, chief Federal Judge of the Fourth Federal District, fifteen years on the Federal bench, member of the Methodist Church, father of three and grandfather of nine, a very prominent citizen of Baltimore, former president of the Baltimore school board, former president of the Board of Trustees of Goucher College, seemed eager, like Richard Nixon, to be liked by everybody. And he created a vastly more permissive atmosphere in his courtroom from the one prevailing in the Boston courtroom in which, a few months earlier, four men who barely knew each other had been convicted of conspiracy. The peace movement had grown in power and in bitterness since the Spock-Coffin trial, the rift in the nation had grown wider since Chicago, its youth had grown angrier. Judge Thomsen, like the government which he served, was intent on pacification. Sitting down every day with a cheerful, affable "good-morning," he remained, throughout the trial, benign, fatherly and painfully courteous towards the angry, ebullient Nine. Slight, spectacled, and gray-haired, with an ingenuous smile, he recalled some proverbially kind and patient Lewis Stone judge out of a 1930's movie.

Whatever impatience he showed was apt to be directed towards the government attorney, a thin and sad-faced young black man who was trying his first political case. The government had provided its own bit of psychodrama by assigning, as chief prosecutor of nine people notorious for their militant work in the civil rights movement, the only black federal prosecutor in the State of Maryland. The government's chief counsel, Arthur Murphy, and his aide, Barnet Skolnik, had to plead their case against four tough and brilliant lawyers who had informally called themselves, in sympathy to their defendants, "The American Four." The defense team was headed by William Kunstler, a tall, suave, leonine man, one of the most flamboyant civil libertarians of the decade, whose clients have included Rap Brown, Morton Sobel, Jack Ruby, the Black Panthers, and who had recently volunteered to defend the Milwaukee Fourteen. Kunstler's colleagues on the "American Four" team were of an unusually ecumenical character: Harrup Freeman, a Quaker from the Cornell Law School who specialized in conscientious objector cases; Harold Buchman, a Jewish labor lawyer from Baltimore; and Father William Cunningham, professor of law at Loyola University, and a colleague of Daniel Berrigan's in the Society of Jesus.

Exhibit "A" proffered by the defense in "United States versus Philip Berrigan et al.," as the case is called in its official abbreviation, was a brown paperback edition of a book called *Vietnam and International Law*, compiled by twelve of the nation's foremost legal specialists, which concluded that the United States' intervention in Vietnam had violated the charter of the United Nations, the Geneva accords of 1954 and the Constitution of the United States. It was a crucial but ill-fated exhibit. It was the hidden premise on which the defense would base its arguments. Yet it was rejected by the government on the basis that it was irrelevant as an exhibit because "reasonable men" could hold such views, and no exhibit was necessary to substantiate the defense's stand upon the war; and the judge would also refuse to consider it, having ruled from the outset, as Judge Ford had in Boston, that no discussion of the propriety of the Vietnam war would be allowed in court. On the basis of the conclusions stated in this exhibit, the Catonsville Nine pleaded innocent to their charges of destroying government property and interfering with the working of the Selective Service System. (A previous charge of conspiracy was dropped by the government on the first day of the trial.)

The Nine freely admitted that they had committed all the acts of destruction of which they were accused, but insisted that they were innocent because they had not committed these felonies with "criminal intent." The defense's strategy was to argue that the Nine had defended themselves by "reasonable force" against "unlawful force"; that they had been entitled to destroy the draft files because they had acted to defend the lives of a collective third party which was in peril. "Confronted with the reasonable belief of imminent peril to the national community," Kunstler had written in his brief in behalf of the Nine, "the defendants were compelled by public necessity to destroy conscription records for the purpose of avoiding a public disaster." Kunstler's statements to the Court, as well as the defendants' testimonies, were replete with dramatic metaphors of situational ethics that illustrated the moral and legal necessity of destroying certain property in order to save lives. (Kunstler: "If a man whose home was adjacent to his draft board was unable to enter his front door because of flames and accordingly broke into the building housing the draft board, destroying its records in order to save a life . . ." David Darst: "If I see a person being asphyxiated inside of a burning car and break the window to save his life, I am not committing a crime by breaking that window . . .") Putting his defendants' case, as he loves to do, on a grandiose historical scale, Kunstler pleaded that the Nine had made the same kind of protest that should have been made in Germany in the 1930's, the kind of protest which Germans were prosecuted at Nuremberg for not making. "They are saying 'We are guilty, but it was not a criminal act . . .' They are not more guilty than Socrates or

Jesus when they were brought before the courts . . . They were making an outcry, an anguished outcry, to reach the American community before it was too late. I think this is an element of free speech to try, when all else fails, to reach the community . . ."

It was a stirring, dramatic, but utopian argument, and the suggestion of a free-speech defense was more of an emotional tactic than a legal device, since the Supreme Court, the previous spring, had even rejected individual draft-card burning as "symbolic speech" protected by the First Amendment. There had been one dissenting opinion, that of Justice William Douglas, who had questioned whether conscription was permissible in the absence of a declaration of war. And Douglas's lone dissent had been the nearest the Judiciary branch of the Government had come to criticizing the Executive's handling of the Vietnam war. The Baltimore Court having refused any discussion as to the legality or morality of this "Executive's war," as Justice Douglas has referred to the Vietnam conflict, it was not apt to be persuaded by the Nine's numerous metaphors which compared American Selective Service Offices to houses, cars or nations on fire, or which likened the defendants' actions to those of the anti-Nazi underground. And so the trial proceeded like a game of shadowboxing, the government taking formidable pains to prove factual evidence which Berrigan et al. readily admitted, the Nine pleading self-defense against a government which the Court refused to consider as aggressor; the government restricting its meaning of "intent" to its traditional definition as "willful act," the Nine pleading a "specific, uncriminal intent" in attacking properties of a government which had violated international law.

As for the Catonsville Nine, already long obsessed by the failure of American institutions, their attitude was one of cynical disdain. They had come to accuse their government of criminally waging—in the words of the Nuremberg Principles quoted in the defense's Exhibit "A"—"a war of aggression in violation of international treaties, agreements and assurances." And since the government which they were accusing of war crimes was permitted to define the nature of the court proceedings, they held the view that their trial bordered on farce; that the more valid events were the forums, the teach-ins, the theaters of protest outside of the courtroom. No current piece of literature more coolly summed up the defense's position than an article by Joseph L. Sax in the *Saturday Review* which the Nine's supporters circulated in hundreds of Xeroxed copies throughout the trial:

> *It is important to demonstrate that the behavior of the American government is illegitimate within the constitutional terms that it formally accepts. If the courts can not deal with these issues, then other forms must be developed that are not so limited by political constraints, that would in this sense be more legitimate than the courts, even though they would not command the same kind of force. The problem of complicity in war crimes, of resistance and civil disobedience, of law and conscience, must be faced by the citizen, whether or not the courts will contribute to this discussion . . . So long as there is no realistic alternative to the present international system, it is important to act in such a way as to contribute to the evolution of more effective institutions and more decent principles of international behavior.*

And as the trial proceeded it grew clear that the nine Catholics had come to court not only to moralize about the iniquities of the Selective Service System, the evils of the Vietnam war, and the excesses of American imperialism. They had come also to protest the chaos of a political morality hovering between the ancient supremacy of national laws and the emergent international codes which increasingly struggle to control the behavior of individual nations. The case of the Catonsville Nine was the quintessence of a political trial.

The defense's first gesture of disdain for the proceedings of Judge Thomsen's courtroom had been not to challenge the choice of a jury. "Just take the first twelve," Kunstler had said with a wave of his elegant hand, not looking up from the brief he was reading. "Any twelve will do . . ." Nevertheless, with a meticulousness which verged on the mischievous, Judge Thomsen spent the first day questioning twenty-six prospective jurors on their vocations, their war records, their emotions about the war and the draft. The story of the Catonsville Nine had been well-publicized in the Baltimore press; and one out of three possible jurors disqualified themselves, looking with outrage at the defendants, as having already made up their minds on the case. After many hours a jury of seven men and five women were empaneled and sequestered for the duration of the trial. It included three housewives, an engineer, a saleswoman, a building inspector, a retired nurse, a truck driver, a steelworker, an insurance agent. The average age of this "microcosm of American society," as Kunstler enjoyed addressing them, was fifty-six. One could not but associate the physiognomy of these twelve men and women with the many profiles offered by the press, in the months preceding the 1968 election, of the typical citizen about to vote the Wallace ticket. Torpid and overfed, bloated with the joyless abundance of the American diet, reminiscent of Kiwanis meetings and American Legion parades, self-righteousness etched on their faces like an addict's grimace, they were a slice of that "somnolent middle class" whose new rightist leanings so obsessed Philip Berrigan and his fellow radicals. They offered little hope for a hung jury.

Like a football team going through the motions of attack on a field devoid of opponents, the Government, on the second day of court, produced its material evidence: the wire baskets in which the draft records were burned; a gasoline can from which the napalm had been poured; the charred remains of the draft records; a film taken by a newsman in the parking lot of Catonsville's Selective Service Office, showing the defendants praying around the burning pile. The first witness for the prosecution was an F.B.I. agent who had arrived at Catonsville an hour after the event and whose cross-examination by the defense counsel drew savage cackling from the war protesters in the courtroom. ("Do you know what napalm is, Special Agent James Anderson?" "I've heard of it.") The defendants smiled condescendingly throughout, like parents watching their first graders put on a Christmas play. Daniel Berrigan stopped scribbling—for he wrote poetry throughout the trial—and stared at the show with a cynical grin. Philip, chin resting on his forefinger, smiled and chuckled as if he were watching one of his favorite films. The Nine's good humor increased further at the appearance of the Government's two material witnesses, Mrs. Murphy and Mrs. Mosberger, the two clerks who had been in charge of the Catonsville Draft Board the day the Catholic protesters staged their raid. Confused and drawling, models of outraged respectability, the two matrons provided the first comic relief of the courtroom drama.

"Mrs. Murphy," asked the Government attorney, "how many floors does the building have in which you work?"

"Well, I think it's three, I've never been up to the top but I think it's three."

"Please explain to the jury what a 1-A is."

"Well, a person is 1-A when he really is not eligible for any other classification. Really, there's nothing else we can find to put him in, frankly."

"The type of work you do, Mrs. Murphy, would you say its prime purpose is to serve the government?"

"Yes sir, the Army of Defense. I serve the Army of Defense."

Next came Mrs. Mosberger. "What happened on the afternoon of May 17th 1968, Mrs. Mosberger?"

"Well we had a little visit. I happened to notice a lady pass one of our desks. I noticed it was a lady because it had a skirt on. I saw this skirt go by the desk . . . then I heard someone say something about clergy. I saw this man with a wire basket. When this man came through the door with the wire basket it went through my mind that something was not right, that I should call the police . . . We had a little scuffle . . . I saw two men out of the window who hang out at the Knights of Columbus Hall . . . I threw the receiver of the telephone through the window . . ."

"What did you see these persons do, after they left the building?"

"They were out in the parking lot, burning records . . ."

That night, at the evening rally, twenty-five young Americans burned their draft cards in the basement of Saint Ignatius Church. As each held up his piece of paper, the flames flickering here, there, everywhere, like fireflies on a summer night, hundreds of priests and protesters clapped rhythmically, chanting "Hell, no, we won't go . . . Hell, no, we won't go . . ." But there was something cruelly jaded, tired, blasé about the gesture. For suddenly the bold sacrificial gestures of the Baltimore Four, the Catonsville Nine, the Milwaukee Fourteen, made card-burning seem as old-fashioned as the Charleston. Even the F.B.I. men leaning against the wall of the church hall attempted to look bored. "Hey, hey you Feds," one of the speakers shouted into the microphone, "do any of you Feds want to burn *your* credentials?" The F.B.I. men smiled nervously, outnumbered, unable to obtain any identifications in the frenzied crowd, trying desperately to look cool. One could not help but recall a harsh statement that Daniel Berrigan had made, the previous fall, when he defended his brother's action: "Draft-card burning has become establishment . . . it's not the time to burn draft cards anymore, but draft files."

"We want Dan! We want Dan!" the crowd stomped as the charred remains of the draft cards lay littering the floor of Saint Ignatius. And the expert seducer of young souls went to the speaker's podium in his blackest mood on that second day of the trial, flaying his anarchic wit at the individuals who were judging him. "I'm caught in the bind of sitting through four days of fly shit at this trial, a process not worth its weight in that commodity. The Boston Five never conspired and they convicted them for conspiracy. We conspired like mad and they dropped the charge. If you've got any complaints, see your local F.B.I. agent. So we burned some trash. Have you ever seen a jury representative of our nation? None of these twelve people are black, none of them are students, none of them are poor. They've all been through three wars and they lump them into one. Sunday they go to church. Monday they go to the National Guard, Tuesday they go back to church, Wednesday they go to the Rotary Club where someone is waiting with a fly net to catch them to sit in the jury box, and as for that poor guy in the black bathrobe who needs a retirement thing, he's going to give us a slow death by drowning us in Karo Syrup . . ."

·   ·   ·

William Lloyd Garrison, who had been, in his own time, as disillusioned about the viability of American institutions as the Catonsville Nine, once said that although politics is the art of the possible, agitation is "the art of the desirable." And the Nine's agitational tactics, in Garrison's sense, created the most desirable political climate, and the most desirable trial, they could have hoped for. For although the government dropped its charge of conspiracy presumably to narrow the scope of the defendants statements, Judge Thomsen's desire to mollify the peace movement led him to permit a startlingly wide airing of antiwar views. Judge Thomsen was intent on restoring faith in American institutions to the angry mobs of protesters, bandaged in mourning for the Vietnam dead, who milled around his Courthouse. He was said to be painfully aware of them. And his leniency in allowing the Nine to include in their testimony every detail of their lives which they considered relevant to their "intent" in Catonsville was precedent-breaking in the history of political trials. This permissiveness was the main bone of contention between the Court and the prosecution. "Your honor," government counsel Arthur Murphy said as he interrupted one of the Nine's rambling testimonies, "we keep using that word 'intent,' and I fear that this little word will get us into an awful lot of trouble." "They can use the words 'motive' and 'intent' the way they wish," the judge had suavely answered, "I shall charge the jury later about the legal meaning of those words." Judge Thomsen would reserve his severity for the last hour of the trial.

If one could have read the minds of the jurors, interpreted the slight tremors that passed over their stern faces, their most frequently recurring emotion would surely have been one of amazement at the wholesomeness, the handsomeness, the poise, the all-Americanness of the Catonsville Nine. Middle-class respectability imbued each and everyone of these parochial school graduates, and the defense exploited respectability to the hilt. Like doting relatives, the Nine's counsels had their clients dwell at length upon their solid and tender family backgrounds, their high scholastic achievements, their patriotic army records, their piety, their works of mercy among the poor. The accused also presented the Court with a formidable array of literature which, they insisted, had been instrumental in their decision to attack the United States' machinery of war. This bibliographical approach was an important new tactic. For it was being increasingly stressed, by the gurus of the peace movement, that the chief conspiratorial agent in Americans' resistance to the war was not any group of persons, but the various media of the press and of free discussion reaching an increasingly enlightened generation of citizens. "Those who have persuaded young men to resist are those who have brought forth evidence regarding the history and character of the war in Vietnam," Noam Chomsky had recently written in a *New York Review of Books* article widely read, that fall, by opponents of the war. "If the government wishes to put a stop to the substantive act of 'persuading young men to resist,' it has only one resource: to block the flow of information and prevent discussion of such information as reaches the public."

The biographies and bibliographies began. Christian Brother David Darst, twenty-six years old, youngest of the Catonsville Nine, summa cum laude graduate of a prestigious Catholic college and recipient of a two-year scholarship to Harvard Divinity School, said that he had started on his road to Catonsville by reading Senator Fulbright's *The Arrogance of Power,* Theodore Draper's *The Abuse of Power,* and Senator Mansfield's congressional testimony on Southeast Asia. Ingenuous, trim, rosy-cheeked, with the spruced handsomeness of a bridegroom on a Victorian daguerreotype, Darst was as dazzlingly respectable as were his parents, pillars of their Church and of Memphis, Tennessee, society. The Darst parents sat in the front row throughout the trial, smiling proudly, championing their offspring as did most of the families of the Catonsville Nine, typifying the remarkable phenomenon of contemporary Americans who have been radicalized by their children. Mr. Darst, a glacially distinguished man who had been a Lieutenant Colonel in World War II, kept saying, at court recesses, "I have a son at Harvard, a son at Yale, another at Notre Dame, and I'm prouder of David than of all the others." Mrs. Darst, a fine-boned woman attired in Chanel-style tweeds and many pearls, had often murmured: "Our David is so Christ-like."

"I have been living and teaching in the poorest black ghetto in Saint Louis where little children don't get enough to eat," Darst said towards the end of his crisply delivered testimony. "I was appalled that our country could be spending eighty billion dollars a year chasing imaginary enemies around the world and raining down destruction on hundreds of thousands of innocents when it couldn't even bother to feed its own children . . . I went to Catonsville after a number of steps, all of them within the law, had proved useless in actually raising the voices of dissent . . . basically my intent was to raise an outcry over what I saw was a very clear crime . . ."

"Did you say 'crime'?" Judge Thomsen asked, deadpan, his pencil poised over the yellow legal pad on which he took meticulous notes throughout the trial.

"Yes, 'crime,'" Darst repeated, "a very clear and wanton slaughter. I saw myself as a man who sees a crime being perpetuated, someone being attacked, and his human impulse is to help, to call the police. How do we all judge the Genovese case, in which thirty-seven people heard her cry in one hour and did not lift their finger? The judgment of the community has been that it was a crime not

to call out. My intent was also to do a very tiny bit to stop
the machine of death from moving. I am comparing it to
Czechoslovakian citizens who throw bricks at tanks to
stop one more tank from perpetuating unfair aggression,
to hinder the effort of destruction in an actual physical
way . . . The non-violent tradition of our religion has
always drawn the line between people and things. It said
that material things are for the use of people, but that
people are sacred, they are absolutely ends in themselves,
they can never be used as means. Jesus Christ beat the
moneychangers and threw over their tables because these
were properties which were desecrating a more sacred
property—the Church. Our point is that we're destroying
property which is desecrating the most sacred property—
life. Was Jesus Christ guilty of assault and battery?"

And with those words Darst had arrogantly turned
towards the members of the jury, whose pale and flabby
faces, in the afternoon light, seemed made of unrisen
dough.

Thomas Melville, thirty-seven years old, former Maryknoll
priest, as beefy and burly and Yankee as the Federal
marshals lining the courtroom, looking like the most popular guy at the Firehouse's Saturday night poker game, had
achieved his revolutionary epiphany by reading General
Eisenhower's memoirs. One of his brothers was a Marine
Corps pilot; his father, after a career of supervising food
store chains, had been foreman of war-equipment plants
during World War II. Like the rest of the Nine, Melville,
who had spent ten years working as a Catholic missionary
among impoverished Guatemalan peasants, had joined
the Catonsville action "to protest United States imperialism,
not only in Vietnam, but all over the world." And as most
of the Catonsville defendants, Melville's testimony offered

a Vista-Vision travelogue, often blithely simplistic in its rage, of the excesses of United States interventionism, of racism at home, of the Catholic Church's resistance to social change. Judge Thomsen, like a film editor trying to splice reels, urged the defendants as politely and soothingly as he could, throughout the statements, to stick to the point.

After being sent to Guatemala as a Maryknoll priest in 1957, Melville testified he realized that his job was not to talk to his parishioners about "the life hereafter," but to improve their standard of living. He established cooperatives and, without permission of the local bishops, put up the titles of his church property to form credit unions on behalf of the peasants. Cooperatives in Guatemala, Melville said, had a bad name because they had been pioneered by the government of Jacobo Arbenz, who had distributed to peasants 230,000 acres of land which had previously belonged to the United Fruit Company. Arbenz's government, according to Melville, "was later accused by our government of being a Communist government, and overthrown with the help of our government." This overthrow was denied at the time by the United States, Melville testified, but President Eisenhower subsequently admitted to the overthrow in his memoirs. These memoirs of Eisenhower's had been a turning point in Melville's life. Melville inquired more deeply into the question, and learned that the man who had headed the U.S.-sponsored overthrow of Arbenz, Castillo Armas, had taken the land away from the peasants and given it back to the United Fruit Company; and that 3,000 peasants were killed by the Armas government in the process of being forcibly evicted from their new land. The outraged Father Melville, along with his brother Arthur Melville, also a Maryknoll priest, had then made a personal visit to a subsequent President of Guatemala, Ydigoras Fuentes, and asked for restitution of land to the peasants. "He was very nice and courteous, but he said that there was not any land for these peasants, because they did not have capital, and they did not know how to work the land . . ."

The government prosecutor made one of his frequent objections about the scope of the defense's testimony. "Your honor, the government believes that the government and this Court are being extremely patient with these defendants . . . we have a sequestered jury . . . we are now hearing a detailed, subjective history of the past twenty years of Guatemalan history . . ."

"We are not trying the government of Guatemala, nor the Catholic Church in Guatemala," Judge Thomsen agreed. Defense attorney Harold Buchman insisted that Melville's experiences in Guatemala were essential to his "intent" in burning draft records in Catonsville. Melville was allowed to resume.

"I took part in that action in Catonsville, sir, because of what happened to me in Guatemala . . . eighty-five per cent of the people in Guatemala live in misery. You don't, so perhaps that is why you don't worry about it. They live in misery because two per cent of the population in Guatemala is determined to keep them that way. This two per cent is aligned with big-business interests in Guatemala, especially the United Fruit Company. The United States government identifies its interests in Latin America, specifically in Guatemala, with the interests of U.S. big business, and the two per cent. So any movement on the part of the peasants, if it does not go . . . according to the way they want it . . . they start screaming, 'They are all a bunch of Communists,' and they begin executing these people."

"You say the United States Government screams and they execute people?" Judge Thomsen said with some alarm. "You mean the United States Government is executing Guatemalans?"

"Yes, your honor."

"The United States Government?"

"Yes, your honor."

"Has the United States sent troops into Guatemala?"

"Yes, your honor."

"When?" the judge asked firmly.

"About the end of 1966, and in January of 1967."

"And you say that the United States executed people?"

"Yes," Melville said triumphantly, "it is in *Time* Magazine."

"All right," Judge Thomsen said, defeated.

"You know, our Ambassador was just killed, your honor," Melville continued.

"I know that," Judge Thomsen said grimly.

"And in January of this year," Melville went on mercilessly, "our military attaché was also assassinated, and so was our naval attaché. Perhaps people in this country should begin to wonder."

"We are not trying the Guatemalan series of revolutions," Judge Thomsen said suavely. There was another objection from the government about the scope of the defendant's travelogue. Judge Thomsen again gently prodded Melville to stick to the point. "It is an extremely interesting story, and I understand you have written an extremely interesting book about it which I look forward to reading. But we just cannot try the last ten years in Guatemala . . . if this experience that you had . . . caused you to have certain views, you can say what they were. This is what we are waiting to hear." And Melville got to the pith of his intent with ferocious intensity.

"We decided that we would join the revolutionary movement in Guatemala . . . myself, Marjorie, my wife, who was a nun at that time, John Hogan who was also expelled with us . . . thinking that perhaps one of us would get killed; and it would not look too good for the American Government if an American priest or an American nun had gotten killed in Guatemala by an American Green Beret. We wanted to complicate things for the United States Government in Guatemala . . . we did not want to see another slaughter in Guatemala as is occurring in Vietnam . . . when we came back I was very pleased that there were people in this country who were very upset about what was going on in Vietnam. We had not heard about it in Guatemala in the papers. I said that we have to speak to the peace movement in this country, so that they know, if we sign those papers in Paris tomorrow . . . all it will do is release 548,000 American boys to start working in other countries in Latin America. We discussed among ourselves what we could do to bring some of the focus to Latin America. We knew that we did not want to turn it away from Vietnam, but we did want people who are upset about the morality of our government to exercise some of their concern towards Latin America, and specifically Guatemala, where we had lived. So we participated in the Catonsville action, hoping to bring the attention of the peace movement to Guatemala, and in that way, avoid another Vietnam . . . I had read Roger Hilsman's book, our Under Secretary of State for Southeast Asia, who resigned over what we are doing in Vietnam. There were other men of conscience who were coming out, such as John Kenneth Galbraith . . . I was trying to distinguish these issues for the American people in as dramatic a way as humanly possible, where there is no court of appeal, including the United Nations, because this government does not want to face these issues in the United Nations. There is no court of appeal for the Vietnamese people, or for the Guatemalan people, or for any other people, in facing the United States military might. So I performed this action, hoping to bring these issues into court . . . and, perhaps, avoid another Vietnam, and to bring to a close, as fast as humanly possible, the war in

Vietnam. I think writing letters and parading are great when you want to enlarge the sewer system or put in a new highway. But when people are being murdered, you have to take dramatic action. I wish there was a magic button that we could have pushed, instead of the action in Catonsville. But there is not."

And this jovial, red-faced Boston Irishman had returned to his seat looking like the head of the local Elks. "Reading the papers, you'd have thought they were a bunch of kooks," a Federal marshal was overheard saying to a colleague during a recess of the trial. "But they're not, they're a great bunch of regular guys."

When Marjorie Melville took the witness stand a member of the courtroom audience murmured "Oh, how could *she* burn anything?" Very short and dainty, with the kittenish smile of a sexy teenager, the former Maryknoll nun who had recently married Thomas Melville looked like the all-American sweetheart, the girl most often pinned at college fraternities, the cheer-leader at the Rose Bowl. Wholesome and rosy-cheeked, crisply dressed in navy blue and white, flashing an irresistible smile, she took the stand like a schoolgirl about to recite Wordsworth's "Daffodils," and spoke with a pert, faint Spanish accent and with devastating shrewdness of her overwhelming love for the United States.

"I think, because I was born in Mexico, I grew to have a great love for my country . . . My father is an American, and he was working for an American company at the time I was born . . . I had to defend the United States against the attacks my Mexican friends would bring forth. I was really so proud to be an American. I went to the American school in Mexico and then to high school in the States when I was fourteen . . . I was assigned in 1954 to work in Guatemala as a teacher . . . I got in when the new president had taken over the country. His name was Castillo Armas. I was really very proud of the fact that this was the only country I had ever heard of that had been able to free itself of a Communist government . . . I was very happy that my country had helped this country to be free from Communism . . . It was not until much later that I found out that it was not exactly the way I had seen it. Finally President Eisenhower admitted that it was a C.I.A. overthrow, and I found out that the reason was that the government that had been overthrown by Armas had taken away quite a bit of United Fruit land, and paid for it, and distributed it among the peasants. But the United States didn't like this, and that is why the overthrow came. When I began to find out little things like this, it was really a shock to me, to realize that my country was not exactly the great ideal that I had always pictured . . . It might have been a little bit like when a child finds out that Santa Claus does not exist . . ."

Marjorie Melville paused, bit her lip, looked forlorn. Judge Thomsen looked at her with compassion.

"In 1962," she continued, "I took a course on Christian social doctrine that the Jesuit Fathers gave . . . it was after I took this course that I began to take the girls I worked with out into the slum areas of the city to show them what life in their own city was about . . . At the same time I got involved with a group of university students . . . I began to realize that my country's involvement in Guatemala was much deeper than what I had expected. Several times we asked for help from the Alliance for Progress for special projects which they could finance with AID money . . . they were very simple projects like putting water in a village, or helping to set up a cooperative—we found out that funds were not available for these things. I found out later . . . that the Alliance for Progress was giving all the anti-guerrilla police in the city new police cars. They were the same make of car, all U.S. donated. Then it came out in the newspapers that two thousand new policemen were being trained in Guatemala, and the salaries, uniforms, barracks, food, the whole thing, were being paid for by the Alliance for Progress."

"Your honor, we think we have been very, very patient," the government attorney interrupted. "But if we could get from the police cars in Guatemala to Catonsville, we would appreciate it."

"We simply cannot try the history of Guatemala," Judge Thomsen agreed. "We have been over it twice already."

". . . I felt my role as an American very important," Marjorie Melville continued, "because I could see the image of my country in Guatemala, and I certainly did not want to permit that image of imperialism to continue . . . Our superiors and the American ambassador in Guatemala got a little nervous about our desire to work with the peasants, and they thought it would be better if we left the country before the thing got too big for them . . . When I came back to the United States in April of this year I was determined to do something . . . I just could not stand back and permit more U.S. troops being sent to Guatemala. There were too many men there, Green Berets, and equipment, arms and helicopters. I think the thing that impressed me most, and the reason I used napalm to burn those draft files, is that napalm has been dropped in Guatemala, as well as in Peru. In Guatemala, an eyewitness told me about it . . ."

The courtroom was hushed. There was an amazing lack of interruption by either the Court or the prosecution as the adorable little former nun coolly continued her inventory of American terrors, of planes missing their targets, of peasant villages being hit.

". . . to me, Guatemala is Vietnam beginning again . . . I know that burning draft files is not an effective way of stopping a war, but I certainly can't find any other way of stopping this war . . . I have really racked my brain, and I have talked to all kinds of people. I can't face the military power of this country. We wrote to Senator Bobby Kennedy and to Senator Teddy Kennedy, and we wrote to Senator Morse. We talked to Senator Hatfield . . . they say yes, yes, yes; but that is it. There is no real answer to stopping it. The thing continues. We have been talking about the war in Vietnam for six years, and it is getting worse all the time. When I read the newspapers and see the television programs where it says so many thousand Vietnamese killed, I know that in Guatemala the numbers are going to be like that. And I know these people. They are not statistics to me. They are just looking for a piece of land to support their children. They are not trying to overthrow the United States. That is the last thing in their minds. I wanted to make as effective a protest as possible to U.S. military intervention across the world, not only in Vietnam, but in Guatemala where I had seen it."

Marjorie Melville rose from the witness stand smiling pertly, and, under the astonished glances of the jurors and the Federal Marshals, went back to her seat like a schoolgirl who had given a perfect recitation. "Underneath it all," her co-defendant George Mische had said, "she's a tigress."

Like all of the Catonsville Nine, Mary Moylan, thirty-two years old, a registered nurse-midwife with a degree from the Johns Hopkins school of nursing, daughter of a former court reporter for the Baltimore *Sun*, was the image of middle-class American wholesomeness. Affable and impeccably groomed, with a luminous skin and soft red hair, dressed in green cashmere, she looked, that day, like a genteel young suburban matron about to pour tea at a garden club meeting. She looked like Mrs. Miniver. She looked like the smiling young women who praise, to television audiences, the benefits of some new brand of instant coffee, or the boons of Ivory Soap for perfect complexion care. But Mary Moylan was filled with the rage of the newly awakened Catholic conscience. Her term in Uganda as a lay worker with a religious order—the White Sisters of Africa—led her to believe that the "present set-up" of the Catholic Church's missionary work was totally irrelevant to the needs of the people it should serve. Her interest in foreign policy had been triggered by her wrath at seeing that in the summer of 1965, while she was in Africa, "American planes piloted by Cubans bombed Uganda, supposedly by accident." The Catonsville travelogue in Mary Moylan's testimony, focused on racism at home. She had been led to burn draft records at Catonsville, she said, by her outrage at the United States' government breaking of the law on many levels, which she had witnessed most poignantly during her work with black communities.

". . . through my involvement in various activities in Washington, it became obvious that we had no right to speak to foreign countries about their policies, when things at home were in very sad shape. I was involved in the militant black community in Washington. It became obvious that . . . in instances which I know of personally, the law was broken by the government; and that, in fact, justice for a black person in the court system is just about impossible . . . through my work in Washington it became obvious to me that . . . our foreign policy is indeed a reflection of our domestic policy. In Washington one of the black youths was shot by a white policeman, and a verdict of justifiable homicide was handed down. A protest was staged by a young leader who had a juvenile record. A Southern Congressman then read into the *Record* of Congress this man's juvenile record. This is absolutely illegal. Juvenile records are available to no one. This congressman was called, and it was pointed out to him that this procedure was illegal. His answer was: 'I did it once, and I will do it again.' . . . We have done this all through our history . . . Today we see people dying in Vietnam . . . We see the Latin American situation, with the Green Berets there. Napalm has been used and reported in the press at least four times in Latin America . . . When you look around and see the imperatives placed on you by the amount of lives lost openly in Vietnam, lost openly here in America, then it is time that you stand up. This is what it means to be a Christian . . . to not only talk about things, but to be willing to do something about it. Now marching and protesting, as a viable or effective form of protest, died shortly after Selma. It has been institutionalized and legalized, and it is no longer effective . . . To pour napalm on pieces of paper is much preferable to using it on any human being. Human life is sacred . . . what I really want to do, by pouring napalm on draft files, is celebrate life, not to engage in a dance of death that the American Government seems intent upon . . . some property, as we have said in our statement, has no right to exist. By this we mean the gas ovens of Hitler's regime, or slum properties, or the files of conscription which continue the imperialistic policies of the American government; which continue the slaughter of people overseas . . ."

"If there were any one way in which you could sum up your intent in doing all of these acts you are accused of doing on May 17th, 1968?" the defense counsel, Father Cunningham, asked.

"It would be to celebrate life," Mary Moylan answered.

"It would be what?" Judge Thomsen asked, pencil poised over his notes.

"Celebrate life," Mary Moylan answered. And the outrage on this respectable young woman's face recalled the long tradition of dissent and of Utopian moralism which has led Americans, since the beginning of their history, to take the law into their own hands to further a cause which they believed morally righteous—be it to repeal a tea tax, to preserve or to abolish slavery, to preserve or to repeal racial segregation. For good or for bad, the Nine's politics of conscience seemed, in this courtroom, as American as apple pie.

Thirty-two-year-old George Mische, cocky, massive, flamboyant in a bright orange sweater, swaggered to the witness stand as into a boxing ring. He sat leaning forward, his elbows resting on his knees, fiercely poised. His slanting, cold blue eyes, the eyes of the young Lenin, stared mercilessly at the prosecutor. He talked in machine-gun style, loudly and sharply, at dizzying speed. His wide cheeks frequently twitched in a sucking motion, like a professional speaker controlling thirst, as he expounded on the piety, the poverty, the patriotism of his family. His father, a former labor organizer, had been the supervisor of the Veterans' Hospital in Saint Cloud, Minnesota. George Mische's childhood had been marked by the suffering of men crippled by war. One of his brothers had founded a Catholic Worker house of hospitality in Chicago. Another of his brothers had founded the Association for International Development, which trained Catholic laymen to work with the poor abroad. George Mische himself had worked with delinquent youths in New Jersey, Harlem, Minnesota. He had scored highest in his major studies' comprehensives at the Jesuits' Saint Peter's College in Jersey City (major in sociology, he specified, minors in economics, philosophy and history). He had served two years in the army, and stayed on for eight years in the National Reserves. During college vacations he had worked with the Maryknoll Missionaries in the jungle areas of Yucatan, establishing cooperatives for the Indians. After graduation from college he had attended the State Department's Foreign Service School, and had been sent to Latin America as an employee of the Alliance for Progress, from which he had later resigned because he was outraged by its "support of military dictatorships." With Mische's testimony the Catonsville Nine's travelogue accelerated to dizzying speed, for Mische loved to travel, Mische had traveled more on his road to Catonsville than any of the well-traveled Nine.

"I worked in all of Central America and the Caribbean . . . in all of the Central American countries, I believe, except Nicaragua. My role was to go in and draw up an economic development program for each country there, trying to make a study of the country, what that country needed most. I would then have to go and negotiate with the presidents of those particular countries, and the cabinet members. I had gone down there with the idea that all of the Latins would be there, waiting at the boat to greet us, because I was an American . . . Then after I became involved with negotiations at a higher level, I started to understand why bricks were being thrown at us. I was involved particularly in two countries where revolutions had taken place. I should not say 'revolutions,' I should say 'coup d'états,' military overthrows of governments. These were two democratically elected governments that were overthrown by the military with Pentagon support. At that point, I felt that I could not, in conscience, go on with this.

Because John Kennedy, himself, had said that we will not have any relationships with any other countries where a military dictatorship takes over, that, at the overthrow of democracy, we will stop all military and all economic support to them . . . Well, when I saw it deliberately done twice, I resigned. Where it had the most impact was in the Dominican Republic, because that was such a tragedy that it was unbelievable."

And then came Mische's shining moment. His friends had predicted that this brilliant and most bellicose member of the Nine would manage, at some moment in the trial, to "blow those guys' minds," "shake up the system." And like an opera star working up to his most virtuoso passage, singing faster than ever, Mische did his thing.

"A man like Trujillo had run that country for thirty-two years. He was kept in power because when anybody talked about social change or social reform, they would go into the house of a person in the neighborhood, take the male head out of the house, cut off his penis, put it in his mouth, cut off his arms and legs, drop him on the doorstep . . ."

A tremor passed over the jury box. The marshals' med-aled chests made a violent thrust forward. There was an anguished tittering of nuns. The government prosecutor leapt to his feet like a terrier out of his den.

"I have to object your honor," prosecuting attorney Arthur Murphy moaned, "I am trying to be patient, your honor. I would suggest, again, that we get to the issues to be determined . . ."

"We are not here," said Judge Thomsen with admirable delicacy during the discussion that ensued at the bench about the 'relevance' of Mische's testimony, "to try the history of the world in the twentieth century."

"I came back to the United States and went all around this country," Mische continued triumphantly, savoring his aria. "I drove 75,000 miles in a year and a half by car. I talked at university levels. I talked to religious groups. I talked at businessmen's clubs. I talked to anybody who wanted to hear about what is happening abroad . . . I spoke to eighty bishops in the United States, Catholic bishops, from one to five hours, trying to have them understand what was going on overseas; what the problem of white racism in this society was doing to separate people from each other; and trying to tell them: Look, if you are moral leaders, speak out. The Holy Father, when he came to this country, said, 'War never more.' The Holy Father talked about peace among men. He talked about racism. He talked about the responsibility of rich nations towards poor nations. The Bishops only get hung up on birth control, but not the other encyclicals . . . We asked them, since they have eighty billion dollars worth of property, and ten times as much in investments, that, if they were really going to live in the spirit of the stable that Christ came from, then, get rid of the buildings. Give to the poor. The man who wanted to build the churches in Christ's time was Judas. And Christ kept saying . . ."

There was another interruption, by the government counsel, to complain about the panoramic scope of Mische's testimony. The discussion ended with Judge Thomsen saying: "We are not here to try the Catholic bishops of the United States."

"Unfortunately," Mische quipped. ". . . I wanted to explore all the avenues to work out these problems . . . I saw, then, that the government, the Church, all of them were writing it off . . . I got involved in the peace program, because I felt that, with the rioting in the streets and all the problems of the domestic violence here, we are not answering these problems . . . it seemed to me that the war in Vietnam, first of all, was illegal, because only Congress can declare a war, not a President like Johnson can take us into a war. We should never have let him. He should be on trial here today."

Led by priests and nuns, a thunderous round of applause surged from the spectators' gallery. Judge Thomsen ferociously gaveled the audience back to order.

"This is the unbelievable thing," Mische went on, "that this society is getting uptight about some paper that we burned . . . and yet each day napalm is put on flesh of human people . . . one of the most powerful things that affected me was Philip Berrigan's first trial for the blood-pouring; again, a six-year sentence for pouring blood on files. Men walk around the street spilling blood continuously . . . the United States, I think, reached its apex of morality in 1945, when they came across with the Nuremberg trials. I said: 'It is good. You are right. Every German citizen had the responsibility to stop Hitler. All of us, as Catholics and Christians, share the responsibility of why they put those Jewish persons in the ovens.'"

Defense counsel William Kunstler asked George Mische what his intent had been in destroying draft files in Catonsville.

"If a sergeant and a major in the Army give you an order," Mische said, "the major's order is more important and supersedes that of the sergeant all the way up the line. So maybe there were some laws involved here, Mr. Murphy, about draft records . . . But there is a higher law we are commanded to obey . . . the intent was to follow the higher law of conscience that all of us have, as human beings, as whatever we consider ourselves: humanists, Christians, Jews, Buddhists . . . That was our responsibility, that was our intent. The double intent was to save a lot of lives, Vietnamese, North and South American lives, everybody, to stop the madness."

There was a recess. There was an elated exhaustion among the supporters of the Nine who milled in the hall outside of the courtroom. Mische embraced his wife and baby and held court with much panache among his admirers. The spectators were jubilant about the variety and the vehemence of the anti-war views being aired at the trial. One of them asked the defense attorneys how they explained Judge Thomsen's permissiveness in hearing the Nine's testimony. "He can't risk the possibility of a mistrial by restrictive rulings on this one," Harold Buchman said. "Also he's painfully aware of the peace sentiment in the community, of the division in the nation . . . he wants to deescalate the confrontation." "I also think," William Kunstler said with an impish smile, "that he's absolutely fascinated to hear what these defendants have to say."

John Hogan, thirty-three years old, a former Maryknoll brother, was the quietest and most retiring of the Nine. A gentle, laconic man educated in Connecticut by Dominican Sisters, he was trained as a carpenter while studying for the Maryknoll order. Upon his assignment in Guatemala he had become business manager of the Pope John XXIII colony, a Maryknoll cooperative run by the then Father Thomas Melville. John Hogan had been recalled from Guatemala at the same time as the Melvilles for being sympathetic to the Guerrilla movement. He had settled down, upon recall, to write a book against United States intervention in Central America. He had decided to make a militant protest against the Vietnam war after reading Seymour Mellman's *In the Name of America* and *Vietnam: Crisis of Conscience*, a collection of anti-war essays by American theologians. "I have an analogy," John Hogan said, ". . . if there were a group of children walking along the street . . . and a car was coming down the street and was out of control . . . and if I were coming along in a car, and if I could divert that car from crashing into those children, then I feel as though I would have the obligation to divert that car from the children . . . Of course, the car is property. The car would be damaged . . . And it is also possible that something would happen to the individual in the car. But I would be thinking ten times more of these children whom the car was going to hit than I would be thinking of the individual in that car."

The defense counsel asked John Hogan to sum up his intent in Catonsville. "I just wanted to see people live," John Hogan said, with that blunt idealism of the Nine in which morality frequently triumphed over intelligence.

The genial and boyish Tom Lewis, who, in the company of Philip Berrigan, traveled handcuffed every morning to the trial in the custody of Federal marshals, had been the star halfback on his high school football team. He had turned down a college football scholarship to go to art school, had studied art at the Uffizi in Florence and at Johns Hopkins in Baltimore. Twenty-eight years old, son of an executive of the Nabisco Company, he had served for eight years in the Maryland National Guard. A devout Catholic intent on works of mercy, he had taught art and led spiritual retreats at inner city schools, Veterans' hospitals, homes for the aged, Catholic colleges. He had been an early and militant member of Baltimore's civil rights movement, and had been arrested before for participating in sit-ins demanding open occupancy in Baltimore County. He had been led to militancy against the war when his brother had left for Vietnam in 1965, soon after the full-scale bombing of North Vietnam began. He had come to the conclusion, after hearing Pope Paul's message to the United Nations later that year, that the Vietnam conflict was "a genocidal war." Tom Lewis had been a co-founder, with Philip Berrigan, of the Baltimore Interfaith Peace Mission. He reviewed, during his testimony, the tactics which he and Philip Berrigan had used, during the first two years of their collaboration, to protest the government's Vietnam policy: peace marches, fasts, and demonstrations, visits with congressional representatives, vigils in front of the homes of the Joint Chiefs of Staff—an escalation of tactics which had culminated, the preceding year, in the blood-pouring action which had brought both of them a sentence of six years in Federal Prison. Tom Lewis's mother, an exuberant and militant member of the Baltimore peace movement who had taken part in many of the earlier protests, sat in the front row of the courtroom smiling proudly at her son. "Tom and Phil are the freest men in the world," she often said during the trial. "How I envy them."

"What were your views on civil disobedience?" the defense counsel asked Tom Lewis towards the end of his testimony.

"The civil disobedience of the early Christians," Tom Lewis answered intensely: ". . . the Apostles walking through the grain field on the Sabbath; the Apostles taking the food that was in the temple to be offered, and giving it to the poor. Jesus disrupting the temple, chasing people out of the temple because of the way the temple was being used. It was no longer used for the good of the community."

Tom Lewis was asked to enlarge upon the significance of his first protest at the Customs House.

"This blood was poured on these records, the symbolism, of course, of blood being, in Biblical terms, a symbol of reconciliation, relating to the blood that is being wasted in Vietnam, not only the American blood, but the blood of the Vietnamese."

He was asked how he decided to engage in the Catonsville action while awaiting sentence for his first protest.

"In a sense," Tom Lewis answered, "it was a choice

between life and death. In a very Christian sense, it was a choice between saving a man's own soul."

Daniel Berrigan had gone to the witness stand dressed in clerical black, all whimsy suspended.

"Once in 1964 when I was invited to the Republic of South Africa by the Archbishop of Durbin," Daniel Berrigan said midway through his biography, "the question was raised, in a large audience by an anguished group of laymen: 'What happens to our children if things get so bad in our society that we have to go to jail?' I remember saying: 'What happens to us and our children if we do *not* go to jail?' I had visited Eastern Europe twice in the course of 1964, visiting and traveling and exchanging with Christians ... I was realizing, from the point of view of very difficult church conditions, what it might cost to be a Christian, and what it might cost, even at home, if things were to change in a direction that I felt we were quite near, even then. I returned in the summer of 1964 ... I was quite convinced during that summer, both from my exposure in France and from my knowledge of what Americans were by being an American, that the war in Vietnam was inevitably going to worsen. I felt that that cloud, which was no larger at that time than a man's hand, was going to cover the sky. I remember reading Demosthenes at the time. I felt that, in the autumn of 1964, I must begin to say 'no' to the war ... So I began to do those things that were very new then ... we marched and fasted and started the teach-in programs and sat in at the United Nations and spoke on campuses across the country and spoke in Harlem ... I underwent a very deep kind of boot-camp in the new man, becoming a peaceable man in a time of great turmoil. Some may be aware that New York was not the most auspicious place to be a peaceable Catholic priest at that time. Cardinal Spellman was still alive. The Cardinal believed that the highest expression of faith for an American Christian was to support military efforts. By his annual Christmas visits to troops across the world and specifically in Vietnam, he was placing an official seal of approval upon our military adventures. And I had to say no to that, too. I had to say 'no' to the Church . . . so much so that in the autumn of 1966, by the conjunction of powers that remain mysterious to me even now, I was exiled from the United States to Latin America."

Judge Thomsen interrupted. Had the *government* exiled Father Berrigan, the judge asked with alarm? No, no, Daniel Berrigan said with his first, elfish smile, an agreement between the Cardinal and the Jesuit Superiors had exiled him, a conjunction of powers which, he repeated, still remained mysterious to him. Judge Thomsen was reassured.

"My decision to go to Catonsville was not taken in a vacuum," Daniel Berrigan went on to say, ". . . I was realizing at Cornell that one simply could not announce the Gospel from his pedestal . . . when he was not down there sharing the risks and burdens and the anguish of his students, whose own lives were placed in the breech by us, by this generation that I and others belong to. I saw suddenly, and it struck me with the force of lightning, that my position was false, that I was threatened with verbalizing my moral substance out of existence. That I was placing upon young shoulders the filthy burden of the original sin of war. That I, too, was asking them to become men in a ceremony of death. At that point I realized that, although I was too old to carry a draft card, there were other ways of getting into trouble with a state totally intent upon war . . . that one could not stop within the law while the moral, social condition deteriorated . . . structures of compassion breaking down, neighborhoods slowly rotting, the poor slowly despairing, social unrest forever present in the land, especially among the young people, who are our only hope, our only resource . . . I must say that there was one other event that was almost unbearably moving to me in the spring of 1968, and which also helped me understand the way in which I must go. It was the self-immolation of a young high school student in Syracuse, just about a month before Easter. This young boy had come to a point of despair about the war and had gone into the Catholic Cathedral in Syracuse, drenched himself with gasoline, and immolated himself in the street. He was, however, still living a month later. On Easter Sunday I finally was able to gain access to the boy . . . There, I visited with him shortly and smelled for the first time in my life the odor of burning flesh and understood what I had seen in other ways in North Vietnam. The boy was lying in total torment upon his bed, and his body looked like a piece of meat that had been cast upon a grill. He died very shortly thereafter, but I felt that my sense had been invaded in a new way, and that I had understood again the power of death in the modern world, and that I must speak of this and act in the opposite direction . . . So I went to Catonsville. And I burned some paper because I was trying to say that the burning of children was inhuman and unbearable, and, as Brother Darst said, a cry is the only response . . . I did not want the children or the grandchildren of the jury to be burned with napalm . . ."

The government prosecutor leapt to his feet. "Now your honor," he moaned. He sat down again and added, in an exasperated tone, "Oh, go ahead."

There was another discussion at the bench. Judge Thomsen suggested that defense counsel Harrup Freeman, a Quaker who taught law at Cornell University, was "coaching" his witness. Mr. Freeman indignantly denied it. Daniel Berrigan was asked by his counsel to state, "beyond anything you have stated to this point," what his intention was on May 17, 1968.

". . . I did not wish that any innocent people should be subject to death by fire, I did not wish that my flag be dishonored by my military and by my men of power and by my President," Daniel Berrigan said very slowly and angrily, leaning forward in his chair, his gaunt face as grim and condemning as that of a medieval inquisitor. "I did not wish that the American flag be steeped in the blood of the innocent across the world . . . I was trying to be concrete about death, as I have tried to be concrete about the existence of God, Who is not an abstraction, and about Whom I read in my Testament."

He said those last words very loudly, slowly, with a fanatic intensity. The defense counsel asked the defendant where man finds his God, according to Jesuit theology. Daniel's face lost its sternness, he sat up in his chair proudly, and there was a sudden lightness, an elation in his voice.

"Well, in the sixteenth century, a Spanish soldier decided to lay down his arms and dedicated himself to a kind of Christian brotherhood. And around him, in his own lifetime, seven or eight other men gathered around the very simple ideal, which, of course, had been a kind of constant in the Church, that the Christian thing to do was to live among the poor and serve in the hospitals and live the life of actual poverty and actually be dependent upon others by begging and by manual labor for their livelihood. Then, this thing grew and grew. Finally, before his death, this man, who was also an extraordinary man of the spirit . . ."

"We can not have a history of the Jesuit order . . ." Judge Thomsen interrupted gently.

"Could I say three sentences about his writings?" Daniel Berrigan insisted. ". . . Shortly before his death, he set down a few, very simple principles, upon which we have been trying to live ever since. They had to do with the idea that we were not monks, and we did not return to monasteries, and our lives were not dedicated to hidden prayer. But that we belonged actually in the society, in the culture, in the schools, in the ghettos among the poor, as the servants of men. And that it was there that we would find God or nowhere."

"I ask you, Daniel Berrigan," said defense counsel Harrup Freeman. "Was what you did on May 17th, 1968, at Catonsville, carrying out that philosophy of the Jesuit order?"

The Quaker and the Jesuit stared briefly at each other.

"May I say that if that is not accepted as a substantial part of my action," Daniel Berrigan said very slowly and somberly, "then the action is eviscerated of all meaning; and I should be committed to insanity."

When Daniel Berrigan walked back to his seat minutes later, he resumed pencilling on a piece of paper a poem which he had started to conceive on that third day of his trial.

> *Everything before was a great lie.*
> *Illusion, distemper, the judge's eye*
> *Negro and Jew for rigorists,*
> *spontaneous vengeance. The children die*
> *singing in the furnace. They say in hell*
> *heaven is a great lie.*
> *   Years, years ago*
> *my mother moves in youth. In her*
> *I move too, to birth, to youth, to this.*
> *The judge's tick tock is time's steel hand*
> *summoning; come priest from the priest hole. Risk!*
> *Everything else*
> *was a great lie. Four walls, home, love, youth*
> *truth untried, all, all is a great lie.*

The truth the judge shuts in his two eyes.
Come Jesuit, the university cannot
no nor the universe, nor vatic Jesus
imagine. Imagine! Everything before
was a great lie.
                    Philip, your freedom
stature, simplicity, the ghetto where the children
malinger, die.
                    Judge Thomsen
strike, strike with a hot hammer
the hour, the truth. The truth has birth
all former truths must die. Everything
before; all faith and hope, and love itself
was a great lie.

The appearance of Philip Berrigan on the witness stand
was the most troubling moment of the Catonsville trial.
One had thought of him as indestructible; he seemed exhausted, browbeaten, unsure. It was as if the psychological
violence of prison life, which he had endured so stalwartly
at first, had accumulated to fell him in a sudden blow. The
politics of penance had taken their toll. His face was drawn
and ashen. The brown civilian suit provided by the Federal
Penitentiary System for the occasion of his trial hung loosely
on his large body. Jeremiah's voice was stilled. The lion was
caged. Philip Berrigan's appearance was a tragic reminder
that he had been the central symbol of the Catholic protesters' expiatory liturgies, both their high priest and their
readiest victim. Philip Berrigan looked not so much anguished as he looked indifferent, drained of all energy or
anger. "Despite freedom from uncommon problems in jail,"
he had recently written in a letter to his brother, "I am sus-
ceptible to a common one—tedium. Now, tedium tends to
feed upon drabness and routine, overcrowding, upon steel
bars and body counts, isolation from community, issues and

struggles. In effect, tedium tempts one to quit; to submit gracelessly and imperceptibly to cop-out; to relish appearances rather than reality; to think less, feel less and love less; to suspend life, growth and Christianity for the duration . . . I find myself vainly trying to discover some spark of constructive anger in my fellow prisoners . . . tedium terrifies me as a kind of deadly abrasive which works on a man's spirit like wind and water on loose soil . . ." Philip had ended that letter to his brother with a quote from Saint Paul's letters to the Corinthians: "But the foolish things of the world has God chosen to put to shame the wise, and the weak things of the world has God chosen to put to shame the strong." And yet, that day, Philip Berrigan seemed to be exhausted by the sacred foolishness of the Gospel.

"What is your function at present?" his defense counsel had asked. "I currently have some sort of ministry within the Federal Penitentiary System," Philip had answered. It was said caustically, with a bitterness not expected of a man who had been so willing to serve a term in jail. His voice had a hollow, empty ring. His testimony was long and dragging, with the compulsive loquaciousness of lonely men. His mind seemed to wander; and the judge, afraid as ever of trespassing on an idol of the young, looked both pitying and exasperated.

"Very early in my New Orleans experience," Philip Berrigan said midway in his rambling testimony, "I became deeply involved in what was called the civil rights struggle of those days. We did a lot of voting registration work. We observed the poor in some of the slums of New Orleans. We tried to provide some sort of bridge between the white and black communities in New Orleans. The population of the city is about one-third black there. We tried to attack racism at its roots. It is a far less subtle form of racism in the Deep South than it is here in the North . . ."

"I do not think we need to go into the organization of groups there," the judge objected gently.

"What I was leading to was this," Philip Berrigan continued. "I was in New Orleans during the Cuban crisis . . . the New Orleans people realized that they were within the range of intermediate-range ballistic missiles from Cuba . . . This led me into an exploration of how the peace was being held together these days. I began to investigate what was called the cold war . . . I began to read deeply into the question . . . I was impressed by Pope John's Encyclical called *Mother and Teacher*, and also his later one, *Peace on Earth*, . . . I thought that these two documents gave me a basis for judgment of America's involvement in the world . . . when the bombing of North Vietnam started with the new administration in Washington in early 1965, I became rather militantly involved in opposition to the war . . . I was ordered by my superiors to remain silent, but Pope Paul came to the United Nations and spoke. I considered this as some sort of mandate . . . from that point on, until the time I was jailed, I had been mostly traveling around the country and talking and writing . . . I came to the conclusion that I was in very, very good standing by way of American and democratic traditions in choosing civil disobedience in a serious fashion. There have been times in our history when, in order to get redress, in order to get a voice, *vox populi*, arising from the grass roots, people have had to indulge in civil disobedience. From the Boston Tea Party on, through the abolitionist and anarchist movements, and through World War I, where we had sizable numbers of conscientious objectors, through World War II, and right on through the civil rights movement, we have, perhaps, the most rich tradition in any country of civil disobedience . . . We were prepared for the blood-pouring by the fact that we had practiced civil disobedience down in Virginia; and because my brother and myself, for example, have been practicing civil disobedience for years by signing complicity statements, supporting draft resisters . . . Of course, this carries —I don't know—three years, and a $10,000 fine. It was, generally, the trial under which Dr. Spock and the others were . . ."

"We are not trying the Dr. Spock case here," Judge Thomsen said with more sharpness than usual. Defense counsel Harold Buchman asked Philip Berrigan to describe the "state of mind" that compelled him to become involved in Catonsville.

"I saw no point to my life," Philip Berrigan said, with a rising vigor in his voice, "if it continued in a rather normal fashion in this society. The issue was not my life or my future. The issue was the deepening involvement of America around the world, not only in Vietnam, but in Latin America. The issue was the most powerful empire the world had ever seen, and the most powerful military power that the world had ever seen, and what this had done to us as a people. My life, I judged to be slightly irrelevant in terms of these overriding considerations . . ."

"If someone, feeling just as sincerely and just as deeply and just as conscientiously as you do . . . that the war is in the interests of this country," the government attorney asked in his cross-examination, "broke into a peace action center or some other repository of papers, documents . . . and destroyed and stole and burned and mutilated those objects, would you feel that he had violated the law and should be prosecuted for having done so?"

"Certainly," Philip Berrigan answered. "We violated the law, and we should have been prosecuted, too . . . I think that their views ought to be exposed through testing by the community . . . just as our views are being tested by this community now and by, we hope, a larger community outside."

"Should they be convicted for the violation of the law?"

"I think that is your problem," Philip Berrigan said dourly.

When Philip Berrigan returned, some hours later, to his prison cell in the Baltimore County Jail, he set down in writing, as he did every night of the court proceedings, his impressions of the trial, and of what had brought him to that courtroom. "Our nine lives meshed in Catonsville," he wrote, "we traveled to that draft board and that parking lot on the same road: Service of ghetto and foreign poor; civil rights and peace militancy; trouble with both church and state; risk of reputation, freedom and life itself; lecturing, writing, demonstrating, civil disobedience, nonviolence and slow growth in the Gospel . . . until, so help us God, we could do nothing else." He expressed cynicism, in these notes, about the trial of the Catonsville Nine. "One does not look for justice in this court, one hopes for a forum from which to communicate conviction and anguish . . . the greatest good that can be extracted from that courtroom is conviction, and the greatest evil, acquittal." He pondered over the overriding terror which obsessed his life, and that of the young Americans who had come to Baltimore to support him: "Chances of avoiding nuclear war today are far less than half, and constantly plummeting . . ." He looked up to youth as the only possible redeemers of the world: "There is only one hope! Our young people are coming on, the most superb breed this country has yet produced. And they're saying to the international barons of government and industry, 'You don't represent us, because you don't stand for what we stand for . . . You're ruining our country by threatening the world's peace. You must stop, or you must go!'"

And with the stoicism of Perpetua before the lions, of Stephen before the stones, Philip Berrigan expressed, at the end of that meditation from jail, the core of his fanatic faith and his lack of assuredness in his survival: "Obedience to the Gospel, duty towards history and rational politics lead together to crucifixion—whether imprisonment or death."

The streets of Baltimore had grown more serene on the fourth and last day of the trial. On the steps of the Courthouse, Governor Agnew's sapphire-helmeted police, compared to their colleagues in other cities and other confrontations, seemed relaxed and smiling. Many of the Nine's student supporters had left Baltimore to return to classes, and there was a mood of jubilation among the several hundred young priests and protesters who had remained to picket the Courthouse. The protesters were exhilarated by the generous airing of anti-war views allowed in the courtroom. The government was satisfied that, thanks to Judge Thomsen's finesse, the trial had not further alienated the young. The city authorities were also satisfied, having proved that they could control the peace movement without any Mayor Daley tactics. All sides had had their triumph. Inside the courthouse, defense counsel William Kunstler exulted over a government concession, made during the preceding day of testimony, that "reasonable men" could hold the view that the Vietnam war was illegal. "For the first time in my knowledge since the start of the American involvement in Vietnam," he rejoiced, "the government of the United States has conceded that it is reasonable for a person to believe that this involvement is illegal. At the trial of the Boston Five, the government had conceded that 'sincere' men can believe the Vietnam war to be illegal. In this case, the government seems to have escalated from 'sincere' to 'reasonable.' This is a concession of such far-reaching legal and political significance that it requires considerable thought by lawyers and laymen alike . . . if it is reasonable for an American to believe the war is illegal, then it is equally reasonable for him to take the necessary steps to stop the continuing illegality."

There was the habitual standing ovation, that last morning, for the defendants as they came into the courtroom. It was more elated, more theatrical than ever, having the style of an encore, ending with the rhythmical, measured clapping that celebrates a great performance. George Mische was carrying his baby. He stood for a while in front of the ornate brass bar by the side of his pretty young wife, bouncing the child up and down, and the room was filled with the cackling voice of a six-months old who has just learned to laugh. Daniel Berrigan faced the spectators' gallery, and thanked them, with a luminous smile, for having created "such an extraordinary sense of community in this courtroom." The marshals, in constant awe of the clerical defendants, seemed not to mind this extemporaneous address, and he went on: "We shall continue, by other means of communication, to share the experience which we have shared together in the past four days. I am not allowed by natural law, or the law of the Jesuits, or the law of the court, to say what these means of communication will be, but . . ." He flashed his most mysterious smile. "Hang in," he added. There was more admiring applause, V signs outstretched. The court was called to order as Judge Thomsen came in.

The prosecution began its summation. The Catonsville Nine were accused of willful depredation of government property in excess of one hundred dollars, of willful seizure and mutilation of documents of Maryland Draft Board No. 33, of interference with the Selective Service Act of 1967. "They were candid," government attorney Arthur

Murphy said, "they were frank, they were honest, we even said they were sincere . . . but, members of the jury, for this kind of offense, the social, the religious, the political, or the moral views are no defense." With a pleading look at the defendants, Mr. Murphy went on to name all the activities which the Nine could have engaged in to express their condemnation of the Vietnam war. "You are allowed to speak at public places. You can write all the letters you want to your Congressmen, to your legislators. You can write letters to the editors . . ." His lean brown hand waved approvingly in the direction of the street, where the protests were continuing. "You can picket. You can debate. You can write books. You can write articles . . ." And then the prosecutor went on to dissect a crucial word of the Catonsville trial, "motive." "Motive is that which prompts an individual to do a thing . . . Intent is what you really do, as distinguished from what you may do accidentally, or by inadvertence. I may have a motive to feed my family and to keep a roof over my family, or the person in the ghetto might have that same feeling. The motive there is what? Give his family food and shelter. But that motive may become so strong, because the man is unemployed, that he goes out and robs a bank. Is he to be excused because the motive was good? No, he is not to be excused. And this is the situation you have with these defendants."

"Ladies and gentlemen of the jury," William Kunstler said as he began the summation for the defense, "we feel that this is essentially an historic moment for all of us." Stalking the courtroom like a large sleek panther, a lock of black hair straying over his forehead which he tossed back with a boyish gesture, he was determined to draw the last ounce of emotion from the impassive jurors. "We are present at one of those moments in history that suddenly crystallize for at least one brief and shining moment certain issues. As I and my co-counsel have said throughout this trial . . . we do not think it is just a simple burning case. We feel that it is something quite different. Just as we never really believed that the trial of Socrates was merely a question of whether he was trying to confuse and destroy the youth of Athens; or the trial of Jesus, that he was attempting to overthrow the Roman Empire . . . We agree wholeheartedly with the prosecutor as to the essential facts of the case. The defendants did participate in the burning of records. They produced a substance called napalm . . . They used the cans you saw. They went to Catonsville. They took certain files out . . . and you must have understood, because it was said openly here, that the Selective Service System is an arm of the Federal Government for the procurement of young men to be put into military service . . . to be used, as one defendant said, as cannon fodder, if that be the government's dictates. This is not a question of just records which are independent of life. It is not driving licenses we are talking about here . . . there are no other records which so directly affect life and death on a mass scale, as do the Selective Service records . . ."

He stepped forward, looking compassionately at two stolid, grandmotherly women sitting in the front row of the jury box.

"They affect every mother's son . . . And you can not put that out of your mind, because that was in the minds of these defendants. That was the reason they were there . . . They were there, firstly, to complete a symbolic act, which we claim is a free speech act; and secondly, they were there to impede and interfere with the operation of a system which they concluded—and it is not an unreasonable belief, as the government has told you—which they have concluded is evil, is immoral, is illegal, and which is destroying people around the world . . . You come to a

situation which all citizens have to face sooner or later:
What happens if nobody listens ... Is it not a fundamental
right for us to try to get attention from someone to listen
to us? ... They were trying to make an outcry, an anguished outcry, to reach the American community before
it was too late to reach anyone any more. It was a cry
that could conceivably have been made in Germany in
1931 and 1932, if there were someone to listen and act on
it ... Now ... I think that that is an element of free
speech to try, when all else fails, to reach the community
... The defendants did everything humanly possible to
avoid having to go into that parking lot. They did everything possible to obey the law. But ... nobody listened,
and the slaughter went on. All else has failed to change a
single American policy, with reference to the war in Vietnam; to stop a single useless death; to end the searing and
excruciating pain of burning napalm on human flesh ...
all in the name of a policy so incomprehensible that it
passes all human understanding."

The courtroom was hushed. Daniel Berrigan, a mercilessly cynical expression on his face, solemnly passed a
stick of gum to his brother. The Federal marshals stood
heads lowered, their arms behind their backs. Among the
jurors, whose faces looked like a tray of one dozen un-
baked rolls, a white-haired woman nervously twisted a
handkerchief around her index finger. Father David Connor, Daniel Berrigan's colleague at Cornell, sat with his
head buried in his arms, one did not know whether in
prayer or in tears. Another priest, in the last row of the
spectators' gallery, was silently, uncontrollably sobbing.

"There is, in the government's mind, a fantastic arrogance that goes along with the sincerity of these nine people," said government counsel Barnet Skolnik as he summed
up the prosecution for a final time. "They hold their views
so sincerely and so deeply that they feel they have the

right to impose their views upon people who disagree. Now that, ladies and gentlemen, is not just sincerity. That is an arrogance which the people of this country simply can not abide . . . Ladies and gentlemen of the jury, this is not Hitler's Germany!" His voice reached a tremolo of outrage, and he paused. ". . . It is an empirical fact, ladies and gentlemen, that the anti-war movement in this country has grown . . . because of the legal expression of views protected by the First Amendment . . . The government does not contend that this country is perfect . . . the history of civilization, ladies and gentlemen, shows that people progress by fits and starts . . . We will progress. We will get better, the country will get better." He spoke pleadingly now, as if to an angry child. "But the problems of the United States are not going to be solved by people who deliberately violate the duly enacted laws of the United States of America upon which all of the people of the United States rely . . . by people who deliberately violate the law under which we all live."

Judge Thomsen ordered a recess before charging the jury. And looking more benign than ever, enchanted with his trial, he stepped down from the bench. The spectators milled out into the hall outside the courtroom. Two Jesuits, history teachers at a midwestern school, discussed the significance of the trial with a group of seminarians. "It is an historic case," one of them said, "because it seems to be expanding the Judiciary's discussion of the Executive's handling of the war. The Executive has been taking far too much power in this war, and after all, if the Judiciary does not check the Executive, we're heading towards . . . towards . . ."—he held his hand threateningly up in the air. "Dictatorship and revolution?" the other Jesuit asked. His colleague, looking forlorn, shook his head in the affirmative.

· · ·

An hour later, on the afternoon of Thursday October 10, having calmed the dissenters for four days with his Machiavellian affability, Judge Thomsen told the jurors, as he charged them, to forget most of what they had heard in the last two days of testimony. "The law does not recognize political, religious, moral convictions, or some higher law, as justification for the commission of a crime, no matter how good the motive may be," he said softly, gently, as he began to charge the jury. "People who believe that the Vietnam war is illegal, or unconstitutional, or morally wrong, have the right to protest in various ways, such as by demonstrations, parades, and legal picketing . . ." and his hand waved approvingly, as had the government prosecutor's, towards the clamorous, picket-filled street. "The protester . . . may, indeed, be right in the eyes of history, or morality, or philosophy. These are not controlling in the case which is before you for decision. It is the state's duty to arrest and try those who violate the laws designed to protect private safety and public order . . ."

There was a tense, electric atmosphere in the courtroom as the judge continued with his charging. The number of Federal marshals had been more than doubled since the morning, as if news had leaked out, during the luncheon recess, that there would be some form of civil disobedience in court. The marshals, some forty strong now in a room that only held one hundred twenty spectators, stood shoulder to shoulder along the wall. They scanned the courtroom nervously, their insignias gleaming on their businessmen's suits, their pistols lurching in their side pockets, seeming suddenly hostile. They glanced anxiously at the door, which was frequently opening and closing with a sharp creak. Familiar members of the Baltimore peace movement, who had stayed in the streets for four days to marshal the demonstrations, were coming in and out of the courtroom to make contact with their colleagues inside. Reporters were rushing through the clanging doors to file their stories to evening papers. There was a faint tinkling of metal recurring every few minutes, and a rumor spread through the spectators' gallery that the Nine were perhaps planning, if convicted, to chain themselves to each other in protest and would have to be carried out of the courtroom. The spectators' heads kept turning and turning, looking around the courtroom to find an explanation for the noise. The tinkling was finally discovered, with relief, to be caused by a piece of costume jewelry, a miniature bell, pinned to Mary Moylan's scarf. But the tension continued to grow. The doors of the courtroom kept swinging open. A crowd of the Nine's supporters, kept out for lack of space, were nervously chatting in the hall outside. More marshals poured into the courtroom, until their shoulders finally overlapped along the walls. And the expressions on the defendants' faces, which, throughout the trial, had been one of cynical and amused resignation, had suddenly become one of grim reserve.

"If you find that the defendants under consideration intended to remove, destroy, and attempted to do so, these records filed or deposited in the office there," said Judge Thomsen towards the end of his charges to the jury, "then it is no defense that he or she also had one or more other intentions, reasons, purposes or motives, such as to make an outcry or a protest against the Vietnam war, or that he or she intended to make a test case, or that he or she acted from high religious motives . . ."

When the charging was finished the jury filed out to deliberate. And the defense counsel, as expected, made their exceptions to the charges, protesting, in particular, that Judge Thomsen had failed to charge, as he had been requested to by the defense, that "if the jury found the acts done by the defendants were done with a reasonable belief as to the invalidity of the war in Vietnam," the jury could find that the defendants had acted without criminal intent. The defense lawyers finished making their exceptions, and the court, in normal procedure, should have been recessed until the jury was ready to deliver its verdict. But the normal course of procedure was altered at this point by a totally extraordinary event. William Kunstler stepped towards the bench and said that the defendants asked permission to address the Court directly.

"All right," Judge Thomsen said amiably. A mutter of amazement spread through the courtroom. However, the shock, the surprise of this unheard-of proceeding was restricted to the spectators and the press. For Judge Thomsen, in one more admirable tactic of pacifying the peace movement, had agreed earlier in the day, during a meeting in his Chambers with the defense, to allow the defendants themselves to take exception to his charges—a privilege which, traditionally, is strictly reserved to lawyers. Judge Thomsen thoughtfully rubbed his spectacles with his handkerchief, put them back on, leaned his elbows attentively on his desk, and smiled. The Catonsville Nine rose to their feet as a single man, and there ensued a forty-minute colloquy between the judge and the defendants which, as Judge Thomsen himself admitted later with some pride, was totally unprecedented in the history of legal proceedings.

"Your honor," Daniel Berrigan said early in this dialogue, "we are having great difficulty in trying to adjust to the atmosphere of a courtroom in which the world is excluded, and the events that brought us here are excluded deliberately by the charges to the jury."

"They were not excluded," Judge Thomsen pleaded, "the question . . ."

"They were," Daniel Berrigan insisted, "the moral passion was excluded. It is just as though we were in an autopsy, and we were being dismembered by people who were wondering whether or not we had a soul. But your honor we are sure we have a soul!"

These words came out weightily from the boyish man in black, spoken with the fanatic intensity of an inquisitor probing a heretic's faith, turning the judge into the accused.

"It is our soul that brought us here," he continued, "it is our soul that got us in trouble. It is our conception of man. We really can not be dismembered in such a way that it can be found eventually that our cadavers are here, and our soul is elsewhere, and our moral passion is outside the consideration of this Court, as though the legal process is an autopsy on us."

"Well I can not match your poetic language," Judge Thomsen said, and was interrupted with frenetic applause. He stiffened. "Any further demonstrations and the court-room will be cleared," he barked out with uncharacteristic fierceness, "and I mean that, the whole crowd!"

The noise stilled, and he continued: "I think that you all for some reason, either because your lawyers have not gotten it over to you or for some other reason, simply do not understand the functions of a court . . . I happen to have a job in which I am bound not only by an oath of office, but by a long tradition of which we are proud in this country."

"Yes sir," Daniel Berrigan said.

"We are proud of the Constitution of the United States," the judge continued crisply. "If this had happened in many countries of the world, you would not have been sitting here. You would have been in your coffins long ago."

"Your honor," said Daniel Berrigan, "may I ask just one more question, and then I will be silent?"

"Yes indeed," the judge said.

"I think you spoke very movingly of your conception of your vocation," Daniel Berrigan said softly, "and I wish merely to ask whether or not one's reverence for his tradition of law or of religion or of any worthwhile human inheritance does not also require us constantly to reinterpret this and to adjust it to the needs of the people here and now; in order that this does not remain a mere inheritance which is deadening us, but a living inheritance which we offer to the living here and now. So that it may be possible, even though the law has excluded certain very enormous questions of conscience, that we admit them for the first time and, thereby, rewrite the tradition for the sake of our people."

The Jesuit had suddenly gained control of the courtroom. The Berrigan magic had scratched through the black carapace of the law to touch the judge's naked conscience. For Roszel Thomsen took off his glasses, looked wistfully at the Jesuit, and began to talk about his distaste for the Vietnam war.

"You speak to me as a man and to me as a judge," he said softly. "To me as a man, I would be a very funny sort of man if I had not been moved by your sincerity on the stand and by your views. I doubt if any of these jurors has great enthusiasm for the Vietnam war. It seems to me that most of the people in the United States now want to terminate the war . . . I am as anxious to terminate it as the average man, perhaps more than the average man . . . Because I agree completely with you, as a person, that we can never accomplish what we all would like to accomplish in the way of giving a better life to people in this country, if we are going to keep on spending that much money. We certainly are not going to do it. We have not done it, and I do not believe that we will be able to do it."

The courtroom was hushed in a moment of exquisite satisfaction. The Jesuit's teach-in had exposed the nation's schizophrenia. And Roszel Thomsen, realizing that he had gone awfully far as a man, swiftly urged everyone to deal with the nation's disease by voting for the right candidate.

"I propose to vote in the elections for people who may be able to do it . . . the answer, it seems to me, has to be that you work on your Congressman; you organize and try to get elected the people who will do it. There will be another Congressional election, and the Congressmen are going to be very responsive. You can work on your congressman . . ."

There was a cynical, savage cackling among the young war protesters sitting in the spectators' gallery, and the judge added pleadingly: "Everything can not be done at once! People can not take the law into their own hands! We either have a rule of law, or we do not!"

"You are including our President in that assertion also?" Daniel Berrigan asked. "That he must obey the law?"

"Of course he must obey the law," said the judge.

"He hasn't, though," Tom Lewis quipped.

"If the President has not obeyed the law," Judge Thomsen said wistfully, "there's very little that can be done about the President, except not to re-elect him. Well," he added with an air of satisfaction, "he is not up for re-election."

And so they conversed, before the amazed eyes of the Federal marshals, who, startled by this total innovation in courtroom procedure, swung their heads back and forth from the judge to the defendants as if they were watching a tennis match. The colloquy lasted for some forty minutes, once more pitting the nine Catholics' visceral idealism against the rationales of their society.

"It is my feeling," said Brother David Darst, "that the instructions which you gave to the jury bound them to a very narrow letter of the law; and that their judgment, according to the spirit of the law, was very strictly prohibited. It is my feeling that the spirit of the law is important, particularly in American legal tradition and in American life. It is the spirit which counts."

"Well many books have been written on the difference between the letter and the spirit of the law," the judge said pensively. "There are certain situations in which the Constitution gives the Judge a good deal of leeway. There are other situations in which it does not. Unfortunately, in this case I concluded that I did not have very much leeway."

"Your honor," said Philip Berrigan, "I think that we would be less than honest with you if we did not say that, by and large, the attitude of all of us is that we have lost confidence in the institutions of this country, including our own bureaucratic Churches . . . we have no evidence that the institutions of this country, including our own Churches, are able to provide the type of change that justice calls for, not only in this country, but also around the world."

"If you are advocating revolution," Judge Thomsen retorted with a sharpness he had not yet displayed towards men of the cloth, "I suggest that you consult your counsel before you say it . . ." He softened a little. "Let me say that they will not do it as fast as you would like, but within the next four years the young people of this country are going to have a tremendous percentage of the vote. I would imagine that that is going to make a substantial difference on a good many issues."

"But how much time is left in this country," said Philip Berrigan, and suddenly the habitual impatience was restored to his worn face. "How much time is left in this country, as our casualties inch towards 20,000 men, and Vietnamese casualties, perhaps 175,000 civilian casualties every year, and then nuclear war, of course, staring us in the face . . ."

"Well, I assure you that I am concerned about it," Judge

Thomsen said, looking increasingly helpless, "selfishly for my grandchildren, as well as for everybody else. It is a serious thing . . ."

It was Daniel Berrigan who stepped forward, and, with a grim courtesy, put an end to the colloquy.

"We do want to thank you, your honor. We do not want, however, the edge to be taken off what we have tried to say by any implication on our part that we are seeking mercy in this Court. We welcome the rigors of this Court. And we do not wish that primary blade of intention to be honed down to no edge at all by some sort of gentleman's agreement whereby we would conclude that you have agreed with us, and we with you. We do not, and we thank you."

"All right," Judge Thomsen said in a tone of relief, seeing an end to the situation. But it wasn't the end. The Nine, refusing, as ever, to be defined by any system, had a few more improvisations to add.

"Could we finish with a prayer, your honor?" Daniel Berrigan asked. "We would like to recite the 'Our Father' with our friends."

Judge Thomsen sat back in his chair, eminently shaken, and a few seconds passed before he answered.

"I will be glad to hear from the chief legal officer of the United States as to his advice," he answered curtly.

There was a flurry at the back of the courtroom. Several Federal marshals who had been patrolling the hall outside swung through the door to observe this new improvisation of the Nine's living theater. The Chief District Attorney for the State of Maryland, Stephen Sachs, a short, dark young man who had been standing at the back of the room for the last few minutes of the colloquy, walked towards the bar, his head thoughtfully lowered, his hands jammed in his pockets.

"The government, your honor, has no objection whatsoever," he said quite amiably when he reached the bar, "and rather welcomes the idea."

The Catonsville Nine made the sign of the Cross. Then they joined hands, as they had on that May day in Catonsville, and in grave, heavy voices, began to recite the 'Our Father.' The spectators and both teams of attorneys rose to their feet like one man and joined in the prayer. The judge stood motionless in his black robes, suddenly transformed, by the Nine's dramatics, into a Congregational minister, his bench metamorphosed into a pulpit, his ornate courtroom into an affluent suburban Church. There were stifled sobs from many young priests and students, and from a large black woman, a former parishioner of Philip Berrigan's, who sat in the front row, a "Free the Nine" button pinned to her coat. The marshals, more stupefied than ever, confused as to whether they should participate in the prayer, joined in at every second word, looking pleadingly at the judge to follow his lead. And the words of the Lord's Prayer—boldly trespassing upon the separation of Church and State, brazenly intruding into the formal language of the law—seemed, in that courtroom, like the marvelous tongues given to the Apostles at Pentecost. The Nine led the prayer on to include the Anglican formula: "And thine is the kingdom, and the power, and the glory, forever and ever, Amen." "We thank you very much," Daniel Berrigan said in his friendly, boyish voice, turning towards the judge's bench. Judge Thomsen fled down from his pulpit, his black robes flapping like the wings of a startled bird. The audience filed out of the courtroom to await the jury's verdict. A bevy of priests and students clustered, as usual, around Daniel Berrigan, who looked arrogant, triumphant, amused. "Did you ever see so many marshals?" he said. "They were guarding Our Father."

. . .

"Members of the jury, what say you, is the defendant Philip Berrigan guilty of the matters whereof he stands indicted, or not guilty, as to Count no. 2?"

"We find the defendant guilty."

"Members of the jury, what say you, is Daniel Berrigan guilty of the matters whereof he stands indicted, or not guilty, as to Count no. 2?"

"We find the defendant guilty."

"Members of the jury, what say you, is Thomas Lewis guilty of the matters whereof he stands indicted, or not guilty, as to Count no. 2?"

"We find the defendant guilty."

A half-hour after the end of the Lord's Prayer, the foreman of the jury, in a soft, timid voice, was giving his group's verdict to the court clerk. Twenty minutes passed in the Elizabethan language of the court as the verdict came in count by count, defendant by defendant, three counts per defendant, twenty-seven times in a row. The twelve jurors seemed more impassive, more imperturbable than ever. One was only aware of their feet shifting uncomfortably beneath the bench on which they sat, of the stockings wrinkled around the women's ankles, of the pale flabbiness of their excess flesh. A final poll was taken of each individual juror. "Juror no. 11, Mrs. Helen Perkins," the court clerk asked, "have you heard the verdicts of your foreman as to each of the defendants?" "Yes, I have." "Are they also your verdicts?" "Yes, they are." "Juror no. 12, Mrs. Anna Paradee," the clerk repeated, "have you heard the verdicts of your foreman as to each of the defendants?" "Yes." "Are they also your verdicts?" "Yes." "Members of the jury," the clerk said, "hearken to your verdicts as the Court hath recorded them. Your foreman saith that each of the defendants are guilty as to each of the counts, and so do you say all, after being polled?" The jurors nodded their heads limply, like rag dolls, to indicate their agreement. "The verdict is recorded," the court clerk said.

And then the courtroom, for the third time that afternoon, was shaken by a totally unexpected event. As the clerk spoke her last word to legitimize the verdict passed upon the Nine, a deep and powerful man's voice boomed out from the spectators' gallery:

"Members of the jury, you have just found Jesus Christ guilty!"

In the total silence of the courtroom, all eyes shifted quickly to the middle of the spectators' gallery. The actor sat calm and immobile, face turned up towards the jury, a serene expression in his eyes, his lips curved in a cryptic, Buddha-like smile. Five seconds passed in total stillness. The marshals, bristling, ready to pounce, stared helplessly at the judge. Then a young woman with long blond hair, holding a baby in her arms, rose and said "Agreed, agreed, injustice . . ." George Mische's wife broke into sobs. The spectators stood up and there was a mayhem of murmurs, of accusations, of arms stretched out in the victory sign. "Let the man be escorted from the courtroom," Judge Thomsen finally barked, fiercely pounding his gavel, "clear the courtroom!" Four marshals rushed to the man and seized him, while the other marshals began to push the spectators out into the hall. The jurors gave one last limp, cottony look at their accuser and tumbled hurriedly out of the courtroom. "That was Art Melville," someone blurted out in the pandemonium, "Tom's brother, the one who was thrown out of Guatemala by the C.I.A. . . ." As they were being escorted out of the courtroom, the spectators began the first stanzas of Martin Luther King's liberation song. The chorus grew, and the strains of "We Shall Overcome" filled the halls, the elevators, the staircase of the Federal Courthouse as the spectators were marshaled out into the street. Inside the courtroom, Daniel Berrigan, as usual, was having the last word, Daniel Berrigan was saying extraordinary things. "I would like to thank the Court and the prosecution," he was saying, "I think we agree that this was the greatest day of our lives." That is the last recorded sentence in the 888-page transcript of the trial of the Catonsville Nine.

It was seven fifteen, a warm, dark fall evening in Baltimore. Facing the Courthouse, standing on the ledge of the monument which commemorates the dead of the War of 1812, some three hundred grave young priests and students, decorated with bandages of mourning and talismans of peace, were holding a candlelight vigil for the Catonsville Nine. They stood very still, the candles close to their faces, looking like the neophytes in some liturgy of the catacombs. And they were as akin to the early Christians of the Roman Empire, these young protesters, as were the Berrigans whom they had come to honor: Bad citizens, refusing induction into armies, rebelling against all national power and military might, fearful of an Apocalyptic destruction of the world, asking for nothing less than a total reorganization of society, acting with the same irrationality and intolerance with which the absurd Christians, the "fools for Christ's sake," had acted towards Imperial Rome, longing for that central utopia of Christianity and of modern youth: the non-violent revolution. These acolytes who had so loved the Berrigans, and been so loved by them, stood facing the Courthouse, the candles to their faces, singing the "Battle Hymn of the Republic": "In the beauty of the lilies Christ was born across the sea . . . As He died to make men holy let us die to make men free . . ." Facing them, on the other side of the narrow street, several hundred policemen stood on the steps of the Federal Courthouse, their riot helmets as sapphire blue as the ocean on a calm summer evening. They stood looking at the young, as they had throughout the week, with a certain tense benevolence . . . protests, marches, pickets, demonstrations seemed, suddenly, anodyne compared to the acts of the new martyrs who had been found guilty that day.

Four weeks later, when the Catonsville Nine returned to Baltimore to be sentenced, the students, the teachers, the clergymen, the nuns, were at it again, mourning and celebrating in their liturgy of penance. The living theater of protest continued. The night before the sentencing, a peace torch was lit by Daniel Berrigan ten miles from town, and carried by relay runners to the Federal Courthouse. In a raw November rain, two hundred young people held an all-night candlelight vigil for the Catonsville Nine. And while the Nine were being sentenced, inside the Courthouse, to their prison terms, a theatrical troupe—professional, they said, but who could tell anymore?—performed mock army inductions in the streets outside.

Judge Thomsen's sentencing of the Catonsville Nine was said to be lenient. The terms ranged from two to three and a half years in Federal Prison, shorter than many terms being received by young Americans for refusing induction into the army. Two years were given to David Darst, Mary Moylan, Marjorie Melville and John Hogan—the same sentence as had been originally imposed on Benjamin Spock and William Sloane Coffin for "conspiring" to abet young men to refuse the draft. Daniel Berrigan, Thomas Melville, and George Mische were given three years. Philip Berrigan and Thomas Lewis each received a sentence of three and a half years, to run concurrently with their preceding terms of six years. All were free, that day, pending appeal, save

Philip Berrigan and Thomas Lewis, who would be given bail by Judge Thomsen six weeks later. (Most of the Catonsville Nine were imprisoned in April 1970, a few weeks after the Supreme Court rejected their appeal. Daniel Berrigan, George Mische, and Mary Moylan defied authority and remained underground for many months.)

cheerful Nine, dressed in black, like the dark stamen of a bright-petaled flower. A few of the Milwaukee Fourteen accompanied him, jovial Boston Irish priests awaiting their own trial who were certain, as were the Berrigans, that they were beginning to discover the true meaning of the Gospel. "We seek a life-style to match the Church's rhetoric." Daniel stood at the steps of the Courthouse, the kids cheering, the cameras whirring, enjoying it all, an arrogant serenity illuminating his face. "What do you say, Dan?" the kids hollered. "It was like Brecht, wasn't it?" he said with his proud and luminous smile. "What do you say, Dan?" other students cried out again. "The bread is rising," he said, "isn't that good enough?" The nuns, the priests, the students cheered, wept, sang, made their V signs, wept again. A young Jesuit, standing on the Courthouse steps, sobbed like a child. "Who's free?" he said. "You're as free as your conscience is free. Are we free? We're not. They are." And then he stopped weeping, sang along with the students and cheered. Thus the crowds had danced, the preceding year, around the mule-drawn hearse of Martin Luther King caught in that primitive matrix of emotion where mourning and celebration, sacrifice and redemption, death and resurrection are fused. Some of the purest, sternest Christians in the country were going to be buried in jail for some time, and who could predict what wholeness of body and of spirit they would retain? Only their blind and arrogant faith could sustain their trust in the value of their sacrifice, that faith which also made them believe that "God is a concrete reality," that they would, after death, "see the Father, and those we love." Those of little faith went on crying, singing, cheering, crying again, feeling small, crude, guilty, angry, impure. How many more such orgies of guilt and sacrifice would this war call forth? How cruel these martyrs to make us suffer so! How cruel of them to torture us with their purity, their diabolical freedom!

Mendez Arceo and
Ivan Illich:
THE RULES OF THE GAME

*Aussi, mon vray mestier, c'est
de n'épargner l'homme,
Mais ces vices chanter d'une
publique voix.*
—Joachim du Bellay

*Noi volemo altro che guglie e fontane
Pane volemo, pane, pane, pane!*
—anonymous, Rome, sixteenth century

I

Close to the sumptuous palaces of the Vatican, near a corner of the Piazza Navona, there stands a personage to whom the Roman populace, for many centuries, have brought their pleas for justice and reform, and their sarcastic diatribes against all those who usurp their power. His name is Pasquino. He is a statue. Tradition has it that Pasquino was named after the fifteenth-century tailor who unearthed him, a tailor whose mordant wit was renowned for cutting men's reputations apart. Erected on a pedestal in front of the Braschi palace in 1501, Pasquino the statue continued to broadcast the sarcastic humor of his human namesake. Romans flocked to Pasquino to affix to his torso, to his pedestal, and to the wall behind him a multitude of quatrains, epigrams, satirical lampoons in prose and verse against the venality of Popes and cardinals, against indulgences and simonies, against the vainglory of princes, against any person or institution considered unjust. These *pasquinades,* as the satires were called, were written in a variety of languages—Latin, French, Spanish, the Roman vulgate. The Borgia Pope Alexander VI deserved the following verse: "Alexander sells keys, Christ, altar, well/He bought them first, so has the right to sell." The Medici Pope Leo X: "He pretended to be a sheep, he took lion as his name, he was in fact a wolf, he died like a dog." Pope Julius II: "A fraudulent merchant, he has sold so much heaven that none remains for him." Some centuries later, Napoleon received the following pun from Pasquino: "*Tutti i Francesi sono ladri? Non tutti, ma buona parte, Buonaparte.*" Few men in power escaped Pasquino's barbs, for wit is Rome's true character. "*Moritur et ridet,*" it has been said of the Romans—they would laugh on their deathbeds, they would laugh the world apart. And throughout the centuries the loquacious Pasquino has been a symbol of resistance to pomp, solemnity and especially clericalism. Some Romans say that Pasquino is the last true Roman left: "*Noialtri siamo dei fessi*" ("All the rest of us are horses' asses").

On a sunny June morning in 1968, Monsignor Ivan Illich of the New York Archdiocese, one of the most admired, feared, controversial priests in the American continent, sat breakfasting in a café in front of the statue of Pasquino, a personage whom he had much admired during his years of study in Rome. After enjoying three cups of *cappuccino* Ivan Illich, tall, lanky, handsome, hawk-featured, an enigmatic smile on his face, rose from his seat and walked across the Tiber towards the Vatican. Monsignor Illich had a nine a.m. appointment at the Holy See, for which he had dressed in a secular grey suit, a secular white shirt, a secular black tie. He walked with a swift and feline stride towards the building just to the left of Saint Peter's basilica lodging the Congregation for the Doctrine of the Faith, an offshoot of the Sacred Congregation of the Universal Inquisition founded in the thirteenth century to suppress the heretic sects flourishing in mountain regions of medieval Europe. Ivan Illich, forty-one years old, a naturalized United States citizen of part Spanish, part German, part Yugoslav, part Catholic, part Jewish descent, the youngest cleric on our continent ever elevated to the rank of Monsignor, had been called to the Vatican to answer certain questions about his faith classified by the Congregation into four categories: "Dangerous Doctrinal Opinions"; "Erroneous Ideas Against the Church"; "Bizarre Conceptions About the Clergy"; and "Subversive Interpretations Concerning the Liturgy and Ecclesiastical Discipline."

It is only fair to note some differences between Ivan Illich's forthcoming inquisition and those of the fourteenth century. Six hundred years ago the subject was dragged to his interrogation in chains. Monsignor Illich had been summoned to Rome in 1968 with the reason that he had become *"una cosa di curiosità, di maraviglia, di scandalo"* ("an object of curiosity, bewilderment, and scandal") to the Roman Catholic Church. He had arrived a free man, by plane, from Mexico, where he had directed, for seven years, a center of higher learning whose progressive character had come to alarm the Vatican.

Ivan Illich, a man of obsessive punctuality, arrived ten minutes early for his appointment at the Congregation for the Doctrine of the Faith, formerly and better known as the Holy Office. After ringing the doorbell and being ushered into a small vestibule, he was led through a set of double doors—one of them padded with leather for soundproofing—into a large reception room which he recalls as rather stuffy. The windows were shuttered and partly

covered with triple sets of curtains. The gilded chairs were
of a high-Baroque style and covered with red plush. In
front of a large sofa stood an imposing marble table. On
it was a ballpoint pen chained to a green plastic holder
which was, in turn, glued to the table. Monsignor Illich
walked to the largest window and opened it wide. He
leaned upon the window sill, looking out upon the con-
struction site of a new building, planned to serve as meeting hall for future Vatican Councils. A group of men
in yellow helmets were directing the placement of twelve-
foot-tall precast cement modules. Behind the building site,
partly hidden by the constructors' cranes and cement
mixers, stood the splendid medieval Church of Camposanto
Teutonico. Monsignor Ivan Illich sat down at the pink
marble table, and, with the chained green pen, wrote
a letter in Portuguese—one of the eleven languages he is
fluent in—to a close friend, a Brazilian archbishop. He
described, in that brief note, the furniture in the reception
room of the Congregation for the Doctrine of the Faith,
and expressed his grave doubts that any part of a church
could be built with precast cement blocks.

Very punctually, at nine a.m., Cardinal Seper of Yugo-
slavia, the head of the Congregation and, after the Pope,
the second-highest ranking prelate in the Roman Catholic
Church, came out of a back door to greet Monsignor
Illich. The Cardinal, after receiving a kiss on his ring from
his visitor, vigorously shook his hand. After a few phrases
of greeting in Italian, the two men talked for twenty
minutes, in Serbo-Croatian, about the weather in Dalmatia.
Cardinal Seper, as Ivan Illich describes him, seemed "very
kind, very correct, most humane, rather apologetic . . .
acting like a man obligated to proceed in a transaction
which embarrassed him profoundly." After this pleasant
interlude in their native tongue the two men went back to
Italian to discuss the business at hand. Cardinal Seper called

into the room an unsmiling official of the Congregation dressed in a worn and austere black cassock—whom he introduced as Monsignor de Magistris—and whom he assigned to escort Ivan Illich to a subterranean level of the Congregation's headquarters.

On their way out of the reception room Monsignor de Magistris picked up a heavy silver inkwell with a pen in it —Ivan Illich is struck, to this day, by the preponderance of pens in his recollection of this visit—and the two men walked down some back stairs to a very ancient creaky elevator which cranked them down several flights deeper into the caves of the Vatican. They emerged into a musty corridor lined from floor to ceiling with bookcases filled with ancient leather-bound volumes. They crossed three more such narrow rooms lined with bookcases covered, Ivan Illich assures one, with "real chicken wire." They arrived at a fourth room. It was dominated by a heavy oak table on which stood two candle sticks, a Bible, a black wooden crucifix with a white figure of Christ, and a large dossier of newspaper clippings, one of which Ivan Illich recognized as a clipping from the French weekly *Paris Match*. Behind the table sat a small, rubicond man in his fifties. Monsignor de Magistris deposited the silver inkpot on the table. Ivan Illich walked up to the Monsignor seated at the table, and the following conversation (in Italian) ensued:

"I am Illich."

"I know."

"Monsignor, who are you?"

"Your judge."

"I thought I would know your name."

"That is unimportant. I am called Casoria."

The three monsignors then all made the sign of the Cross to signal that the judicial procedures had begun. Ivan Illich was asked to put his hand on his chest and to swear to tell the truth. He obliged. He was then asked to keep secret everything that transpired in the ensuing conversation and was warned that a special excommunication would be issued to anyone who revealed the proceedings of the Congregation. Ivan Illich, in very rapid Italian, replied that he refused to take any oath of secrecy on the grounds that such an oath would be "against the natural law of self-defense and the divine law of honesty in the Church"; that it would contradict the Second Vatican Council's reforms of the Congregation's procedures; and that it would violate, in particular, the recent Papal edict *Integrae Servandae* of 1965, which stated that the rules of procedure of the Congregation should be a matter of public record.

The secrecy of the Catholic Church's inquisitional branch, which was the foundation of its power, had seldom before in the seven centuries of its existence been contested on such reasonable grounds. And a certain pandemonium prevailed, for the next hour, in that section of the Vatican's caves.

Interrogator: "If you don't want to swear to secrecy this is over."

Ivan Illich: "In the name of the Father and the Son and the . . ."

Interrogator: "What are you doing?"

Ivan Illich: "I am putting an end to this session."

Ivan Illich recalls there was some very excited shouting. "*Mamma mia,*" the gentlemen cried, "*Non c'è precedanza,*" "*Bisogna appellare al Santo Padre.*" "We have other means at our disposal," Monsignor Casoria exclaimed throughout this, waving many papers. The discussion lasted heatedly some forty-five minutes, at the end of which time the judges agreed that Ivan Illich would not have to answer any accusations until he received a written copy of all the charges against him. Monsignor de Magistris disappeared upstairs to confer with Cardinal Seper, during which time the two remaining monsignors had a strained but polite conversation. Casoria asked Illich whether it was true that he had once written that the Pope lived in a palace of a thousand rooms. Illich, in turn, asked his judge what his official post was at the Vatican. Monsignor Casoria disclosed a few of his official titles: Judge of the Congregation for the Doctrine of the Faith, Under-Secretary of the Sacred Congregation for the Discipline of the Sacraments, Counselor of the Sacred Congregation for the Clergy, Deputy to the Monasteries of Rome, and—a specialist in the physical details of non-consummated marriages.

In the middle of this disclosure Monsignor de Magistris returned and glumly announced that with Cardinal Seper's consent, a written copy of the Congregation's questions would be brought to Monsignor Illich that afternoon, as he had requested. And Ivan Illich, after emerging from the caves and chatting with a progressive Belgian theologian, an old friend, whom he had met quite by accident at the exquisite fountain in front of the Congregation's building, went off to have an excellent lunch with other friends in the Piazza Navona.

Ivan Illich, on this trip to Rome, was staying at the Capranica, Rome's oldest and most prestigious ecclesiastical residence, where he had lived while studying for the priesthood. It was to the Capranica that a messenger brought the Xeroxed copy of the Congregation's questionnaire. The document was delivered to Ivan Illich at three thirty. Very shortly after he had begun to read it, he started laughing. And Illich's crystalline laughter pealed for several hours of that afternoon as he perused this extraordinary document. For he found that most of the questions were not only theologically absurd, and based on the vaguest of anonymous innuendos, but also very funny:

"What do you think of heaven and hell, and also of Limbo?"

"Do you deny the distinction between shepherds and sheep among the people of God on earth?"

"What are your thoughts on the peaceful co-existence of East and West?"

"What did you have to do with the kidnapping of the Archbishop of Guatemala?"

"What is the nature of your relations with Octavio Paz and Carlos Fuentes?"

"Is it true that you would like to see women go to confession without a grate in the confessional box?"

"Is it true that beginning in 1960 there has been in you a dangerous general development of new ideas and disintegrating tendencies of a humanitarian and libertarian nature?"

"What would you answer to those who say that you are petulant, adventurous, imprudent, fanatical and hypnotizing, a rebel to any authority, disposed to accept and recognize only that of the Bishop of Cuernavaca, Mexico?"

After a few hours of joyous Roman laughter, Ivan Illich decided not to share his amusement with the world because this document, as he put it, "was so profoundly embarrassing to the Church." He chose, for the time being, to keep it secret, and to answer the Congregation in the most affable, humble, and formal terms. That evening, sitting at a *trattoria* in front of the Teatro di Marcello over a dinner of *Carciofo* (artichoke) *alla Romana*, *Cervella alla Milanese*, *Bieta* (a uniquely Roman type of spinach), and three carafes of Frascati, Ivan Illich composed the following letter (in Italian) to Cardinal Seper, finishing it in the early hours of the morning:

> *Most Reverend Eminence, following upon the interview which your Eminence granted me yesterday morning with so much pastoral feeling, I find myself obliged to report to your Eminence all that took place during and*

after the interrogation conducted by Msgr. de Magistris and Msgr. Casoria, and to give your Eminence my own view of the situation as it now stands.

Let me start by saying that, faced with authoritative procedures which, at least in my opinions, are so very questionable in both substances and style, I am left—as a Christian and as a priest—with a single, clearcut choice.

I can, on the one hand, simply withold any defense of myself, without claiming my most reasonable rights or advancing my most lawful defense. Or, on the other hand, I can (not for my sake but for the sake of defending the divine constitution of the Church and the honorable status of its ecclesiastical institutions) set myself systematically in opposition to everything which I recognize as a distortion of the Gospel, contrary to the divine principles which govern the Church, contrary to what has been decided by the Councils, and even contrary to the most recent and repeated statements of the highest ecclesiastical authorities.

Eminence, I must acknowledge to you that I have decisively opted for the first way, and that I have resolved to take as my watchword, "If a man asks you to lend him your coat, then give him your shirt as well."

In this letter, Ivan Illich added that many of the questions put to him were phrased to elicit defamatory information about other priests, laymen and even bishops, information which he suggested the judges should "ferret out by other and more correct channels." And he stressed the fact that his refusal to answer the Congregation's questionnaire was in no way a personal defense, but had the purpose of "contributing to the greater splendour of the Church." The letter ended in that tone of contrite subservience to Rome which is Illich's style, and which annoys many of his progressive friends. "Trusting in Your Eminence's continued understanding, I declare myself Your Eminence's most humble son."

The following morning, before boarding a plane home to Mexico, Ivan Illich returned to the Vatican to deliver his letter personally to Cardinal Seper, who received him more cordially than ever. "I had the impression," Ivan Illich said later as he recollected their last meeting, "that his feelings were somewhere between perplexity, incredulity that such a procedure was possible, exasperation, and humorous annoyance. As we parted he gave me an *ab-braccio*, most affectionately. And then a most extraordinary thing happened. We were speaking in Croatian, and as the Cardinal led me to the door his last words to me were '*Hadjite, hadjite, nemojete se vratiti!*' which means 'Get going, get going, and never come back!' In other words, 'Beat it!'"

"It wasn't until I was going down the stairs from his office," added Illich, "that it struck me that he was quoting from the Inquisitor's last words to the prisoner in Dostoievski's story of *The Grand Inquisitor*."

The Illich inquisition had been plotted by a vast international network of secular and religious reactionaries whose machinations were as devious as they were medieval. It did much to heighten the already considerable reputation of its victim, a man looked up to by many as the most brilliant and prophetic, albeit enigmatic, Catholic thinker of his generation.

Let us note that some time after this interlude in the caves of the Vatican, Monsignor de Magistris and Monsignor Casoria were relieved of their posts at the Congregation for the Doctrine of the Faith.

II

In 1952, Father Ivan Illich, a young European recently ordained in Rome, had arrived in the United States and been assigned to a church in New York's Washington Heights, a conservative Irish neighborhood which was receiving a startling influx of Puerto Rican immigrants. He was welcomed to his parish by its pastor, Monsignor John Casey, an Irishman who had once served as secretary to Cardinal Spellman. "Ivan Illich?" Monsignor Casey asked incredulously as he greeted his new curate. "What kind of a name is that to go around with?" "Ivan is Johann, Jean, John," the young priest answered affably, always enjoying his control of many languages. "Ivan sounds Communist," said his superior, "we'll call you Johnny." Whereupon Monsignor Casey immediately took Johnny Illich downtown to the Berlitz School, where Monsignor Casey had been studying Spanish three times a week, for three years, with little results, in order to attend to his growing flock of Puerto Rican parishioners. John Illich's performance at Berlitz staggered Monsignor Casey; he covered seven lessons in one session. Within three weeks John Illich quit Berlitz. Within three months he spoke Spanish faultlessly, having learned it by standing on the street corners of Washington Heights, asking questions. Where had they come from, he asked his Puerto Rican parishioners, what were their native customs, what could the Church do to make them more at home? John Illich was staggered by the fact that in the brief span of a decade, one fourth of the Catholic population of the New York Archdiocese had become Puerto Rican, and he was interested to hear that the problem of integrating them into American-style religion was one of Cardinal Spellman's biggest headaches. Within another two years, John Illich was revolutionizing the New York Archdiocese's approach to the Puerto

Rican problem, having documented himself on the issue more thoroughly than any other priest in New York. His methods were unorthodox. During his vacations, he had walked, ridden horseback and hitchhiked throughout the entire width and length of Puerto Rico with a knapsack on his back. "The first Mass I said at about six in the morning," he wrote, describing one of those ascetic journeys, "after I had slept on the altar steps of the chapel. Then I traveled on, by horseback, to the next chapel. I heard confessions, baptized, married, and off I went to the third chapel, on horseback still, where I arrived after noon . . ."

The genial, dynamic Father Illich puzzled his colleagues. His background was uncomfortably different from those of the Irish curates who staffed Incarnation Parish and much of the New York Archdiocese. His father, who came from a titled Dalmatian family, had been a wealthy landowner and engineer in prewar Germany. Many of the languages in which Illich was fluent had been learned at the knees of governesses. His internationalism was such that he was once overheard, at a reception for AFL-CIO executives, conversing in voluble Yiddish with David Dubinsky. Born in Vienna, Illich had lived in several parts of Europe throughout his youth. By the time he was twenty-four he had earned master's degrees in theology and in philosophy from Rome's Gregorian University, and a doctorate in the philosophy of history from the University of Salzburg, where he had written his doctoral dissertation on Arnold Toynbee. He had also completed doctoral studies in natural science at the University of Florence, where his specialty had been crystallography. Illich's family were intimate friends of such European intellectuals as Rudolf Steiner and Rainer Maria Rilke, and, since his teens, Illich himself had been a close friend of Jacques Maritain, whom he considered to be a central influence on his life. Illich disdained classification into any nationality, but when asked what country he felt most kinship for he answered that he was, at heart, a Roman. The Holy See had wanted him to enter the Collegio di Nobili Ecclesiastici, where the Church's most gifted men are trained for prestigious careers in the Vatican's diplomatic corps. It was therefore a source of bewilderment to all why this high-strung, suave, dazzlingly brilliant aristocrat with the looks of a Hapsburg had chosen an obscure position in New York City's most conventional Irish territory, rather than accept the high posts for which the Holy See had intended him. "What in heck did you come here for?" one of his colleagues at Incarnation Parish, Father Joseph Connolly, once asked him. "I came," John Illich answered, "because my friends in Rome ribbed me about not being able to make it in an American parish." John Illich always evidenced a need to test himself, to accept the toughest challenges, which some said bordered on the masochistic.

According to Father Connolly, living in the same parish with John Illich was "like riding a Piper cub with an atom bomb under the seat." Illich climbed stairs three at a time and never walked through the rectory, but swept through it like a tornado. He rose earlier, questioned more, worked harder for the Puerto Ricans than any man in the diocese. His ability to recruit people was nothing short of extraordinary. When he pioneered camps for Puerto Rican children dozens of Irish bus drivers gave up their Sundays to drive the kids to camp. He encouraged young social workers to live in *cuartitos*, small apartments in the Puerto Rican slums, to observe better the needs of the people. He started employment agencies for the Puerto Rican immigrants. "The Puerto Ricans idolized him," Father Connolly says, "he was Mr. Puerto Rico, their Babe Ruth." Father Connolly also describes John Illich as "the most prayerful and ascetic priest I've ever known." He was in the church before six a.m., before anyone else, saying his breviary and his rosary. He forgot to eat when there was work to do. His broken-down car, "held together with scotch tape," was the consternation of his conformist colleagues. He was zealous in visiting the sick, the aged, men in jail. He was also notorious for his rigorous, sometimes pedantic orthodoxy. He researched the most difficult and ancient sources to clear up a doctrinal point. He insisted on frequent confession and frequent communion. Illich's colleagues criticized him only for an overabundance of zeal —he encouraged too many women, for instance, to enter convents. "Lay off that stuff," Father Connolly would say. "You're pushing them in." Yet, throughout the four years in which he was the idol of New York's Puerto Ricans John Illich suffered from his inability to integrate with the Irish priests around him. He once turned to Father Connolly, a man from Hell's Kitchen who had worked as a slaughterhouse butcher, and said wistfully: "I wish like you I had been a slaughterhouse butcher, because I could be closer to the other priests." "You were not cast for the role of shepherd," Father Connolly answered cordially, "but for empire."

Illich was to learn everything about the American clergy except how to be one of them. He began, early in his career, to criticize the American church for its smugness, its bureaucracy, its chauvinism, especially for its way of imposing Yankee values on minority groups such as the Puerto Ricans. He voiced his criticism in essays published in theological journals under the guarded *nom de plume* "Peter Canon." "A critical attitude is precisely one of the areas in which Christian love for the Church can develop," he wrote in one of his first essays. "Criticism is the fruit of hard work and prayer." Soon, irritated by the Yankee "ecclesiastical conquistadores" whom he saw working as missionaries in Puerto Rico, angered by their ignorance of native idiom and their indifference to native tradition, he began to agitate for a radical transformation of American missionary methods. The missioner must not only become indifferent to possessions and material comfort, he wrote, but to all the values and customs of his own home. The American priest working with people of a foreign culture should cultivate a spirit of "total cultural indifference." To the international Illich, any feeling of cultural superiority is as powerful a manifestation of original sin as the confusion of tongues at Babel. The process of obtaining grace, he stressed, might involve a total stripping of cultural values, "a beatitude of cultural poverty." The missioner is the man "who is willing to witness with his life, to a foreign people, the relativity of human convictions in front of the unique and absolute meaning of the Revelation." This was a tough doctrine for the average Irish priest to accept.

John Illich was fond of pointing out that many Puerto Ricans failed to attend mass in the United States because it started on time. And if he had had his way he would have totally transferred the church of the *campesinos*, with its unpunctuality, its semi-pagan rituals, its great community feast days, to the streets of New York. He wanted to forget all formalities to meet their needs. His crusade to give church weddings to the numerous Puerto Rican families who had only had a civil or consensual marriage was the nightmare of Incarnation Parish. "The rectory bell would would ring at any time of day or night," Father Connolly recalls, "and there would be a bridal party, bride and groom all dressed up holding flowers, accompanied by all their children and friends, asking for Father Illich to marry them on the spot. Well, he was ready to marry them without any papers or certificates; we had to hold him back. How did we know the groom wasn't already married to someone else? We had to curb him—he was like a wild horse. I'd say to him 'Form them first, don't just get them to church.' He simply wanted to bring all the Puerto Ricans into church and make them feel they were wanted. It was a very aristocratic concept—the aristocrat's complete trust in the people. He had a wing-ding, bread-and-games approach to the poor. I'd say to him: 'John, you're getting at them through their stomachs.'"

In 1955, in what turned out to be a very successful bread-and-games approach, John Illich decided to pioneer a national feast day for the Puerto Ricans of New York. The Italians had their Columbus Day and the Irish had their Saint Pat's. Why shouldn't the Puerto Ricans have their San Juan's day? A San Juan Mass, drawing a few thousand persons, had already been held in Saint Patrick's cathedral since 1953. But Illich wanted his people's day held in a grandiose outdoor space which would recreate a native plaza on the *Fiesta patronal*. Permission was asked of Cardinal Spellman to hold the Fiesta in the great quadrangle of Fordham University and to have the Cardinal be a star guest. "The boss says all right," the message came back from the Chancery, "but he says he doesn't like to play to empty houses." And Illich saw to it that the house was full. He took ads in Spanish language newspapers, persuaded Madison Avenue magnates to promote the event, and traveled through the city for weeks on a sound truck announcing the Fiesta. "You might get five thousand people," a police official said the day before the event to Father Joseph Fitzpatrick of Fordham, who was master-minding San Juan's day with Illich. "I've been watching Father Illich and I think there'll be thirty thousand," Father Fitzpatrick said. The police chief assigned a detail for a crowd of eight thousand. But Father Fitzpatrick's own hopes were exceeded. He was awakened the next morning at six a.m. by an excited babbling of Spanish voices under his window. Although the event was scheduled for noon, streams of Puerto Rican families were already converging at dawn towards the Fordham football field. And by noon, they were thirty-five thousand. It was a turning point in the life of New York's Puerto Ricans, the first time they had gathered together in traditional native fashion. Illich had arranged for national flags, dozens of roast suckling pigs, and native bands, had programmed speeches in Spanish by Puerto Rican leaders and New York officials. He had also provided hundreds of the traditional *piñatas*, gaily colored paper vessels which when broken with poles spill out hundreds of gifts for which children scramble. The *piñatas* were broken open by Cardinal Spellman and brought the Fiesta to its climax. The Cardinal knew what happens when a *piñata* is broken, but the Irish police—uptight because of the crowd's unexpected size—did not. As the gifts spilled out of the *piñatas* thirty-five thousand Puerto Ricans seemed to converge on Cardinal Spellman. The police, thinking that a riot had broken out, whisked a reluctant Cardinal out of the Fordham quadrangle. "Puerto Rican crowds mob Cardinal Spellman" was a front-page headline, the following day, in numerous newspapers. "What did the big boss think?" one of Illich's friends asked a chancery official the next morning. "He's thrilled," came the reply, "without Illich's mob scene the story would barely have made page 17." By that time the Cardinal, for many other reasons, had realized that Illich was a key man in his diocese, and a key man in the American Church. He had already named him, the year before, to be coordinator of the Archdiocese's Office of Spanish-American Affairs. A few months after the mob scene at Fordham, Spellman appointed Illich to be Vice-Rector of the Catholic University of Puerto Rico, where he was to pioneer a center for the training of American priests in Latin-American culture. A year later the Cardinal made Illich, at twenty-nine, the youngest Monsignor in the United States. The *nom de plume* "Peter Canon" disappeared. The new Monsignor began to sign his essays "The Very Reverend Ivan Illich, Ph.D."

The Spellman-Illich relationship was fascinating. The champion of Catholic traditionalism and the adventurous thinker, whose ideas would radicalize thousands of American Catholics, had deep trust and respect for each other. Illich describes Spellman as "a simple man rigorously true to himself, for whose consistency I had the most profound admiration." Spellman trusted and admired Illich, used him for many delicate diplomatic missions, sanctioned all his projects, and protected him until his dying day. Out of the many meetings the two men had together, three out of four times they disagreed. "So you know better than the Archbishop of New York," Spellman would say with a big smile, "well you'd better succeed." A colleague of Illich's describes the relationship between the straight-forward Irish prelate and the suave young cosmopolite as "too close for comfort. . . . Illich could get anything he wanted out of Spellman."

With typical efficiency, Illich, within three months of his arrival in Puerto Rico, had organized a conference of the heads of all Catholic universities in the United States to discuss the problems of Latin American studies. By the following summer, he had started the most intensive crash program ever devised to teach Spanish to American priests. The training center was called the "Institute of Intercultural Communications." Its purpose was to steep American priests in various aspects of Puerto Rican and Latin American culture; or, as a Brooklyn priest put it, "to stop the Irish malarkey of imposing our ways on other people." Cardinal Spellman sent half of his clergy there for training.

The center was often crowded to overflowing. When rooms were scarce Illich slept on a cot in the kitchen, reading arcane European journals of theology late into the night. In the daytime he tortured his students. He made them live on simple native diets, inspired them to travel on foot and on horseback to the wildest mountain regions of Puerto Rico, gave up his own punctuality to accustom them to the Latin Americans' sense of time, and grilled them with rigorous cross-examinations. Father Edmund Burke, a priest of Brooklyn's Ocean Hill–Brownsville district, recalls that he was "ready to throw Illich into the Caribbean." "He ran a disorganized Latin American shop," Father Burke says, "never appeared anywhere on time, and at midnight he came into my room and psychoanalyzed me until dawn. What he was doing was forcing Burke to take a good look at Burke, and get him rid of all the Yankee hang-ups." Father Burke, after the shock of initial therapy, returned to Puerto Rico for three years in a row and became one of Illich's most devoted friends. Twelve years later another Brooklyn priest trained in Illich's anti-colonial philosophy, Father Powis, was instrumental in helping to set up the independent school board in Ocean Hill–Brownsville. The impact of Illich's ideas upon the progressive clergy of Ocean Hill–Brownsville, who were fervent supporters of Rhody McCoy throughout the 1967–8 school crisis, is subtle but real.

Illich has been aptly described as "a bizarre mixture of profound piety and high diplomacy," and the second of those traits was in evidence during his five-year term in Puerto Rico. Throughout the nineteen-fifties, the Catholic Church on the island had been increasingly inimical to the progressive government of Muñoz Marin. Illich immediately made friends with the highest officials on the island and worked for five years, with much criticism from the local hierarchy, to reconcile the Church to

Muñoz Marin's government. His relations with the island's hierarchy came to a head in the election year 1960, when the Bishop of Ponce, the Most Reverend James Mc-Manus, formed a Catholic political party to oppose Muñoz Marin's birth control program and threatened excommunication for any Catholic voting for Muñoz. Illich became the Catholic party's fiercest opponent. "As a historian, I saw that it violated the American tradition of Church and State separation. As a politician, I predicted that there wasn't enough strength in Catholic ranks to create a meaningful platform and that the failure of McManus's party would be disastrous on the already frail prestige of the Puerto Rican Church. As a theologian, I believe that the Church must always condemn injustice in the light of the Gospel, but never has the right to speak out in favor of a specific political party." And as a satirist, Illich found that a political party organized on the birth control issue, campaigning under a banner decorated with a crucifix and a rosary, was downright comical. He ridiculed the Catholic party, lectured against it, and incited the growing animosity of Bishop McManus.

An event reminiscent of seventeenth-century court intrigues precipitated Illich's departure from Puerto Rico. In October 1960, when the election campaign was at its peak, Cardinal Spellman was expected in San Juan to consecrate a new bishop. A few weeks before he was due, a prominent Puerto Rican layman with wide influence in his government came to New York to ask Cardinal Spellman if he would lunch with Governor Muñoz—Bishop McManus's arch-enemy—on the day of the consecration. Cardinal Spellman readily agreed. With fervent Irish consistency, Bishop McManus not only refused the invitation, but also forbade any of his clergy to attend the lunch. Illich blithely overlooked the ban, and went to

lunch with his Cardinal. The very next day Bishop Mc-
Manus—who to this day is said to be convinced that
Illich had arranged the Muñoz-Spellman reunion—wrote
Illich a stinging letter ordering him to leave the is-
land. Illich returned to New York to an ever sympathetic
Cardinal Spellman. The Jesuits immediately appointed
him to the political science faculty of Fordham University.
Bishop McManus was shortly thereafter relieved of his
post.

For several weeks after his return, Ivan Illich studied a
map of Latin America, searching for "a valley with excellent climate, with a town not more than an hour away
from a great library and a good university, where housing
and food would be cheap enough to accommodate many
students." And then Illich flew to South America, and
proceeded to walk and hitchhike from Santiago, Chile,
to Caracas, Venezuela, a distance of some three thousand
miles.

Illich avows a deep nostalgia for medieval times, which
he looks upon as "the high point of man's spiritual life."
And throughout his career, in moments of crisis or decision,
he has imposed on himself many austere disciplines—fasts,
retreats, pilgrimages—considered outdated by many of his
contemporaries. At the age of eighteen, when he had decided to be a priest, he had gone into a thirty-day retreat
under a Jesuit spiritual director to decide whether he
should become a Jesuit. In 1959, he had spent his vacation
from the University of Puerto Rico in a forty-day meditation at a monastery in the Sahara desert. His four-month
walk from Santiago to Caracas in the winter of 1960–1 was
a form of pilgrimage in another turning point of his life.
When asked what he learned on that walk, he smiles and

answers: "I learned the meaning of distance." But one may assume that he was also searching for a place to start a new center of missionary training; and that during his trip he observed, with growing alarm, the contingents of Yankee priests who were beginning to migrate into Latin America in response to the crisis of faith on that continent and who were dotting the slums of Lima, Buenos Aires, and Quito with smug brick rectories and parish schools in imitation of those of Chicago, Brooklyn, and Saint Louis.

Central and South America yielded no pleasant valley equipped with a great university and a good climate. Illich continued his search northwards. In the spring of 1961 he found himself in Cuernavaca, Mexico, examining vegetables in the market place, comparing the price of its housing facilities with those of other Latin American countries, and reflecting upon the delights of that city's perennially dry, sunny climate. The bishop of the city, Sergio Mendez Arceo, was known for his open-mindedness. One day Ivan Illich rang the Bishop's doorbell, was ushered into his study, sat down on his couch, and announced: "I would like to start, under your auspices, a center of de-Yankeefication." The two men talked, without interruption, for nine hours. And Ivan Illich settled in Cuernavaca because he found, in its bishop, "a man for whom *le bon ton, le bon goût*, were of supreme importance, a man with whom I could communicate on my own wave length . . . I knew from the start that we could please and even surprise each other." The Bishop, on his part, found Ivan Illich to be "an extraordinary man with startlingly lucid ideas, who I knew would live in a state of perpetual renewal." And Bishop Mendez Arceo, a passionate nationalist who has an unshakeable faith in the adventurous free play of the Holy Spirit, sanctioned Ivan Illich's educational venture.

The center of de-Yankeefication, with Illich's great gift for public relations, was launched under the most respectable Yankee auspices. It had the approval of Cardinal Spellman, and was looked upon as a continuation of the missionary training center Illich had pioneered in Puerto Rico. It had the joint support of Fordham University and the American Bishops' Committee on Latin America. Various Catholic hierachs, such as Cardinal Spellman and Cardinal Cushing, who described Illich's venture as "by far the best training center we have," helped to get it off the ground by funding scholarships for their priests. It was first called CIF, for "Center of Intercultural Formation," and later CIDOC, for "Center of Intercultural Documentation."

CIF's second opening session was attended by representatives from CELAM, Latin America's most prestigious episcopal group. The keynote address was given by Bishop Helder Camera of Rio de Janeiro, Brazil, who translated Illich's previous epithet into Portuguese, and approvingly called the school "*o centro do desgringalização.*"

Nineteen sixty-one was the year that the Alliance for Progress was launched and also the year that the Pope issued a call for the North American Church to send ten per cent of its personnel—some thirty-five thousand priests and religious —to Latin America to help offset the critical shortage of clergy on that continent. Ivan Illich saw an ominous conjunction between the two projects. He was cynical about the Alliance for Progress, which he labeled "an alliance for the progress of the middle classes." He predicted that the kind of Yankee missionaries who would respond to the call would be "pawns of United States cultural imperialism." And he was determined to block their flow into Latin America. Illich's CIDOC—part language school, part conference center, part free university, part publishing house —was not so much designed to train missionaries, as to keep all but the most progressive of them away.

III

It is ironic that Ivan Illich should have chosen to settle, for this phase of his career as priest-educator, in a country which has bred the continent's most reactionary brand of Catholicism. Mexico was the first of the new lands to be evangelized in the missionary zeal of the Counter-Reformation, and it became the most powerful theocracy in Latin America. The spirit of dedication and of poverty preached by the first wave of Franciscan, Dominican and Augustinian friars was quickly perverted by the Church's material enrichment. By the end of the eighteenth century the Catholic Church controlled more than half of the money in circulation in Mexico and owned over half of its land. During the revolutions which swept through Latin America in the nineteenth century the Mexican Church aligned itself closely with the wealthy landowners and sought alliance with the numerous foreign powers which periodically invaded the country to combat its movements of liberation.

The Church in Mexico was more violently persecuted by the nineteenth century's revolutionary governments, and the twentieth century's progressive governments, than it was in any other nation on the continent. Not only were its funds, lands, schools, and hospitals expropriated; its libraries were confiscated and its seminaries closed. It was deprived, well into the twentieth century, of most means of scholarship and of theological research. The number of priests in the nation was decimated, in the 1850's, to a mere five hundred. For most of the past century, Mexican priests have been forbidden by the government (rather prophetically) to wear clerical clothing in public. In the 1920's, under the regime of President Plutarco Calles, church worship was severely restricted. And as recently as

1928, a prominent and duly elected public official, Governor Tomas Canagal of the state of Tabasco, publicly flaunted his hatred of Catholicism by naming his two sons Lucifer and Lenin, decreed that only married priests could reside in his state, ordered every church in his province torn down, and commanded his troops to shoot any group of peasants who might congregate in the ruins of church buildings.

The Mexican hierarchy has emerged from these persecutions bitter and impoverished, nostalgic for its lost power. It ranks today, along with the Colombian hierarchy, as the most conservative of any Latin American nation. The tenor of its theology is cautious and retrogressive, and its popular religion is still steeped in a worship of the Virgin and of various saints which verges on idolatry. Mexican Catholicism today is marked by what theologians call integralism—that wedding of reactionary politics with reactionary theology which has played a large role in protecting the interests of oligarchies in many parts of the Latin American continent. Yet within the stridently conservative group of men that compose the Mexican episcopate there is one maverick exception. Bishop Sergio Mendez Arceo of Cuernavaca was to startle the world in 1962—a year after Ivan Illich had settled in Cuernavaca—by emerging as a leader of the ultra-progressive ecumenical wing of the Second Vatican Council.

It is quite clear by now that Ivan Illich's inquisition in the bowels of the Vatican was not only aimed to remove him from Mexico, but to remove Bishop Mendez as well. For since the Council, Mendez Arceo has been the plague of Mexico's powerful reactionary forces. In recent years many walls of Mexican towns have been periodically decorated with the slogan *Muerte a Méndez Arceo* ("Death to Mendez Arceo"). One would think, in the context of

Mexican history, that the motto would have been painted on by the passionate anti-clericalists who have persecuted clergymen for a century. But in fact they are the handiwork of devoutly reactionary Mexican Catholics who believe that Mendez Arceo is out to destroy the principles of the Catholic faith—principles which, in the integralist vision, are unchanging through time.

Sergio Mendez Arceo, seventh Bishop of Cuernavaca, is a portly, erect, courtly man with warm, thoughtful, witty brown eyes, a luminous smile, and a most informal manner. His frayed cassocks, worn shoes and modest way of life evidence his profound disdain for comfort, for worldly goods, and for any outward show of authority. The son of a prosperous lawyer of Southern Mexico, he studied in Rome, wrote his doctoral dissertation on early sixteenth century humanism, and is the leading authority in Mexico on the thought of Erasmus. He lives by the side of the Cuernavaca cathedral in two austere, high-ceilinged rooms which recall the lodgings of some scholarly *grands seigneurs* one meets in ancient manors of the European countryside. Bishop Mendez's study is stacked high with advanced intellectual journals in numerous languages and sparsely furnished with a few pieces of worn furniture. On the walls hang a large painting, left over from a previous occupant, of a saint whose name the Bishop can't quite remember; a portrait of Pope John drawn by a Protestant lay theologian; another drawing of an Indian-featured Madonna by the Mexican painter Siqueiros, a former leader of Mexico's Communist party and a long-time resident of Cuernavaca. On a chest of drawers stands a large television set which helps the Bishop to satisfy his enormous interest in international affairs. On a simple oak table that serves as a desk there is an Olivetti portable typewriter on which he writes his essays and correspondence. "I could not stand a secretary," he says, "I am too much my own man."

In these simple rooms which breathe of serenity, scholarship, and a very aristocratic kind of poverty, the Bishop lives alone, without a secretary, cook or housekeeper, unaided by any personal staff except for a seminarian who arrives at uncertain hours of the morning to answer his phone. He shares his meals—frugal fare brought in by nuns from a neighboring convent—with the twelve clergymen of the city in a little room off the cathedral cloister, or else he drops in to friends' homes at dinner time and takes pot luck. As one sees Mendez Arceo driving his little Opel car through the twisting roads of Cuernavaca one is reminded that his diocese, in the state of Morelos, was the terrain of Zapata's revolution, and that the Bishop has always declared himself to be a staunch "Zapatista." "To say that I am a Zapatista is to say that I am a citizen of Morelos. He was the only leader of the 1910 revolution with a coherent social program." Mendez Arceo's style is democratic in every way. He is "Don Sergio," never "Your Excellency," to acquaintances old and new. If it is difficult to get a message to him on the phone, it is because the seminarians assigned to answer it are changed from day to day in order that the Bishop may become "intimately acquainted with the wishes of the young generation." However it is not hard to see him. He is likely to open the door of his humble residence himself. Bishop Mendez's diocesan staff is composed of two priests who help him with some paper work. "In that," he says slyly, "consists my Curia." Bishop Mendez's comment on the Catholic Church in the United States is biting: "Its tragedy is its huge human organization and its horrible riches." Unlike most of his colleagues Bishop Mendez takes enormous pride in the poverty of the Mexican church. "Our poverty and our total lack of political muscle is our greatest glory, a providential gift of our nineteenth century reformers." The Church, in his view, has too long encouraged reverence for civil authority because of its vested material interests. Its messianic task is rather to serve as the constant critic of secular power. "*L'Église est le lieu privilégié de la critique*" ("Criticism is the prerogative of the Church"), he says.

Mendez Arceo, before being appointed to the diocese of Cuernavaca, was spiritual director of students at the largest seminary in Mexico, and he is distinguished from other bishops by his immense interest and trust in the young generation. He spends two days a month in retreat with the sixty priests of his diocese to "receive their impressions" of the work that has to be done—in fact to allow them a free hand in the running of the diocese. In the same spirit, he urges his priests to write their sermons in teams of four or five because he believes, in the strictest orthodox tradition, that the Holy Spirit works better through communities of men than through single individuals. And he has encouraged weekly meetings at which his young priests meet without him to discuss means of part-time secular employment in order that they adapt to what the Bishop calls "the inevitable secularization of the future clergy."

Mendez Arceo is loved by his priests as few bishops are; but he is gently criticized by the older ones for one fault: he does not direct them enough. "He is so simple, so approachable," one of them comments, "too simple. He does not satisfy our people's regressive need for authority, their need for pomp, for formality, for great personages." But an authoritarian manner is not in the character of Mendez Arceo. He is a man who believes that "the desire for human power over others is demonic, the clearest manifestation of original sin." His conception of what a bishop should be? "The bishop must preside with the greatest simplicity, he must advise rather than direct, he must respect the free spirit of scientific investigation. The bishop is the humble coordinator of the work of the Holy Spirit."

There is a Mexican proverb, dating to the more evangelic spirit of the early sixteenth century, which says: "*Báculo de palo, obispo de oro; Báculo de oro, obispo de palo*" ("Wooden staff, golden bishop; golden staff, wooden bishop"). Bishop Mendez's staff is a simple oak stick which he confiscated, one Christmas week in Cuernavaca, from a child dressed as a shepherd for a Christmas procession. "That's just the staff I've been looking for!" the Bishop exclaimed as the boy came down the street. "May I have it, brother?" The shepherd relinquished his possession, looking a little sad to be deprived of it, and this is the same staff which Bishop Mendez uses at every one of the extraordinary Masses in his Cathedral, which he celebrates dressed in a chasuble of rough Indian hemp and a mitre of white cotton.

It is hard to say which element of Mendez Arceo's character annoyed his Mexican colleagues first: his informality, his great disdain for raising funds for his diocese, his advanced views on social reform, his friendships with a variety of intellectuals of all ideological coloring, or his theological and liturgical modernism. The last factor was the first to make news. When he began the renovation of his Cathedral—the oldest in Mexico—in the late 1950's, he stripped the interior of its Baroque altar and nineteenth-century ornaments, and stripped it too, to the fury of the conservatives, of all its statuary *santos*. He retained, at the left of the altar, one lonely statue of the Virgin Mary. The interior of the Cathedral as he has restored it has the grandiose ruggedness of the early Franciscan missionary style. Its furnishings have a severe modern elegance. The monolithic stone slab that serves as altar is dominated by an austere bronze ciborium,

flanked by stark bronze lecterns and a filiform wooden cross.
"A Cathedral, like a bishop, must be stripped and denuded
of all material wealth," the Bishop says. "One hears the
Lord best in the desert." Portions of the basilica's coarse
walls, wherever the architects were able to restore the original seventeenth-century frescos, depict the martyrdom
of the missionary priest, Saint Philip, Mexico's only saint.
The Bishop points with a pixyish smile to the image of Saint
Philip, hanging, thin and cerulean blue, from a Japanese gal-
lows. "We are too poor to have more than one saint. Our
poverty is our greatest asset."

However controversial the Bishop's style, his Sunday
Mass has become—to the added discomfort of conservative
Mexicans—the chief tourist attraction of the state of
Morelos. Its music is based on native folk melodies of
Mexico, Chile and Brazil, and is played, from the Angelus
to the last Alleluia, by a native *mariachi* band of violins,
drums, guitars and trumpets. The Mariachi Mass originated
at CIDOC, where Illich had commissioned it from a young
Canadian musicologist-priest. The Bishop had heard it
there, had liked it and, as the Americans in Cuernavaca say,
had brought it to Broadway. The Cathedral is filled for
hours before the 11 a.m. service. The milling crowds join
lustily in the syncopated singing. In between refrains, the
Bishop frequently engages in a dialogue homily with his
congregation. Some of the younger worshippers literally
dance to the altar at communion time to the rhythm of a
Chilean folk song. Communion is offered not only at the
altar but at the back of the church, at both of its side
entrances, seemingly everywhere, because of the great
numbers who desire it. It is an animated, Pentecostal atmosphere—for the Bishop is a great admirer of Pentecostal
sects, and of their "trust in the Holy Spirit." He believes
in creating—his arms flay the air powerfully as he says
this—"an explosion of the Gospel through liturgy." The

practice of Catholicism in Bishop Mendez's diocese—in a country where religion is considered a woman's thing, and where a bare ten percent of Catholic men attend mass—is spectacular. One young Cuernavacan explains that he and his friends go to Mass because Bishop Mendez has restored masculinity to religion. And many United States Catholics have burst into tears from the excitement and the beauty of the Cuernavacan liturgy. "It is evident," one young New York priest said, "that under such a Bishop no underground church would ever need to exist."

"The air of Cuernavaca," a Mexican remarked, "seems to stimulate our men of the cloth." Bishop Mendez had become a source of bewilderment and scandal to the Mexican Church long before the Vatican applied that epithet to Ivan Illich. The modernism of his Cathedral had already startled conservatives. But Mendez Arceo grew even more puzzling when he sanctioned, in the town of Cuernavaca, the use of psychoanalysis by a whole community of Benedictine monks. The experiment had been started by the rector of the monastery, Grégoire Lemercier, who had settled in Cuernavaca in 1951 after being chased out of his former abbey in southern Mexico at gun point by a monk turned bandit. Lemercier, who arrived at Cuernavaca the same year as Mendez Arceo, and quickly became a close friend of the Bishop's, was a maverick from the start. His community of Benedictines began to sing Mass in the Spanish vernacular in 1951, the year they settled in the rugged hills above Cuernavaca. They are said to be the first religious group on the continent to have discarded the Latin liturgy, and their avant-gardism was a major influence on Bishop Mendez's evolution towards modernism. For Mendez Arceo, until his arrival at Morelos, had been a very middle-of-the-road man renowned for his rigorously classical Roman training.

Lemercier, an intelligent, humorless Belgian with icy-blue eyes, had gone into psychoanalysis after experiencing a vision one night, while lying in bed after compline. He describes the vision in his recent book *Dialogues with Christ:* "I saw a multitude of lightning shafts of all colors, an excessively beautiful spectacle . . . A sort of screen then appeared on the wall of my cell, on which I saw a rapid succession of human faces. This kaleidoscope focused on a very beautiful face of great kindness. I started to weep with extreme violence, invaded by the profound consciousness of being loved by God, and of not deserving His love because of my sins." Lemercier entered into psychoanalysis to allay his sense of guilt and to "purify his vocation," as he put it, particularly to aid him with the problems posed by celibacy. The monks, experiencing similar problems, followed their rector's example. Therapists came from Mexico City twice a week to the little monastery of Santa María de la Resurrección above Cuernavaca to hold group therapy sessions with the community of monks. Lemercier, with a typically Benedictine concern for productivity, observed that his monks worked faster and better under therapy, tilled more land, grew more vegetables, produced more stained glass. The experiment had flourished in the dry sage-covered hills above the town of Cuernavaca, to the outrage of the Mexican hierarchy and of many laymen, who labeled the experiment sanctioned by Mendez Arceo as "a repugnant immorality . . . *aggiornamento*, and progress converted to heresy." Criticism of the psychoanalytic experiment was aggravated by the growing notoriety of Illich's neighboring CIDOC, which by the mid-sixties was becoming a freewheeling seminar center on political and social change in Latin America. Bishop Mendez hardly redeemed his reputation when, upon the fourth session of the Second Vatican Council, he chose Lemercier to accompany him to Rome as his special theological adviser.

The hostility of the Mexican hierarchy towards the Bishop of Cuernavaca was much aggravated by the spotlight turned on him at the Council. An infinitely more sophisticated and mundane man than his Mexican colleagues, with more erudition and showmanship about him, Mendez Arceo was the only Mexican bishop who spoke at the Council. He spoke a great deal. And he startled observers by agreeing with the progressive northern European bishops on most items of the agenda. The Mexican hierarchy's triumphalist view that the Church has never erred, and has nothing to learn or be sorry for, epitomized the traditionalists' resistance to ecumenism. Whereas Mendez Arceo's concept of a sinful pilgrim Church (*semper renovanda, semper reformanda*), which should apologize towards all those whom it had estranged throughout history, put him into the vanguard of the ecumenical movement.

There is a very Platonic turn to Mendez Arceo's mind that sees truth as attainable by a great amount of civilized discourse between those of opposite opinions. It is important to note that Mendez Arceo was the only bishop at the Council's first session—and the very first bishop at its second session—to ask for that "forgiveness" of the Jews which the Council Fathers finally declared. "The purification of the Church by the Council," in Mendez Arceo's words, "could not proceed without a humble declaration of regret at all the injustices committed throughout history against the Jewish people." His crusade for rapprochement with Protestants was equally intense. For Mendez Arceo has often said that he would like to be known as "a bishop of both confessions" in the same sense as Karl Barth has been called "the theologian of both confessions." Since anti-Protestantism is much stronger in Mexico than anti-Semitism, the Bishop's sympathy for Protestants was even more controversial in his country than his crusade for the forgiveness of Jews. In few parts of rural Mexico can

Protestants live without physical and psychological harassment, and for some years the state of Morelos, thanks to Bishop Mendez's great popularity in his own diocese, had been one of the few areas of the country where Protestants could live in peace.

It is a tribute to the stubborn consistency of the Mexican reactionaries that even Mendez Arceo's plea for reconciliation with Freemasons became a subject of heated controversy in his country. When he urged that the ban of excommunication be lifted from all North and South American Freemasons, the Mexican paper *Gente,* official organ of the Opus Dei organization, urged immediate excommunication for Bishop Mendez. Opus Dei, or Opus *Daemoni* as the liberals call it, is led in Mexico, as in Spain, by prominent millionaires and military leaders who seek to influence national policy by having secret members in the highest government circles. Its efforts to defame Mendez Arceo were to grow throughout the 1960's.

Bishop Mendez Arceo was progressive on many other points. He was a staunch supporter of collegiality, the decentralizing philosophy which aims to democratize church structures by giving bishops a voice equal to the Pope's. Some of his speeches on religious liberty were Quaker-like in their disdain for cultism. In one declaration, after belittling such legalisms as the observance of fasting and definitions of venial sin, he described Christ's teaching as "a deliverance from the servitude of the law, in such a manner that the veritable Christian law is not one written in stone, but one written in hearts. Love is the plenitude of the law." His views on relaxing celibacy laws were also liberal. He believed that priests who had returned to the lay state should be allowed to marry. "The consciousness of a possibility of a return to the lay state, and of the dispensation from the vows of celibacy, would not be a peril, but a source of greater fidelity and serenity among priests." And seldom was Mendez Arceo more sensation-making than the time he took the floor, during the debate on religious liberty, to urge the Church to recognize the benefits of psychoanalysis.

MEXICAN BISHOP ENDORSES FREUD is the way *The New York Times* headlined this speech of Mendez Arceo's on its front page in October of 1965. "The Church has assumed a position towards psychoanalysis that recalls the history of Galileo," the Bishop said. "This has been due in part to the anti-Christian dogmatism of some psychoanalysts; but because of her distrustful approach the Church up to now has had no influence on those engaged in this science . . . the genius of Sigmund Freud is as great as the genius of Darwin and Galileo." Mendez Arceo went further. He suggested that the methods of psychoanalysis might be used in clerical circles "to purify vocations." He praised it as "a precious tool for the spiritual and psychological liberation of man" and as "a most efficacious tool for discerning religious vocations and for elevating souls towards the way of evangelical virtue and Christian holiness."

Although he has warned that psychoanalysis may become harmful if it "becomes overconfident of its own methods," Bishop Mendez still believes that it is not only useful to the mentally ill, but can be widely used as a preventive general treatment by those of sane mind. Healthy men, he says, profit more from psychotherapy than the ill, "just as healthy people profit more from their vacations than the sick." He is interested in group therapy techniques, and believes that many people would benefit from two weeks' vacation each year spent in a community for group therapy. "It is like a trip to the mountains or to the seashore, it is like taking the sun for two weeks. We must clarify our interior life to the utmost degree in order to be better integrated."

However advanced his views on the care of modern souls, nothing the Bishop said at the Council shocked his compatriots more than his attempt to de-emphasize the cult of Mary. One must remember that the dispute on whether a chapter on the Virgin Mary should be included in the schema "On the Church in the Modern World," or whether Mary deserved a document of her own, was one of the most heated debates of the Council. As the progressives saw it, a separate schema on Mary would encourage further excesses of devotion to the Virgin and thus widen the cleavage between Catholics and Protestants. In the traditionalists' view, as held by the hard line Roman curialists and most Spanish-speaking Fathers, Mary should have a schema to herself because "the mystery of Mary is greater than the mystery of the Church." The conservatives wanted to see the Church in the context of Mary, the progressives wished to see Mary in the context of the Church. The dispute raised such passions that an aid of the arch-conservative Alfredo Cardinal Ottaviani, a Yugoslav Franciscan who was not even an observer at the Council, did not hesitate to use the Vatican press to run off a pamphlet which solicited the Fathers' votes in favor of a separate schema on Our Lady, and led them to believe that the vote was a matter of taking sides "for" or "against" the Virgin Mary. The pamphlet was distributed in Saint Peter's Square with scandalous repercussions.

Throughout these arcane debates, Mendez Arceo sided fervently with such progressive Northern European Fathers as Bernard Cardinal Alfrink, saying that Marian worship must be restrained to correct excesses in popular devotion and to further ecumenical reunion between the Catholic Church and other Christian bodies. "Devotion to Mary and the saints," Mendez Arceo said, "especially in our countries, at times obscures devotion to Christ." He was angrily rebutted by a Spanish bishop who stated that by not having a schema of her own, Mary would be seen "in a passive role as the Church's eldest daughter, not as the Mother of the Church." At which point Mendez Arceo took the floor again and exclaimed: "If the Virgin Mary is the Mother of the Church, then she must be *our* Grandmother!" He elaborated with rigorous Thomist reasoning upon his opinion that the epithet "Mother of the Church" was nonsense. Since Mary is a member of the Church, he said, can she be her own mother? Since, as Saint Thomas said, the Church comprises its angels, is Mary the mother of the angels? Let us just say that she is the one closest to Christ, the first of the saved. Mendez Arceo's progressive faction won with a mere fifty votes. Mary was included into the larger schema on the Church. As the American Protestant observer Robert McAfee Brown said, it was unnerving to see the Holy Spirit win by such a narrow margin.

Mendez Arceo's attack on "the excesses of Marian devotion" in his country had violent repercussions in Mexico. Because of the fervid anticlerical emotions of progressive Mexicans and the equally fervid Catholic passions of its conservatives, the issue of the Virgin Mary can polarize that country as radically as a law and order issue polarizes the United States. Bishop Mendez's put-down of Mary was thought scandalous in a country where the cult of the Virgin still persists on the idolatrous, passionate levels of ancient fertility cults, and where the saying "Mary came to save us, Christ came to condemn us," is a popular proverb of the people. In recentering Catholicism upon the person of Christ, the Bishop was not only masculinizing and modernizing his nation's religiousness, as he had in his Cuernavaca liturgy, he was also subtly threatening the fabric of Mexican society. For psychologists have often noted that the dictatorial sexual *machismo* of Latin men, and the passivity of Latin women, are very much structured upon the sentimental cult of the suffering Mother Goddess. "To do away with the cult of Mary would mean to emancipate Mexican women and make us ready to act in social change," a progressive young Mexican sociologist, a woman, recently said. "That's why Mendez Arceo is considered so revolutionary, and so feared."

Mendez Arceo took many more courageous steps into the twentieth century in the years succeeding the Vatican Council. In 1968, he was the only Mexican bishop who refused to sign a declaration drawn up by his colleagues which supported the Pope's new ban on artificial contraception. That same summer, he was the only member of the Mexican hierarchy to express sympathy for the students in the bloody and red-baiting riots at the University of Mexico, and to deplore the Mexican government's repressive measures. Later that same year, he published a stronger condemnation of the United States' Vietnam policy than any prelate in the entire Catholic Church (save for Cardinal Lercaro of Bologna.) "The prestige of the United States," Mendez Arceo wrote, "would be to renounce its role of world police, consecrating itself instead to the common good." This statement drew fervent praise from the liberal former President Lazaro Cardenas, whose support was without precedent. Such had been the vicissitudes of the Church in Mexico in the past century that no head of state—or former head of state—had ever before backed a member of the Church hierarchy on any subject whatsoever.

By that time a group determined to relieve the Bishop of his diocese had burgeoned in Mexico. It called itself

"*Comité pro Reindivicación de la Iglesia Católica en Cuernavaca*" ("Committee for the Recovery of the Catholic Church in Cuernavaca"). This emergency group was supported by Catholics in the states of Guadalajara, of Puebla, of Michoacan, in provinces two thousand miles from Cuernavaca, by Mexicans who had never been to Cuernavaca and had no intention of ever going there, but who considered the Bishop's modernism a threat to national security. The committee gathered enough momentum to publish defamatory statements against the Bishop throughout the right-wing Mexican press. Some articles stated that the Bishop's "amicable relationships with atheists, Freemasons and Marxists" were proof that he was contributing to the infiltration of Communism into the Church, evidenced everywhere in the world. Another denounced the Bishop for playing "music of dangerous folkloric character" in his Cathedral, and for allowing his liturgy to be attended by "theatrical personages of doubtful moral character." An editorial in the Opus Dei paper *Gente*, quoting the Bishop's statement at the Council: "we must establish a dialogue with all men, notwithstanding how much of Marx or Freud they have in them, for Christ is in all men," concluded that "the only fitting music for the Cuernavaca liturgy would be the *Internationale*." Still another article, after denouncing the Bishop's stand on the Virgin Mary, on Protestantism, on Jews and on Freemasons, concentrated its fire on his friends, and on the serious harm that the Bishop was doing to Catholicism by harboring at his side "*eso personaje extraño y sinuoso, escurridizo y reptante de nationalidad indefinible, que se llama, o dice llamarse, Ivan Illich*" ("That strange, devious and slippery personage, crawling with indefinable nationalities, who is called, or claims to be called, Ivan Illich"). In a letter to the Holy See published in the form of a paid advertisement in Mexican dailies in October 1967, the Committee for the

Recovery of the Faith in Cuernavaca complained of "the shameful events concealed under the veil of Freudian psychoanalysis at Grégoire Lemercier's Benedictine monastery," and of "the heretic ideas of the enigmatic Ivan Illich," and it urged Pope Paul VI to "give a final end to this fearful drama which threatens with such danger the faith of so many souls and which has so harmed the prestige of our Church."

Mendez Arceo had undoubtedly taken dangerous steps in offending the Mexican right. He had created, in one of the continent's most reactionary Catholic nations, an Arcadia of the Church where experiment and dialogue could thrive as they had in few Catholic communities in our century. But he remained serene and undaunted under the barrage of his compatriots' criticism, for he was totally sure of himself, devoid of all ambition except to purify his people's faith and to spread his very spiritualized conception of the Gospel. Mendez Arceo had acted on his belief that "the Church must retain, within her unity, the diversity of the Holy Spirit." And the Bishop's love for diversity is perhaps most clearly evidenced by the fact that the two chief sources of scandal in his entourage, Grégoire Lemercier and Ivan Illich, have a profound dislike for each other. Lemercier considers Illich to be *"un génie détraqué en grand besoin de psychanalyse"* ("an unbalanced genius in great need of psychoanalysis"). Illich refers to Lemercier as "that son of a Belgian officer." His comment on psychoanalysis is that "it's for those who want it, rather than those who need it." Illich, who knows at least as much about the science as Lemercier does, had always looked askance at the Benedictine's experiment because he is "vigorously opposed to any religious community being used as a base for a psychoanalytic experiment." The two men have hardly seen each other five times in the past ten years though they live less than three miles apart. As Lemercier says in a Belgian idiom, *"Nos atomes ne se sont jamais crochus"* ("Our atoms never hooked up"). And yet the Mexican right had the two men so inextricably linked with each other that the second question in the Vatican's questionnaire of Illich, directly parroting accusations of the right wing press, went: "Is it true that beginning in 1960, and especially under the influence of the Benedictine monk and psychoanalyst Grégoire Lemercier, there has been in you a general development of new ideas and disintegrating tendencies of a humanitarian and libertarian nature?" Given the frigidity of the two men's relations, it was one of the Congregation's most comical blunders.

As for Mendez Arceo, he has had to act, all along, as a buffer zone between "the two volcanoes of Cuernavaca," as Mexicans often call Illich and Lemercier, alluding to the two mountains that dominate Mexico City. "I have tolerated, with the greatest diplomacy," the Bishop says, "the mutual dislike of two extraordinary men. I am very pleased with myself."

Mendez Arceo's loyalty to both of his disparate friends remained unswerving. In June of 1967, psychoanalysis at Lemercier's Benedictine monastery was ordered stopped by a direct edict of the Holy See. The edict had come after *"une série d'événements abracadabrants,"* as Lemercier puts it, one of which was Lemercier's own inquisition at the Vatican in 1966. He had sat for eight months in a room of the Congregation for the Doctrine of the Faith answering questions in writing, and never once saw either one of his judges. At the end of the eight months Lemercier had sent Pope Paul a list of his expenses in Rome, and a long letter stating his opinion that he was being used as a pawn in an inquisition which was in fact not aimed at him, but at Bishop Mendez. When the Papal edict banning psychoanalysis at Lemercier's monastery was issued in June 1967, the monks were given the choice of stopping their therapy, or continuing it and being dispensed from their vows. The following Sunday, in his weekly sermon, Mendez Arceo issued an extraordinary pastoral letter. Instead of passing any judgment on his Benedictine friends' experience, he urged his flock, in this address, to be more open than ever to the spirit of renewal and modernism in the Church:

> *I ask you to place yourselves before the Holy Spirit, that Spirit whose action lies deeper than institutions or sociological changes, that Spirit who is present in the hearts of the people of God.*
>
> *The Bishop is required by the Gospel to respect the freedom of each of his brothers. It is the task of the Bishop to be ever more aware of the movements of the Holy Spirit in the midst of the human conditions which ring about us. He must be aware of it especially today, when the whole Church seems shaken to its foundations, when we hear a summons to embrace ever more closely a world in which human change has become a universal experience. Whenever the Christian community faces this experience, and is challenged to reform, two alternatives are open. She can, on the one hand, strive to renew her existing structure. Or she can take a more radical step, and seek creative innovations, new forms of presences to man. By innovation, I mean a new spontaneous growth which the Spirit grants us. I mean a search for entirely new ways, new styles of life. I mean a new sign offered to new times.*
>
> *The Bishop must know that the vitality of the Church does not come through efficient administration or technical planning or authoritarian decision . . . the Church is*

first of all a community of life, for the giving of life. All else, all structures and external forms, exist only to foster a climate of freedom, so that the summons of God may be heard and obeyed in the hearts of the faithful.

What we are now witnessing has a long history. We call it the progressive secularization of religious life. In search of adaptation to new times, men have moved in many directions, they have left the cloister, abandoned older forms of prayer, gone into secular institutions, or ventured to establish community among Christians of different traditions.

And before asking his flock to offer their prayers and brotherly support to the twenty-four monks of Santa Maria, twenty-one of whom eventually chose to leave their order and remain in therapy, Mendez Arceo made the following statement of conscience, unequalled in the Catholic hierarchy for its faith in the future, and in the Holy Spirit:

I feel deeply the pain of breaking with the past, the uncertainty of being far from land on uncharted seas. But I also feel the purifying emptiness of poverty in being stripped of the very riches that the past has given us.

Soon after renouncing his vows in July 1967 and turning his monastery into a secular community for group therapeutics, Lemercier got married with some fanfare, in a manner which Ivan Illich labelled as "extremely incorrect."

IV

Ivan Illich, tall, aquiline, smiling affably, gesticulating with long, gangling arms, conversing in five languages at once, walks swiftly through the rooms of CIDOC, an elegant Palladian villa in the flowered hills above Cuernavaca.

"I would like to help people smile—I mean it in the sense of the French word 'sourire'—smile the social system apart.

"Here at CIDOC we smile violence apart. It is a place where violent people can come and learn a *respeto para la vida*.

"Real revolutionaries are men who look with a deep sense of humor—with sarcasm—upon their institutions. Sarcasm is adult playfulness. Cynicism is its opposite. Instead of freedom and independence it produces the play-acting of revolution, a regressive attachment to slogans and self-worship. Deadly serious revolutionaries—*non merci*.

"Sarcasm is essential to purify ourselves of our illusions. As Marx said, we must go beyond our illusions to change the conditions that made them necessary. That is two paragraphs before the mention of religion as the opium of the people, in his commentary upon Hegel's philosophy of the law.

"I do not really like to use those words violence, nonviolence. At times idols must be shattered. A flower grows through stone and breaks the stone. Is that violence?"

And he rushes out of the room to attend to some business. It is typical Illich tactics to leave the visitor to answer tough questions by himself.

"What makes the place run here is *le bon ton*," he says another day, walking around his luxurious garden, bending solicitously towards his flower beds. "Our basically correct behavior, our concern for the garden.

"I am attacked by both the left and the right because I insist on rigorously correct behavior. I am profoundly opposed to the Underground Church because it is counter-revolutionary. You reform by staying within the system. I believe in good manners, in playing the rules of the game.

If you don't like the rules of chess, stop playing but do not try to reform the rules of chess.

"Your Yankee Underground Church is not civil disobedience but civil unkemptness. I have never seen effective change achieved through means of civil unkemptness.

"I am attacked by my liberal ecumenical friends because I insist on good manners. An American priest comes here and takes a glass, not even a beautiful glass, the ugliest glass he can find, and starts saying Mass in a sports shirt, an ugly black-and-white-striped sports shirt. *Quelle horreur!* Underground churchmen, no thank you.

"*On n'est pas frères et cochons avec le Seigneur.*

"I am theologically profoundly conservative. I could teach with deep relish a course in pre-conciliar theology. I take my stand with Spellman against a married clergy. I would have liked to have lived in the Middle Ages, one of the high points of man's spirit.

"We want to keep CIDOC a free island, an oasis for the free exchange of knowledge and experience. The only rules we hold are, one: you may talk for ten minutes without being interrupted. Two: do not try to proselytize or brainwash. Three: do not organize any direct political, economic or social action, not even religious movements.

"CIDOC is in its deepest sense a contemplative place, not a conspirational place, and this is scandalous to both the left and the right."

He smiles, and throws back his shock of long black hair with a boyish gesture. When smiling Ivan Illich looks like the young Voltaire: long-faced; beak-nosed; the deep-set brown eyes both gentle and cynical; the mysterious wide mouth curving up in a sarcastic, knowing smile, a little kinder and more ingenuous than Voltaire's.

. . .

Excerpts from CIDOC's catalogue of publications, printed under Illich's supervision for the benefit of individuals studying sociocultural change in Latin America:

Peruvian Catechisms in the Sixteenth Century (337 pages).
Socialization of Medicine in Mexico, 1965–1968 (441 pages).
Che Guevara: Reactions of the American Press Concerning the Consequences of His Death, 1967–1968 (438 pages).
Birth Control in Brazil, 1966–1967 (deals with the controversy arising out of the promotion of the intra-uterine spiral as a medium of demographic control; 169 pages).
The Religious Beliefs of the Aymara Indian Tribes of Bolivia (300 pages).
Concubinage in Central America (283 pages).
Pentecostal Sects Among the Puerto Ricans of New York City (150 pages).
Missionary Attitudes of the Latin American Episcopate Toward Indians in the Sixteenth Century (six volumes).
Guerrilla Violence in Peru, Bolivia, Colombia and Ecuador from 1960–1968 (twelve volumes).
Health Education Among Indian Communities in Oaxaca (142 pages).
Student Unrest in Paraguay in 1968 (in preparation).

Also in preparation is a work which will sum up the findings of every diocesan council and synod held in Latin America since the year 1531, and which will include a bibliography of all religious documents, periodicals, pamphlets ever published on the continent. Its editor, Julio Torres, a young Mexican priest, predicts that his work will be at least twenty-five volumes in length and may take him a lifetime to prepare. It will serve as basic text for extensive seminars on the history of the Church in Latin America. It will aim "to provide a pastoral method more deeply rooted in the cultural tradition of Latin America, and to combat the prevailing trend of developed countries imposing their solutions on underdeveloped countries."

As for the twelve-volume work on guerrilla violence mentioned above, compiled by an Argentinian Jesuit, it includes material from a leather-bound volume in the possession of CIDOC entitled *Catálogo de Instrumentos Musicales.* The innocent title enables numerous Bolivians to carry a copy of it casually under their arm in the streets of La Paz. Upon opening the book, one finds it is a highly competent manual for guerrilla warfare, complete with recipes for napalm, diagrams for assembling machine guns and blowing up bridges.

A sampling of the courses offered at CIDOC in the summers of 1968–70, attended each year by some three hundred students from the Americas and Europe:

Manpower and Educational Planning in Puerto Rico.
Social Change and Argentine Literature: 1945–1965.
The Peasant Leagues in Northeastern Brazil, 1955–1963.
Camillo Torres: The Development of His Ideas.
University Reforms and Student Movements in Latin America Today.
Revolutionary Awareness in Brazilian Popular Culture and Contemporary Art.
Theology and Revolution in Latin America.
Cuban Fiction Under Castro.
Attitudes Towards Authority in Mexican Culture.
The Labor Movement in Modern Mexico.
An Analysis of the Haitian Press.
Poetry of Social Protest in 20th-Century Latin American Literature.
A New Concept of Literacy Training.

The last course listed above is taught by Ivan Illich's friend Paolo Freire, a prominent Brazilian educator who was jailed, and then exiled, when he claimed that he could teach fifteen million illiterate Brazilians to read in six weeks if the government allowed all of its trained teachers to use his methods. The Freire method is based on the principle of "conscientization," or "awakening the conscience of the deprived." Freire has already proved, in small experimental groups throughout Latin America, that adults can be taught to read in six weeks of evening classes if the teaching vocabulary is built around emotion-loaded phrases which relate to their social conditions, e.g.: "This land produces our food," "The land must be ours."

Ivan Illich was recently asked to define his theological conception of grace. He replied: "Another form of grace, these days, can be attained through night school." The aphorism has several levels of meaning. Illich believes in adult education, and would like to see all traditional school systems abolished because they favor the privileged middle classes at the expense of the marginal groups; only through a radically transformed system of adult education can the underprivileged rise from misery to the grace of enlightenment. He also believes that wealthy nations create violence by imposing their values on underdeveloped countries; and that priests, social workers or government employees must achieve formidable expertise in the economic, social and political problems of any underdeveloped nation they work in to avoid breeding that violence. CIDOC can be looked upon as a kind of secular monastery where men come for rebirth into Latin American culture, and where all tools of adult education—seminars, civilized discourse, language training, library research—are the sacraments of Illich's secular grace.

CIDOC's library has a collection of material pertaining to social and political change in contemporary Latin America which has few equals on the continent. It has, for instance, the only complete collection in existence of the writings of Camillo Torres, the Colombian priest who was killed by government troops in 1966 when he joined Colombia's guerrilla bands. CIDOC's librarian, Benjamin Ortega, a dry young Mexican who decided "to serve the revolution by making index cards," estimates that there are already some sixty thousand items in the collection, which, according to Illich's wishes, uses the same index card system as the Vatican library. Another unique service offered by CIDOC is its language school, by which the center is largely financed. It uses a modified form of the Foreign Service training system to teach faultless Spanish or Portuguese in twelve weeks, and is said by many to be one of the two best language schools on the American continent. The other one is in Petropolis, Brazil, where CIDOC has set up a small sister organization, and where Illich himself learned to speak impeccable Portuguese in three weeks.

Illich's first site in Cuernavaca was an old hotel on the West slope of the city, which Bishop Mendez preferred to its more grandiose present home for "its spirit of Christian poverty, its so un-American way of life." Although CIDOC's attendance was predominantly clerical in its first years, it grew gradually more secular as Illich sent back half of the priests who came for training with the diagnosis that they could never be "de-Yankified" enough to serve properly in Latin America. The more timid American curates were kept away by rumors of Illich's rigorous intellectual demands and of his sarcastic diatribes at those who could not survive his cultural lobotomies. By the mid-sixties the attendance of religious at CIDOC was only fifteen per cent of its total enrollment, and it had become a progressive free university or think-tank type of organization, a cross between the New School for Social Research and the Center for Democratic Institutions in Santa Barbara. The type of United States clergymen whose devotion to CIDOC grew over the years were tough-minded and brilliant progressives such as Monsignor Robert Fox and Father Robert Stern of the New York Chancery, and Father Joseph Fitzpatrick, S.J., of Fordham's sociology department, who feel that CIDOC serves the important function of breaking down the Savior complex of the American clergy, and who look upon Illich as a prophetic genius pioneering the Church of the future. Students, secular and lay, who survive CIDOC and like it are a mixed bag of sophisticates. Harvey Cox of Harvard, who taught a course in "Religious and Social Change in Latin and North America" at CIDOC in the summer of 1968, describes some of the thirty students who attended his seminar: "There was a very brilliant, very radical French nun who had worked for years in Mexican slums; a Panamanian priest also deeply involved in social work; a young Maryknoll seminarian from the Middle West who was probably the most radical man I've ever met. The rest were laymen: a couple of Belgian sociologists; a Ph.D. student in zoology from Berkeley; another Ph.D. student in sociology —a Nisai—from the University of Chicago; an SDS leader from Radcliffe. It was the most interesting bunch of students I've had in all my years of teaching." At Illich's insistence, Harvey Cox spent part of the summer reading through all the spiritual exercises of Saint Ignatius.

CIDOC's present site, to which Illich moved in 1966, no longer reflects the spirit of Christian poverty which Bishop Mendez had praised in its earlier home, but rather Illich's exquisitely austere and sophisticated tastes. Its main building is a white Palladian-type structure built in "U" shape around a swimming pool in an idyllic setting of pine trees, flowering trees and tropical plants. The rooms are large, white and serene, sparsely furnished with Cor-

busier-type modern furniture designed by Illich's architect
brother. The tiled floors are scattered with starkly handsome Indian rugs in hues of brown and tan. There are
a few abstract crucifixes here and there. CIDOC has
its own printing plant, lecture rooms equipped with ear-
phone systems for instantaneous translation, a movie projec-
tion room, a row of forty cubicles where the language
courses are given to groups of four students per class, and
study spaces for visiting scholars. Its atmosphere of rarified
scholarship evokes the style of the great medieval monasteries where secular men came to steep themselves in study
and in learned dialogues. CIDOC's superefficiency, the
exquisite institutional courtesy of its staff members, the
dazed expression of young Americans in the process of
their cultural *kenosis*, also recalls a luxurious private clinic.
Doctor Illich runs through its white corridors, a grey
Mexican wool serape flapping behind him like the wings
of a jackdaw, finding a few minutes a day—like a surgeon
making his rounds—to administer some devastating aphorism to each of his patients; or to give them short discourses
on Saint John of the Cross, Wittgenstein's philosophy of
language, the relationship between tenth century monastic
groups and twentieth century hippie communes.

Some of CIDOC's personnel explain the center's incredibly smooth functioning by the fact that Illich's charm
casts a spell on anyone who works with him. Illich insists
that it runs smoothly because none of his staff members
received "conventional educations." One of the directors
of the center, Valentine Borremans, is a Sacré Coeur
graduate who worked as a deep-sea diver with Jacques
Cousteau. The librarian never went to college, but has
devised a simplified cataloguing system which is now being
adapted in other underdeveloped countries. The night
watchman is a former peasant leader in Zapata's revolution
who comes at five each evening to guard the center with

his 1910 gun. Illich also insists that CIDOC runs smoothly "because of the flowers," and that it is "a free club for the search of surprise . . . where we are chiefly concerned with becoming humorists."

A friend of Ivan Illich's mother once said to her: "Why did you not have seven sons instead of one Ivan? It would be so much simpler for the world." The public image of the mundane, astringent-witted scholar-priest shelters a Promethean variety of men. Illich is both tough and tender, guileful and ingenuous, devout and cynical. He is a flamboyant exhibitionist and profoundly modest. He is as radical in some domains as he is traditional in others. He is an arrogant aristocrat with a militant dedication to the poor. He is as diabolically sarcastic to his critics as he is loyal to his friends. One of his favorite sayings, taken from Che Guevara, is *"Il faut s'endurcir sans jamais perdre sa tendresse"* ("One must toughen up without losing one's tenderness"). Illich refuses to be categorized, and regales in being controversial. In a church whose members have a very regressive need for authority, he deliberately generates hostility by needling Catholics to be independent, flexible and keenly critical. He often makes himself unavailable to his trainees when they need him the most to force them to work out their own problems—the way they will have to when they are in the mountains of Peru. Keeping an appointment with an American hung-up on Anglo-Saxon punctuality, the scrupulously punctual Illich will arrive an hour late to teach him the Latin American sense of time. To the conventional Brooklyn curate who complains about Mexican cooking Illich will serve a two-week diet of *favos*. He refuses to be anybody's hero and befuddles men on both the left and the right by rigorously adhering to the rules. Underground clerics who have come to Cuernavaca to learn from Illich's progressive thinking are appalled to hear that he rises at six a.m. every morning to say his breviary; goes to confession in an old-fashioned booth; dutifully takes Communion every Sunday; and delights in observing feast days, holy days, saints' days, and other ancient forms of Catholic ritual. As for the traditionalist who once accused Illich of not believing in Canon law, he was equally startled by the reply: "We are called to observe the law, not to believe in it." Illich enjoys teaching by puzzlement, and answers questions in cryptic aphorisms worthy of the toughest Zen master. The young Catholic asking Illich what Christianity is about is told: "Being a Christian is like understanding the joke in the story. A story is told to a group of people. Only the Christian smiles, only he gets the joke. And some men smile who do not know that they are Christians." What is faith about? "Faith is a readiness for the surprise. We must have a sarcastic readiness for all surprises, including the ultimate surprise of death."

("I love the way Illich tortures his missionaries," Bishop Mendez comments. "Sometimes I cry with emotion at seeing aged men, old priests, shed their old selves under his care.")

Illich is as severe towards himself as he is to others. To cure himself of a certain discomfort and estrangement he has felt towards Mexican culture ("I was terrified of their gods, of the devouring eyes of their sculptures"), he frequently goes to spend the night alone on the desolate peak of Xochicalco, a Toltec ruin near Cuernavaca filled with terrifying bas reliefs of sacrificial themes, where he sleeps on top of a flat mountain ledge, wrapped in his serape.

Illich is at his roughest with those who have any romantic notion of revolution, and with those who try to use CIDOC as a center for political proselytizing. When a group of Yankee SDS students picketed CIDOC in protest against the former president of Columbia University, Grayson Kirk, who had been invited to dine at the center, Illich sent an Argentinian Jesuit, an authority on guerrilla warfare, to lecture the picketers. The Jesuit accused the SDSers of Yankee imperialism. How did they dare stop anyone from visiting a Mexican institution?

All proselytizers and romanticists are curbed with the same severity. The Yankee student radical expressing curiosity for Central American guerrilla bands is packed off to the library to read the complete works of Goethe. The progressive priests who express admiration for Camillo Torres (whom Illich knew as "an adorable drinking companion," but never invited to CIDOC,) are coldly reminded that Torres willfully shed his clerical status before joining the guerrillas, which was "the canonically proper thing to do." For one of the most contradictory aspects of the cryptic Illich, given the progressive tone of his institution, is his insistence that priests must abstain from any direct political action. He believes that although through history the Church has participated constantly in the shaping of political change, blessing governments and condemning them, the time has come for Her to withdraw from any specific social initiative. It is a modern rendering unto Caesar. Illich traces it to what he calls "my profound Jewish roots. 'Do not use Yahweh's name in vain.'" A consciously secular ideology must now assume the task of solving social problems. The position is subtle, and sometimes hair-splitting. The Church must condemn all forms of injustice, but never support any specific program. "Your American bishops should all condemn the Vietnam war as Bishop Mendez did," Illich says, "but they must not express their preference for McCarthy or any other candidate. Bishop Mendez came out against the Vietnam war, not for the Paris peace talks."

Within the framework of this logic, Illich has as much scorn for a progressive Catholic action party such as Chile's

Christian Democrats as he has for Colombia's equally Catholic Conservative party. Illich believes—and Bishop Mendez would agree—that the function of the Church is "to recognize the presence of Christ among us through liturgical celebration, and to charge human beings, through these celebrations, with the proper emotions towards social action." "The less efficient the Church is as a power the more effective She is as a celebrant of the mystery." "The priest must continually ask himself if he can abstain from the little social good he can do in order to better lead his people in the liturgical celebration of change." One of Illich's best aphorisms on the subject: "Let us follow the example of the Pope; let us have the courage to allow churchmen to make statements so ephemeral that they could never be construed as the Church's teaching." Another epigram: "I celebrate my faith for no reason at all."

The notion that the priest's role is at the altar is also held by the William Buckley brand of Catholic, and it is disgruntling to the young Yankee clergymen who flock to Cuernavaca in hope of finding a haven of social activism. Two such priests of the Los Angeles diocese came to CIDOC once to complain to Illich that Francis Cardinal McIntyre, the United States' most conservative prelate, had not allowed them to march in favor of civil rights legislation. They did not receive the sympathy they had expected. "If I were your cardinal I would not allow you to march either," Illich snapped. "If you want to parade against discrimination in general okay, but not for the passage of another lousy stopgap law. Or else take off your white collars." When Daniel Berrigan was sent to cool his heels in Cuernavaca after being exiled for his anti-Vietnam activism, he found in Illich "a lot of intellectual violence aimed at our religious left." Much of the left, indeed, looks upon Illich as a cross of Savonarola and C.I.A. man, a cop-out on radical vision. When asked to comment on the Melvilles, the Maryknoll missionaries who had helped Guatemalan guerrillas to arm and who had once spent a night at CIDOC on their way home to the United States, Illich shrugged disdainfully and said: "Dilettantes! Ingenues! One does not take short cuts." Nothing is more foreign to Illich than the type of guerrilla-martyrdom engaged in by the Melvilles in Latin America, or by the Berrigans in the United States. For Illich, the proper way to force an upheaval in society is through a revolution in the educational process. Teach a million Brazilian peasants to read in six weeks of night school, rid a few thousand missionaries of their Yankee hang-ups. Such adult education, in Illich's view, is far more radical than training guerrillas. It is an Apollonian versus a Dyonisiac concept of revolution. As one of Illich's close friends said, "Ivan would never be trampled by the wheels of revolution, he'd be at the hub of the wheel, at dead center."

What the Yankee progressives learn to recognize, if they stay long enough at CIDOC, is that removing the Church from the political sphere in Latin America can be in itself a supra-political act. As recently as 1937, the archbishop of Lima, Peru, had this praise for the Latin American status quo: "Poverty is the most certain road to eternal felicity. Only the state which succeeds in making the poor appreciate the spiritual treasures of poverty can solve its social problems." In a continent where the Church has been such a comfortable justifier of poverty and extreme wealth, the removal of Church support might mean the collapse of an entire network of oligarchies. In the United States, with its separation of Church and State, it is the conservatives who want the Church to remain aloof from social matters, and the progressives who prod Her toward social activism. But in Latin America, with its heritage of theocracy, it is the reactionaries who wish to use the Church's political muscle. Many of the most sophisticated progressives want to deprive Her of secular power. Illich's stand on an apolitical Church—in a typically ambivalent Illich way—is in fact highly political. It is all the more ambivalent because of his expertise in international affairs, and because of his frequent and vitriolic attacks on United States foreign policy.

There is something about the Yankee way of life which evokes more sarcasm from Illich than any other brand of nationalism. He began to make, in the mid-1960's, a series of violent anti-American statements which doubtless played a role in leading him to the caves of the Vatican. He had been frustrated, in 1965, by the inability of his American students to relate the problems of the ghettos and of Vietnam to the Yankee-bred violence in Latin America. He had referred to Guatemala as "Vietlat" in a speech to the Foreign Policy Association in 1966. And he had sarcastically compared our peace movement to "cough syrup given to nineteenth century syphillitics" because of its failure to protest U.S. intervention in Latin America in the same voice as it protested Vietnam. Noting that the Alliance for Progress had tripled the amount of revenue flowing into the United States from Latin America, he had labelled it "an alliance pregnant with violence that has maintained or swept into power military regimes in two thirds of Latin American countries," "a deception designed to maintain the status quo," "a bone thrown to the dog, that he remain quiet in the backyard of the Americas."

Violence in Watts, Vietnam, and Guatemala, he wrote in 1967, all shared the common cause of United States messianism. All three were related to "the failure to win hearts and minds of people by an outpouring of money and human lives that Americans perceive as an expression of heroic generosity . . . It is not the American way of life lived by a handful of millions that sickens the billions, but rather the growing awareness that those who live the American way of life will not tire until the superiority of their quasi-religious persuasions is accepted by the under-dog." He compared the Alliance for Progress to the war on poverty in the United States: "Both programs were designed to have the poor join in the American dream. Both programs failed. The poor refused to dream on command."

A stern religious message is added to Illich's anti-Yankee polemic: "Only God can create values. The United States breeds violence by imposing its values on other nations." For according to Illich, the world is not so much divided between nations or political blocs, but between an international middle class which takes its style and values from the United States, and the billions of under-privileged who are increasingly alienated from that middle class. Illich has the aristocrat's sentimental attachment—recalling Tolstoi's—for cultures of poverty untainted by bourgeois aspirations. As in his early days with the Puerto Ricans, he delights to see the People celebrating in their native fashion. "Peasant cultures provide categories which endow even extreme rural privation with dignity." "I am for those who want to deepen life rather than lengthen it." The peasant is richer and wiser than the Alliance for Progress. Let him enjoy himself at his traditional fiestas and die happy rather than receive powdered milk from the Yankees' sacristy and yearn for the vulgar Coca-Cola culture imported by U.S. foreign aid. It is an ideology shared by many arch-reactionaries, which leads Illich to be attacked more frequently by radicals than by conservatives.

V

"I make a scrupulous distinction," Ivan Illich once said, "between the Church as She and the Church as It."

("That," he added triumphantly, "one can say only in English.")

"*She* is that surprise in the net, the pearl. She is the mystery, the kingdom among us. The identity of the Church-as-She will remain through whatever changes She's presently undergoing, which are no greater than the changes She underwent under Constantine, or in Abelard's time. Those who believe in Her believe in something that cannot be said in words. No pronouncements however stupid, be it on birth control or on clerical celibacy, can lessen my love for Her and my faith in Her mystery. People who leave the Church because of what She says don't understand love."

"*It* however is the institution, the temporary incarnational form. I can only talk about It in sociological terms. I've never had trouble creating factions and dissent towards the Church-as-It. It is the chrysalis, the skin which has to die in order for the butterfly to metamorphose to its true form. Yet there can't be a butterfly without a chrysalis."

Illich was asked whether he meant this to be a metaphor for the traditional distinction between the Church as the mystical body of Christ and the Church as temporal institution. "Let us not make things so complicated," Illich said, and rushed out of the room. But the Jesuit sociologist Father Joseph Fitzpatrick, who frequently interprets Illich to the world, enjoys enlarging on the metaphor. "The Church-as-She is the mystery of God's presence among us. The Church-as-It is the scandal of incarnation, God's presence in human forms. One must use all the human power one has to expose the scandal in order that the presence of the Word can be perceived. Illich's function as a priest is the scrupulous criticism of the Church-as-It for the sake of the Church-as-She."

Jesuits have protected, published, and interpreted Ivan Illich for many years. "Too bad he's not a Jesuit," Daniel Berrigan once quipped, "he's such a caricature of us."

When Ivan Illich began his forays against the Church-as-It, in the mid-sixties, he was writing as a historian, having taken part a decade before in the first methodical sociological survey ever given to the Latin American Church. The Latin American Church was experiencing a crisis in the 1950's similar to that which the French Church had undergone a decade before when it launched its worker-priest movement, concluding that it had lost its working classes and that France had become, as the famous book *France: Pays de missions?* suggested, a pagan, missionary territory. The state of emergency in Latin America, which holds one third of the world's Catholic population, was more acute. The Church there was abysmally poor, some eighty per cent of baptized Catholics on the continent failed to practice their religion, and the shortage of priests was much more drastic than it was in France.

The pioneers in the first massive studies of the Latin American Church were the two European sociologists Father François Houtart and Father Émile Pin, S.J., whose work would have a great influence on Illich. Their surveys revealed that in some regions of Latin America—in areas of the Dominican Republic and Guatemala, for instance— there was one priest for every seventy thousand Catholics, as against an average of six hundred parishioners per priest in the United States; that in some Brazilian dioceses the rate of ordination averaged two priests per year; that only about ten per cent of the Catholic population of Brazil practiced their faith; that in some of the continent's largest cities, like Buenos Aires, only five per cent of baptized Catholics attended Sunday Mass. It is this crisis which evoked the Papal decree of 1961 that had so alarmed Illich. The decree had called for ten per cent of all North American religious to migrate into the Latin American continent. But by 1967, the North American influx to the south had only reached six thousand of the Pope's stated goal of thirty-five thousand. One of Illich's first explosive articles, "The Seamy Side of Charity," published in the Jesuit magazine *America*, rejoiced over the failure of the program, and called for its immediate discontinuation. Like all of his writings, it was polemical, bristling with barbed aphorisms, calculated to needle and provoke.

Illich's central thesis in the article, which infuriated hierarchies on both sides of the border, was that the so-called "Papal plan" was nothing but "part of the many-faceted effort to keep Latin America within the ideologies of the West." Missionaries of the kind that were being sent South of the border, he wrote, were "pawns in a world ideological struggle;" they played the role of "a colonial power's lackey chaplain;" they transformed "the old-style haciendas of God into the Lord's supermarket." Such personnel, in Illich's view, chiefly buttressed private institutions such as Church schools serving the upper and middle classes at the expense of the underprivileged. He related it to the general swamping of Latin America by United States values. "The influx of U.S. missioners coincides with the Alliance for Progress, Camelot and C.I.A. projects and looks like a baptism of these." The article was written, Illich admits, angrily and in a hurry, right after *Ramparts* magazine hit the newsstands in January 1967 exposing the C.I.A.'s backing of the National Student Association. "I wrote the article fast to make it clear that within the

Church there were people who refused to take funds from Alliance for Progress and other similar sources."

Yet the hidden premise in this particular polemic of Illich is more religious than political. For in that shortage of Latin American clergy which had panicked the Vatican Illich saw a rare and precious chance to pioneer new forms of priesthood. Illich's passionate involvement in Latin American affairs stemmed in part from his realization that both its religious crisis and its turbulent rate of political change made it a precious laboratory for the society of the future. What conservatives saw as a crisis of scarcity in the priesthood Illich diagnosed as a surplus and a blessing. "Exporting Church employees to Latin America masks a universal and unconscious fear of a new Church," he wrote. "The promise of more clergy is like a bewitching siren. It makes the chronic surplus of clergy in Latin America invisible and it makes it impossible to diagnose this surplus as the gravest illness of the Church . . . If North America and Europe send enough priests to fill the vacant parishes, there is no need to consider laymen to fulfill most evangelical tasks; no need to rexamine the structure of the parish, the function of the priest, no need for exploring the use of the married diaconate, and new forms of celebration . . ." Beefing up the clergy in any continent, in Illich's view, was a way of maintaining a clerical and irrelevant Church. Illich compared this cure to that of the doctor who prefers aspirins to radical surgery. "They feel no guilt at having the patient die of cancer, but fear the risk of applying the knife."

To diagnose the symptoms of a cancerous structure was Illich's task in another controversial article, "The Vanishing Clergyman" ("*Métamorphose du clergé*," "*Il Clerico Desparecido*" as it was translated for publications in other countries). "The Vanishing Clergyman," which Illich had actually written in German in 1961, remains unsurpassed today for its bold prophecy of new forms of ministry. Its demand for a return to an early-style Christianity untainted by pomp and secular power is similar in message to the romantic longings of the Underground Church. But it is expressed in Illich's rigorously scientific, methodological manner, and cloaked in his Apollonian sarcasm.

"The Roman Church," the article begins, "is the world's largest non-governmental bureaucracy. It employs one million eight hundred thousand full-time workers—priests, brothers, sisters and laymen. These employees work within a corporate structure which an American business consultant firm rates as among the most efficiently operated organizations in the world. The institutional Church functions on a par with General Motors and the Chase Manhattan . . . Men suspect that it has lost its relevance to the Gospel and to the Word. Wavering, doubt and confusion reign among its directors, functionaries and employees. The giant begins to totter before it collapses. Some church personnel react to the breakdown with pain, anguish and fright. Some make heroic efforts and tragic sacrifices to prevent it . . . I would like to suggest that we welcome the disappearance of institutional bureaucracy in a spirit of deep joy."

Illich goes on to call the traditional clergyman "a folk-loric phantom," "a member of the aristocracy of the only feudal power remaining in the world," "a man sentenced to disappear, whether the Church wishes it or not, by the changes in modern society." His clerical science fiction uses Hegelian dialectic. If the Church is to retain men to preach the Gospel, he argues, the traditional antithesis between pastor and layman must be allowed a new synthesis which will transcend present categories. And it is the leisure society of the future, with its reduced working hours and its early retirement ages, which will allow this synthesis to take place. Illich predicts that the leisure society will free ordinary laymen to accept vocations for part-time ministerial functions, men chosen for a "sense of the Church" which they will have cultivated by prayer, scriptural study, a pure life.

"An adult layman," he writes in an often quoted passage, "will preside over the normal Christian community of the future. The ministry will be an exercise of leisure rather than a job. The *diaconia* (an informal community of worshippers meeting in each others' homes,) will supplant the parish as the fundamental unit of the Church. The periodic meeting of friends will replace the Sunday assemblage of strangers. A self-supporting dentist, factory worker, professor, rather than a Church-employed scribe or functionary, will preside over the meeting. Only with the emergence of such a part-time priesthood will the Church free itself from the restrictive system of benefices and from that gigantic bureaucratic efficiency which corrupts Christian testimony more subtly than power." Illich, from the day he was ordained, had consistently refused stipends for any priestly function. He had always been sharply critical of the economics and the institutional pomp of the Church. ("The title of Monsignor," he once said about his own rank, "is rather akin to the sexuality of a mule.")

"The Vanishing Clergyman" goes on to state that celibacy is an admirable way of life which has nothing whatsoever to do with the priesthood. The two states—priesthood and celibacy—had been linked together by custom within a set of historical circumstances that no longer exist. Illich is all for celibacy as long as it is taken as a free choice for the sake of itself, stripped of all magic or ritualistic reasons. And his praise of this type of freely chosen celibacy is a uniquely tender, lyrical passage in the oeuvre of a very abrasive writer, revealing Illich's very profound strain of mysticism. Freely chosen celibacy is a choice taken "for the sake of the kingdom," "a personal realization of an intimate vocation from God." "The Christian who renounces marriage and children for the kingdom's sake seeks no abstract or concrete reasons for his decision. His choice is pure risk in faith, the result of the intimate and mysterious experience of the heart. His decision to renounce a spouse is as intimate and uncommunicable as another's decision to prefer his spouse over all others."

But should the Vatican therefore be petitioned to relax its laws of compulsory celibacy? Certainly not, the mystic says, returning to his most sarcastic vein. Illich is against married priests because the Church already has too many unmarried ones, and such halfway *aggiornamento* would slow up any true revolution of church structures. Once again he is for surgery, not for aspirin. "The clerical mass exodus," he writes, "will only last as long as the present clerical system exists. During this time, ordination of married men would be a sad mistake. It would only delay needed radical reforms." Illich stresses that he has projected a Utopia for the future. For the moment, he is for playing the rules of the game, and for strictly adhering to the Pope's edicts on compulsory celibacy. (It is a somewhat Leninist logic: the worse things get, the better for the revolution.) "I believe that the emergence of a new pastoral Church depends largely on compliance with the Pope's directives during our generation." (One can visualize the sly Voltairean smile on Illich's face as he writes this passage.) "His position helps assure the speedy death of the clergy."

And Illich boldly asks for defections, for an increasing exodus of priests to ensure the speedy death of the traditional clergy. "May we pray," he writes, "for an increase of priests who choose radical secularization? For priests who leave the clergy in order to pioneer the Church of the future? For priests who, faithfully dedicated to and loving the Church, risk misunderstanding and suspension? For extraordinary priests, willing to live today the ordinary life of tomorrow's priests?" And he asks all clergymen to pose themselves a question which has tormented an increasing number of Catholics in the past decade: "Should I, a man totally at the service of the Church, stay in the structure in order to subvert it, or leave in order to *live* the model of the future?"

"The Vanishing Clergyman" enraged many progressive United States Catholics by its rather cynical logic, its haughty dismissal of any possibility of a married clergy in our generation. But it enraged Latin Americans even more, as had "The Seamy Side of Charity," because of its description of the Church as "priest-ridden." That image, in a continent whose overworked clergymen live in squalor, was unjust. Even Bishop Mendez Arceo criticized the article harshly as "a caricature that missed the whole supernatural factor of the priesthood," and commented that Illich had "projected the realities of the United States Church into Latin America." The Bishop's insight, as usual, was very astute. "The Vanishing Clergyman's" sarcasm was triggered by Illich's close observation, in the 1950's, of the wealthy, bureaucratic, and overstaffed United States Church.

If Illich's progressive supporters were annoyed by the two articles, one need not try hard to imagine the rage of the Mexican right wing. A conservative Mexican Jesuit even dedicated the major part of an entire book—later censured by the Archbishop of Mexico City for its fanaticism—to tearing the two essays apart. Illich accepted the criticism with a bemused smile, saying that the Church of the future would be a happening, a surprise, that he had projected just one of many possible Utopias, and that he did not necessarily agree with his articles a year after he had written them. It is interesting to note that throughout the body of his writing and lecturing, whether he crusades against clericalism, the school system, or U.S. foreign policy, Illich uses a very ancient Papal method which one could call the negative principle. He condemns institutions without clearly structuring any alternatives to them. His utopias remain foggy. It is in the great critical tradition of the ban, the interdict, which the Church has used for a millennium. By condemning institutions without suggesting a clear alternative, the Churchman as critic does not commit himself to what is coming next, he does not lose face, he is saved from history's surprises. Illich's radical message of secularization and of letting history take its course was being given in the most orthodox Roman terms. As he chipped away at the walls of the Church-as-It from the inside, Ivan Illich, one of the most rigorously trained theologians of his generation, was using the most traditional Catholic tools.

In September 1967, a few months after the appearance of his two controversial articles, Ivan Illich was asked to give a lecture to a group of students at the National University of Mexico. He took as his theme "The Use and Abuse of Religious Symbols in Present-Day Change." The following article, printed in the Mexican daily *Últimas Noticias* five days before Illich's lecture, announced his talk in these words:

> *Doctor Ivan Illich, from the Congregation of Benedictine monks in the ex-monastery of Santa María de la Resurrección in Cuernavaca, has still not changed his mind about giving lectures on advanced religious themes despite the decree of the Holy See, where the monastery is no longer recognized . . . Doctor Illich is one of the monks who has undergone psychoanalysis in the ex-monastery.*

Illich thought that was hilarious. The Mexicans' paranoia about the diocese of Cuernavaca was such that it had never been able to distinguish one man from the other, despite their non-existent relationship.

As Illich stood on the podium of a university lecture room delivering his talk, he was physically attacked by four members of a right-wing student organization. Somewhere in the middle of a sentence that went "a clear distinction must be made between idealized religion, which makes men feel superior to others, and faith, which is a progressive humanization," shouts of "Apostate!" came from the back of the room. And the priest was bombarded with an assortment of rotten eggs, tomatoes, and bags of ink and red paint. The four disturbers were quickly spirited out of the lecture hall by a group of angry students. Illich, with a dazzling smile, put an artist's smock over his spattered shirt, sat down cross-legged on the edge of a table to avoid the mess by the podium, and serenely resumed his lecture.

The attackers were members of MURO (*Movimiento Universitario de Renovadora Orientación*), a sinister Catholic secret society which was founded in 1962 in the town of Puebla, under the specific auspices of its Archbishop, Octaviano Marquez y Toriz, a man widely acknowledged as the arch-conservative of the Mexican hierarchy, and Bishop Mendez Arceo's bitterest enemy. MURO, a militantly anti-Protestant, anti-Semitic, anti-Masonist, anti-Communist society, soon resorted to such terrorist methods that it was banned, two years after its founding, by the primate of the country, Archbishop Miguel Dario Miranda of Mexico City. He forbade Catholics to belong to it and threatened its members with excommunication.

Members of MURO take their initiation oath with their hand stretched over a crucifix flanked by a dagger and a human skull. Their ideology is that of right wing militants the world over—a Jewish-Communist conspiracy has infiltrated into all organs of society, the press, the Church, the government, banks, big business, and must be resisted, if necessary, by armed force. However, its militancy is more sinister than that of many other groups because of its religious fanaticism, its slogan that "the conspiracy must be crushed for the sake of Christianity." Yet, MURO is nothing but a humble façade, a pawn, for an international network of right-wing movements which make our Birchites look anodyne. It is linked, for instance, with the Fascist Pan-American movement called *Joven América* ("American Youth") which, after having staged a bomb attack on the progressive Mexican paper *El Día* in 1965, issued the following press statement: "We preach and practice the terror of the Crusaders. We shall implant totalitarian states in all of the American continent through the means of non-conventional revolutionary warfare. MURO belongs to our organization. We totally repudiate the free speech system of democratic nations." MURO— whose members had attacked Bishop Mendez Arceo earlier that same year with bags of red paint as he was walking about Cuernavaca—is also linked with more secret organizations, many of them emanating from Puebla—which have contacts with the extreme right wing of the Spanish falangists and with such terrorist organizations as the Argentinian TECOS. Three books that are required reading for all prospective members of these sects are Hitler's *Mein Kampf*, Henry Ford's *International Judaism*, and another bible of the anti-Semitic movement, *In Order that He Reigns*, by the French fascist Ousset, a work long censured by the French bishops for its deviations from doctrine and its advocacy of terrorist tactics.

Within the vast literature which has stated the philosophy of these groups in the past years, there is one position paper by the Mexican right-wing writer Ricardo

Fuentes Castellanos which sums up most lucidly the sentiments of those who have been active in returning "the true faith" to the diocese of Cuernavaca: "We must maintain devotion," he writes, "to the Hispanic tradition founded in Catholicism, in a Devotion to the Virgin Mary, whom we consider the cornerstone of our national identity, and in the repudiation of those Communist principles, be they sociological, political, or cultural, which derive from the ideals of the French Revolution and of the Voltairian Encyclopedists of the 18th century. In the political order, we maintain nationalism and therefore reject all ideas of 'pacific coexistence' with the followers of Marx and Lenin —we proclaim the spirit of uncompromising struggle against Communism and all its traveling companions." In this essay, which is titled "Militant Catholicism," the author goes on to accumulate proof that all American universities, from the United States to Chile and Argentina, are Communist-infiltrated. He offers as example Jacques Maritain, "that apostle of progressive Catholicism," who had taught at Princeton, "a lay university of the same leftist reputation as Harvard and Yale." Princeton, he points out, had gone even further in inviting as lecturer "the traitor Alger Hiss, pardoned in the spirit of appeasement of Camp David by the then President Dwight Eisenhower, who so gloried in his friendship with the Soviet Marshal Zhukov." The document ends on a note of triumphant and messianic Hispano-nationalism: "Those who preach such a North American or European way of peaceful co-existence with the left have no comprehension of the vibrant, clear, and militant Hispanic spirit. Our people, valiant, passionate, and extreme, have never tolerated, and will never tolerate, any nuancing, any human respect, any formalist practices of the Anglo Saxon or Swiss manner . . . Mexico is not England or Switzerland or France! Our blood is not made of grain syrup as that of the frigid Scandinavians or the phlegmatic British! Here in Hispano America we call for clarity in the Spanish manner, we call bread bread, and wine wine . . . For that reason Communists and their appeasers merit, in our tradition, the most brutal epithets of the energetic idiom of Cervantes, of the sonorous Castillian tongue . . . in our tradition, it is not 'against charity' to label and denunciate them as brutally as possible as enemies of Religion, of the Fatherland and of Humanity."

In such fanatic terrain was the conspiracy against Mendez Arceo and Ivan Illich construed. Mexico's militant Catholics quickly lose all respect for prelates who do not abide with the dogmatic triumphalism of the nineteenth-century Church. The epithets being thrust at the Bishop who had asked for dialogue with Freemasons, Protestants, Jews, Marxists, and Freudians, and who had questioned the place of the Virgin Mary at the center of Mexican faith, were not only Cervantesque but obscene. He was called *tapadera*, a word which even the most emancipated and radical Mexican women refuse to translate, but which the dictionary discloses as the lowliest term for a "shameful whore." He was also called *alcahuete,* which can mean, in turn, pimp, cover-up man, underground agent. And in 1967, on the walls of the MURO-infiltrated University of Mexico where Illich had smilingly resumed his lecture, the signs no longer said "*Muerte a Méndez Arceo,*" but "*Muerte a Méndez* Ateo"—"Death to Mendez the Atheist."

The Catholic Gestapo overtly began its concerted attack to remove *el tenebroso Dálmata Illich* from Mexico in the autumn of 1967. It was launched theatrically on October 4 by an open letter to the Pope published in Mexico's largest dailies, and inserted as a paid advertisement by the "Committee for the Recovery of the Faith in Cuernavaca." It was signed by some twenty laymen and priests, including

Father Celerino Salmeron, a man so reactionary that he is described by colleagues as *"un anti-Juarista furibondo."* (Benito Juarez had been the liberal reformer of the 1830's.) "The spectacular and theatrical liturgy which we have seen in the Cuernavaca Cathedral," so the letter ended, "the new so-called Gospel which its Bishop preaches, the psychoanalyzed and degenerate community fostered under him, the touristic hotel run by Monsignor Illich where bizarre things have been witnessed, these are not, cannot be the work of God." The attack was in pincer-like formation. Almost simultaneously, the Archbishop of Puebla, who happens to be a cousin of President Diaz Ordaz, and who was, that year, president of the Conference of Mexican Bishops, was writing to Cardinal Spellman to ask that Illich be recalled to the New York diocese. Cardinal Spellman courteously replied on November 10, stating that "Illich is a priest of excellent standing in my diocese, in every way obedient," and informing the Mexican Bishop that he would not recall Illich to New York, since he had academic contracts in Cuernavaca to which Spellman had explicitly given his approval.

Cardinal Spellman's letter expressing his loyalty to Ivan Illich was one of the last he ever wrote. He died a few days later. Less than a fortnight after Spellman's death the New York Chancery received a new series of letters asking for Illich's recall—some from Mexico, one emanating, with Mexican pressure, from the arch-conservative Roman Cardinal Alfredo Ottaviani. "The timing was totally obscene," an official of the New York Chancery angrily recalls. "Cardinal Spellman was barely buried. They knew that Illich had lost a staunch friend and they did not have the decency to wait."

On December 19, Spellman's provisional successor, Archbishop Maguire, wrote to Illich asking for his immediate return to New York—by order, this time, of

Rome. Illich, in a letter to Maguire postmarked January 6, expressed "profound embarrassment at my present unavailability," and convinced Maguire that his duties at CIDOC made it impossible for him to come to New York at that time. Archbishop Maguire—who turned out to be as staunch a supporter of Illich as Spellman—pleasantly accepted his excuse, and communicated Illich's statement to Ottaviani.

Meanwhile, the liberal factions of the Latin American hierarchy had rallied to the aid of Bishop Mendez and Illich to counteract the intrigues being mounted against the diocese of Cuernavaca. The President of the Conference of Latin American Bishops, the Brazilian Bishop Avelar Brandão, had asked two theologians, Father Lucio Gera of Argentina and Bishop Candido Padin of Lorena, Brazil, to make a doctrinal investigation of CIDOC to clarify Illich's work and to dispel the calumnious gossip emanating from Mexico. The two prelates had spent some weeks in Cuernavaca in November 1967 and had compiled a very favorable report on the center, which they had sent on to Rome at the end of the month. But four months later, on March 7, the report had not yet been studied in Rome. It had mysteriously vanished after being submitted to the Vatican. Not even Bishop Mendez or the Apostolic Delegate to Mexico had been able to see a copy of it after having made numerous requests for it. Rather than rely on the document drawn up by Latin America's most prestigious episcopal group, the Vatican continued to view the Illich case through the eyes of the Mexican hierarchy. "There was a moment," the head of the Latin American Bishops' Conference wrote to Illich from Rome in March, "when I felt that they would not return to an authoritarian style . . . but the path of dialogue was interrupted."

Illich's own attempts to dialogue directly with the Holy See were equally futile. In January 1968, he had written a letter to the Pope in that grand and humble ecclesiastical style which some of his progressive friends would resent because of its attitude of total submission to the Papacy:

"Most Holy Father, I, the undersigned Ivan Illich, am humbly prostrated before Your Holiness . . . With all respect and humility I beg Your Holiness, that if I have failed in any way against faith or morality, to communicate to me how I have so failed, disposed as I am to immediately retract my mistakes . . . I humbly kiss your ring and submit myself to your kindness," the letter ended. *"Your most humble son, Ivan Illich."*

This formal appeal was never answered.

Yet, for a man who plays the rules of the game with such elegance, Illich has a terrible inability to control his sense of humor. Sometime during that year, he was seated next to an elderly South American Bishop on a plane flying back from Brazil. Illich had just visited Bahia, where he had studied the ritual poetry of Voodoo sects, and was reading a dossier on Voodoo culture during the flight. "I have a lot of friends who're witch doctors," Illich said with a mysterious smile when the Bishop inquired about his reading matter. Shortly thereafter this Bishop, at the request of the Archbishop of Mexico City, stated to the Papal Delegate that Illich indulged in black magic in the mountain hinterlands of Brazil. This allegation was immediately added to the other complaints which the Mexican right was sending on to the Congregation for the Doctrine of the Faith.

Another exotic rumor about the diocese of Cuernavaca was soon spread by the traditionalists. On March 16, 1968, the Archbishop of Guatemala was kidnapped a few blocks away from his residence as he rode home from the airport in his black Mercedes-Benz. The Very Reverend Maria Casariego had just returned from a trip to Mexico, which he had concluded with a visit to CIDOC and to his colleague, Bishop Mendez. The nature of the kidnapping was made clear in a matter of days: A group of Guatemalan right-wing extremists who call themselves "*La Mano*" had tried to provoke a popular uprising by this feat, hoping to incite one of that country's frequent military coup d'états. But the admirable serenity of the press statements that issued from the Episcopal Palace, and the total indifference of the population to this event—the right wingers had vastly overestimated the emotional hold of bishops over modern Guatemalans—undermined the intrigue. Four days after his sequestration the Archbishop came home to his palace, excommunicated his kidnappers, and identified them to the government. Shortly thereafter the leader of the group was shot down in a church in which he had sought sanctuary.

In reporting upon this typical Latin American occurrence, an editorial in the official Opus Dei publication *Gente* suggested that Illich, his CIDOC staff, and the Bishop of Cuernavaca had been responsible for the Guatemalan prelate's adventure. Archbishop Casariego, *Gente* explained, had gone to CIDOC to inform himself on its alleged sheltering of the Maryknollers-turned-guerrillas (the Melvilles and company) who had been recently expelled from Guatemala. And Opus Dei implied that the kidnapping was arranged so that the Archbishop would be unable to report to the Holy See the "strange and displeasing things" he had seen at CIDOC. The Opusdeistas went on to suggest that CIDOC was a headquarters, *cuartel general*, for all the chieftains of Latin America's guerrilla bands.

The Opus Dei allegations, although they would go verbatim into the list of questions put to Illich at his inquisition, caused a furor in the moderate Mexican press. They were called "an infamous continuation of the defamation campaign against Bishop Mendez." Bishop Mendez even received unprecedented support from his own Mexican colleagues. The new president of the Mexican Bishops' Conference, the Bishop of Oaxaca, who had recently succeeded the Bishop of Puebla in the post, issued a statement "in the name of the Mexican Episcopate" denying any role his colleague might have played in the Guatemalan affair and asking that the campaign against Mendez Arceo be stopped. But the machine of international conspiracy had gone too far to be reversed. On the tenth of June 1968, the Apostolic Delegate to Mexico, Guido de Mestri, sent Illich a summons to fly immediately to Rome and submit to an interrogation by the Congregation for the Doctrine of the Faith. The Apostolic Delegate had always found Illich's conduct beyond reproach. "Your position is so canonically impeccable," he had once said to Illich, "that I doubt if you are even a Christian."

VI

It is a tribute to Ivan Illich's courtesy that, between June of 1968 and January of 1969, he kept the colorful events of his inquisition in complete secrecy. He kept them secret because, as he said, "I was so terribly embarrassed for the Church." It took one more scandalous move from the Vatican to trigger Illich into exposing the scandal.

At ten o'clock one sunny January morning in Cuernavaca, six months after Illich's interrogation in Rome, Bishop Mendez was in one of CIDOC's conference rooms, giving his third lecture on liberal reform in the Church in the early sixteenth century, comparing the style of that profoundly humanistic period with the more dictatorial style of the post-Tridentine Church, and giving particular stress to the progressive thought of Erasmus. The phone rang in Ivan Illich's study. It was the Apostolic Delegate Guido de Mestri, saying that he had to see Illich, in the presence of Bishop Mendez, with the utmost urgency. "I did a thing which in this center has never been done before," Illich says, "I interrupted something so sacred as a seminar." Bishop Mendez stopped lecturing to speak to the Roman delegate. An appointment was made for five that afternoon. When Monsignor de Mestri came at that hour, he brought an order from the Holy See forbidding all Catholic priests, monks, and nuns to attend courses or seminars at Illich's educational center. No reasons were given for the ban other than the "many complaints"—left unspecified—which the Vatican had received about the center, concerning its "unfortunate effects"—also unspecified—upon the Catholic world.

Ivan Illich then acted in what his friends call his "Roman manner," which is based on the logic of "If they do this, I'll do that." With a superb sense of public relations, Illich called the religion editor of *The New York Times* to give him an exclusive release of the entire questionnaire which had been handed him in Rome six months earlier. He would release it to the world press a few days later. That was Illich's chesslike move against the Church-as-It. His lasting love for the Church-as-She was expressed that same week in a letter which he wrote to Bishop Mendez, made public at the same time as the Roman Curia's questionnaire.

"I am deeply saddened," he wrote, "by this procedure of the Holy See, which is the supreme teaching authority of the Church. I am distressed as I watch the Roman Curia launch a grave and global accusation against a nonsectarian institution of higher learning, without ever mentioning a single charge.

"We shall leave it to others to express their indignation at the precedent-setting intervention of Rome into academic life through the ecclesiastical ban of an entire academic community.

"I am indeed sad, yet hopeful. The roots of my mind and of my heart have taken into the soil of the Roman Church. I am embarrassed by this decree but my embarrassment will fade as it has before in front of Her immense contribution to beauty, truth and awareness."

And there Illich's comments on the ban ended. The only other statement he would make on it was: "I am a priest in good, decent standing, but I am mostly an educator. I love my Church deeply and I am very embarrassed by the thoughtless mistakes of some churchmen." The indignation, as Illich predicted, was left "for others to express." And it was voiced, outside of Mexico, by even the most conservative factions of Catholic opinion. Even the Brooklyn *Tablet*, long considered a most reactionary Catholic paper, came to Illich's support. "The issue is not a dispute between liberal and conservative factions," an editorial in the *Tablet* stated after admitting its opposition to most of Illich's ideas. "It involves the credibility of the Church . . . One need not agree at all with Monsignor Illich, only believe in human dignity . . . This entire controversy must accelerate practical implementation of procedures for due process within the Church . . . to eliminate ecclesiastical procedures which are a scandal to responsible men within and outside the Church in 1969."

There was vigorous applause from the Mexican right, however, which sent a telegram to the Holy Father—again published in the form of a paid advertisement in the Mexican papers—thanking him for the ban on CIDOC. "This comforting news fully confirmed our views," the telegram read, "that any effort to sow confusion into the

Church's dogmatic truths with the pretext of clarifying Her message to modern man will be rejected by the robust and total faith of the Mexican people."

There were three major ways in which Illich's interrogation violated due process and denied all concepts of common law, paralleling the procedures used by medieval inquisitions, current sessions of the League of Soviet Writers, and Puritan witch hunts:

(1) The accused was presumed guilty by the very nature of the questions: "What would you answer to those who describe you as restless, daring, imprudent, fanatical and hypnotizing?" "Is it true that the diverse publications of CIDOC broadcast Communist propaganda frequently and with gusto, and contain qualified commentaries of Protestant and anti-Catholic thinking?" "Is it true that you consider seminaries useless and even dangerous?"

(2) The vagueness of the questions impeded any attempt of the accused to state his innocence with precision. "Is it true that you want a new democratic Catholic Church, without sacraments, doctrine, hierarchy, clergy or pastors?" "Is it true that you want a Church confined to the social class of the poor only, a Church that excludes the rich from its membership?" "What do you think of the right of individual liberty and of individual freedom? What do you mean by dialogue? And how do you wish it to unfold itself between discordant political and religious beliefs?" As Illich said, even the Pope would have to write a book on each of these subjects to come out of it ideologically intact.

(3) The interrogation—and there lies its most scandalous resemblance to inquisitional and totalitarian procedures —made numerous attempts to solicit incriminatory information about other persons. "In what capacity and for

what reason did the apostate of religion Thomas Melville, implicated in the Guatemala guerrilla movement, use CIDOC to defend his apostasy and answer to the canonical censures of his Superior General?" "What can you report of the life and social ideas of Father Ceslaus Hoinacki, who contracted a civil marriage in 1967?" "Who are Fathers Baltasar Lopez, Father Segundo Galilea and Father Casiano Floresta and what are their ideas upon clerical celibacy?" "What do you think of the scandal caused among religious women by Father Jean Lefèvre and his sensation-seeking ideas?" (Neither the nature of the scandal nor the ideas are specified.)

Finally, the theological naiveté of the questionnaire was as crude as its method. "What do you think of hell, paradise and of Limbo?" is the question that made Ivan Illich laugh the hardest as he stood on that June day in Rome reading the questionnaire. Limbo has never been an article of faith, and is considered nowadays as a folkloric, almost heretic, deviation from doctrine. The accusation may have been drawn from the fact that Illich had recently quipped at a theology seminar: "To hell with Limbo! That is a correct statement of Augustine's theology."

Reviewing Illich's interrogation in the light of the ten-year-old campaign against the diocese of Cuernavaca, one is struck by the docile manner in which the Congregation parroted accusations made by diverse branches of the Mexican right wing without once bothering to substantiate one charge. One is also amazed that the Gestapo-like process which led to it was able to occur over the opposition of such men as the highest-ranking prelate of the United States and Latin America's most prestigious episcopal group. In terms of the Roman hierarchy, Illich's inquisition is a sad commentary on the growing current of reaction that has emanated from Rome in the past two years, negating many basic principles promulgated by Vatican II. In terms of the laity, one can see the defamation campaign against the diocese of Cuernavaca only as an hysterical last-ditch stand of the Latin American right wing, a faction made all the more militant because of the enormous radicalization of its clergy in the past three years. Mendez Arceo and Ivan Illich are men who have been eager to hear any point of view, be it from proponents of guerrilla warfare or Grayson Kirk—as long as it is backed with scholarship and intellectual rigor. But such intellectual freedom in Mexico, where the masses live in such extreme poverty that the Mexican population has the second-lowest life expectancy of any on the Latin American continent, is looked upon as dynamite by the wealthy few.

The Church elsewhere in Latin America is changing at a furious pace. In Argentina, Catholic priests are teaching classes in the techniques of strikes and demonstrations to peasants and factory workers. In Chile, it is the militant Catholic clergy who pushed Eduardo Frei's progressive government to the left of its programmed course, and played a major role in his decision to nationalize the country's copper industry. In Paraguay, the bishops are proving to be even more militant than their priests in needling the government for social and agrarian reform. In Recife, Brazil, where Church buildings are regularly sprayed with machine-gun fire, Archbishop Helder Camera recently said that right-wing "death squads," possibly working with the connivance of the government, have marked thirty-two Brazilian clergymen for death, including himself. In Colombia, continuing the tradition of Camillo Torres, an organization of Catholic clergymen called the "*Colgonda*" are said to be using an elaborate biblical code in arranging for supplies and assistance to guerrilla groups. "The United States shouldn't worry about the Soviets in Latin America, because they are not revolutionaries anymore," Fidel Castro said recently to a group of foreign visitors. "But they should worry about the Catholic revolutionaries, who are." In a continent so seething with new Catholic radicalism, the religious and intellectual freedom of the Cuernavaca diocese is as much of a menace, to those Catholics trying to preserve the status quo, as Voltaire was to the French royalty; and the proponents of such freedom are equally in risk of exile.

However, Illich's inquisition may have had its salubrious side. Thanks to the comic light which Illich cast upon the proceedings of the Congregation for the Doctrine of the Faith, and the elegant timing with which he disclosed them, he has probably spared his colleagues from undergoing other such grillings. Monsignor Casoria and Monsignor de Magistris are the ones who were deposed. As Aristophanes, Pasquino, Erasmus, and Voltaire knew, wit reforms. Comedy cleanses. Sarcasm purifies. Ivan Illich had wished to "smile the system apart." However, underneath his exterior of wry irony and good humor, Illich must have been deeply hurt. It demands phenomenal faith in the Church-as-She to survive such an offense from the Church-as-It.

Ivan Illich had always believed that a priest must abandon his clerical status as soon as he becomes controversial.

"It is canonically correct," Illich said one day in March 1969, standing on his sunny terrace in Cuernavaca, "for a clergyman to divest himself of his faculties as soon as he becomes notorious." He circumscribed, with a gesture of his elegant hands, two imaginary rooms, one at each end of the terrace. "The room over here," he said, pointing to the East, "is used for political discussions. The room over there," he pointed to the West, "is for celebrating the Eucharist. Only the ones who have remained uncontroversial in the political seminar should go in there" (pointing to the imaginary chapel) "to preside over the celebration."

Someone protested that in Illich's definition all the imaginative, progressive, and courageous priests would have to remain in the political seminar room, that the ones in the chapel "would be a bunch of dopes."

"Or clowns?" Illich suggested with a wry smile. He walked to the room at the Western end of his terrace where he had said Mass during his less controversial years, opened a closet to show his neatly folded white chasuble, his chalice, his Mass book. "Since the controversy," he said, "I have abstained in order to be canonically correct." There was on his face an expression of sarcasm mingled with deep pain.

The same week, with rigorous consistency, Illich wrote to his superior, Archbishop Terence Cooke, from whom he had already received a temporary permission to live as a layman. In this letter Illich informed Archbishop Cooke (who would shortly thereafter be made a Cardinal) that he had decided to retire permanently from employment of the institution, from the Church-as-It, while remaining an ever faithful member of the Church-as-She.

> *"Your Excellency,"* he wrote, *"By now the press has extensively covered the proceedings of the Congregation of the Faith (the former Holy Office) which were aimed at my work and my reputation. These proceedings have cast over me the shadow of a 'notorious churchman,' and this interferes with my ministry, my work as an educator, and my personal decision to live as a Christian.*
>
> *"In September of 1968, you gave me leave to live as a layman, in other words, as a reserve officer. I now want to inform you of my irrevocable decision to resign entirely from Church service, to suspend the exercise of priestly functions, and to renounce totally all titles, offices, benefits, and privileges which are due to me as a cleric."*

In ending, Ivan Illich stated that he would not ask to be dispensed from two priestly prerogatives: He wished to retain the obligation to say his daily breviary, and his obligation to remain celibate.

News of Illich's half-way withdrawal spread consternation among liberal young clergymen everywhere. "Father Illich felt that he had to resign some of his priestly faculties," said a friend of Illich's who is highly placed in the New York Chancery, "because he couldn't stand the institution's lack of trust. His stance as a Christian is so at odds with that of the Holy See that he felt uncomfortable continuing as an officer, or a field worker, of the institution. He was suffering too much harassment to continue to function with joy as a Christian. Canonically, he remains a priest. It has been very important for us to have Father Illich as a member of the New York Archdiocese even though he lives away. He visits us at length whenever he's in town. We love and admire him, he is a great source of renewal and of inspiration to us. There was profound sadness among us when he renounced his faculties. It was the feeling of 'If he can't make it, how can I?'"

"The teaching, educational function is a crucial aspect of the priesthood," said another close friend of Illich's at the New York Chancery, Monsignor Robert Fox. "And to Illich it has always been the primary function. At times we have to specialize, we have to suspend ourselves from certain faculties of the priesthood to better fulfill other priestly duties. I predict that Ivan Illich will soon be having as much of an impact on the educational system as he's had on the Church."

. . .

Ivan Illich, indeed, was ending the decade by smiling the school system apart.

The myth of universal schooling, he writes, which was spread by the world's rich nations in the nineteenth century, has taken the place of the Church in the inevitable secularization process of society. Schooling began to take religion's place when Christian Churches entrenched themselves in justifying the status quo, lost their religious and educational creativity, could no longer direct society to a humanistic education. "Today universal schooling is accepted as inevitable as was church membership by priests, city fathers, and the great majority in past generations." "Like an established church, the school system is regarded as sacred, is accepted as a symbolic interpretation of the status quo . . . we attend it regularly, conform to its various rituals, and bow to its functionaries in a sacred environment . . . Formerly the Christian shuddered at the thought of unbaptized babies going to hell, today it is dogma that high school dropouts are condemned to the ghetto."

Ivan Illich turns his guns on the schools in Latin America. He is concerned with the fact that the ideal of a twelve-year education, in a continent where no more than twenty-five per cent reach the sixth grade, condemns the dropouts to permanent inferiority. He puts the blame on the United States. "Blind faith in mother school was first exported from North America by missionaries and is now advocated by a variety of technical assistants." Noting that some Latin American governments spend as much as two fifths of their total budgets on schools, he writes: "Everywhere in Latin America the beneficiaries of the school monopoly, the learned, judge each other's status by applying measures for school attendance which are made and revised yearly in the U.S. . . . thus mass acceptance of the liberal consensus on the need for schooling implies worldwide colonialism. The myth of the necessity of schooling convinces most Brazilians that a few technocrats and the idle rich have an inevitable right to run their country . . . it assures that throughout the world two separate societies develop ever more unequally, those schooled below the obligatory level accepting their own guilt and inferiority." He compares compulsory schooling to recent improvements in highways and in parking facilities throughout the world. "They overwhelmingly benefit those who have their own cars—one per cent—and the allocation of the budget in these improvements discriminates against what should be the true goal for a just society: the best transportation for the greatest number." The same school system which was necessary in the last century to overcome feudalism and create the Latin American bourgeoisie has now become, in Illich's view, "an oppressive idol which protects those who are already schooled. Schools grade, and therefore they degrade."

Ultimately, Illich warns, the cult of schooling, like all idolatry, will lead to violence. "The time of reformation, secularization, and the disestablishment of the school with bring processes analogous to those which occur in the breakdown of established Churches . . . we will see struggles for investiture, struggles for local control and struggles for freedom from dogma. We will experience the rise of lay preachers, sectarianism, heresies, inquisitions, and religious wars." He compares today's student rebellions against the "idolatry of the schools" to the numerous movements which, throughout history, have sought liberation from an established Church. "Our present student rebellions have the time-worn marks of all other spiritual insurgency against religion gone stale: enthusiasm, insistence on personal testimony, poverty, freedom, and small community." He compares the New York City school crisis of 1968 to a revolutionary situation at the turn of the eleventh century: "Shanker and his clergy remind one of Pope Gregory VII at Canossa letting King Henry (Lindsay) wait in the cold until he would lift the interdict."

Before sketching a Utopian alternative to the present educational system, Illich makes a methodical separation of the various functions provided by contemporary schools: One: their custodial, baby-sitting function. Two: their selective role, which grades and shades for social role and status. Three: their indoctrination for conformity, which helps keep a population docile. All these functions are part of *schooling*, not *education* in Illich's sense of the world. Only their fourth task—the cognitive process—is educative, and it has suffered much at the expense of the first three.

Illich suggests that the first three functions be radically reduced in favor of the fourth. The poor must be educated without undergoing the selective, custodial, and indoctrinatory processes of the present system. "The disentanglement of education from schooling," he writes, "has become one of the primary 'revolutionary' tasks . . . we must ask ourselves what can be done to prevent schooling from discriminating against the world's majority, which cannot afford it and who, in the long run, threaten with violence those who can."

In Illich's still modest utopia for future schooling he suggests that instead of the nine-month-a-year schedule under which we now go to school, school sessions be radically reduced to two months per year, and spread over the first thirty years of a man's life. Noting that adults, with modern methods such as Paolo Freire's, can be taught to read in six weeks of evening classes at one tenth the cost it takes to teach a child, he suggests that industry begin to assume some of the roles now played by schools. Factories could serve as training centers during off hours. Managers could be obliged to spend part of their time planning this training. We would rid ourselves of the notion that schooling must precede productive work. Labor unions, political parties, professional clubs could also take on educational tasks. The family unit would be given back much of the educative function it had in the past. Illich admits that such a revolution in the school system will be difficult to achieve. "The demand for rational educational innovation affects society like political dynamite, like a call to the subversion of sacrosanct values." Throughout this upheaval, he predicts, "only those who do not take the school itself too seriously will be able to keep the sense of humor which will enable them to educate."

The vanishing clergyman was spending most of his time writing about the vanishing schoolmaster.

Ivan Illich's half-in, half-out position in the priesthood caused much speculation among Catholics the world over. Was he pioneering some new hybrid form of priesthood? How did his actions fit in with his theories? He had prophesied a Church of sacramental laymen, and he himself had ended up an unsacramental priest. As a theologian, Illich had made a rigorous separation between the priest as bearer of the Word and the priest as administrator. As a man he had found that the two are not so easily separable, he had had to disassociate himself, with great sorrow, from the sacramental life in order to leave the administration. And yet he remained a priest. It was all marvelously cryptic, complex, and enigmatic, like the man himself.

As their Church's most agitated decade since the sixteenth century came to an end Illich's quixotic status set other questions into the minds of progressive Catholics. How much could one disdain the Church-as-It without severing relations with the Church-as-She? How much criticism of *It* could one indulge in before losing contact with *Her*?

There were strong parallels between the secular and the religious realm for Catholic liberals in the United States in 1970. The decade of the sixties had begun during the years of John Kennedy, John XXIII, *Gaudium et Spes*, and *Pacem in Terris* in a mood of enormous hope and joy. Under Paul VI and Richard Nixon, in the years of *Humanae Vitae*, the continuing Vietnam war, and the century's darkest mood of national crisis, it ended in an atmosphere of cynical despair. The Catholic hierarchy was stiffening on many levels. In the summer of 1969, the most progressive Catholic Bishop in the United States left the Church amid a scandalous campaign of defamation that closely recalled the harassment of Mendez Arceo and Ivan Illich. The United States Bishops—behind closed doors—had censured their colleague James Shannon for his "outspokenly progressive beliefs"; there was a Vatican reprimand for his blunt stand against the Vietnam war; his written appeal to the Pope, like Illich's, had remained unanswered; and there had been a plan—also implemented by an Apostolic Delegate—to get him out of the United States to work abroad. In October 1969 the Synod of Bishops in Rome had raised little hope for the democratization of Church structures promised by Vatican II. In this context of retrogression, the leadership of United States Catholics in the movement protesting the Vietnam war and the Latin American clergy's powerful new leadership in social reform seem the clearest sign of the enduring vigor of the Catholic faith.

For the Underground Church is now at a low ebb. Catholics who had rushed to each others' apartments in 1967 to share rye bread and California wine to the strum of badly tuned guitars have either dropped out of the Church altogether or have gone back to their parishes in resignation, staring jadedly at the familiar announcements of Bingo games and Daughters of Isabella card parties. The Underground Church had been a form of civil disobedience. But civil disobedience, in both church and state, is based on the hope that the system is reformable without the psychological or physical violence of schism. It had been nourished, in the Church of the mid-sixties, by the immense hopes offered by Vatican II. Hopes for true reform have waned in the past two years as it became evident that Paul VI would fail to implement the spirit of the last Council; the Underground Church, and the theology of civil disobedience upon which it had been based, waned with them. Emmaus House today is as secularized as Illich's CIDOC, and more conventional. It has turned its sights quite away from reforming the Church and towards social work, counseling, vocational advice. It is calling itself "A community for putting people in touch with alternatives to traditional life-styles." Emmaus House has ceased to be a cell of the Underground Church rebelling against the hierarchy; it has become a "parallel structure" totally indifferent to the institution, an occasional meeting place for stimulating and poetic interdenominational worship, too secularized to be either underground or schismatic.

For the Catholic progressives who still desire to keep some fidelity to the institution, the decade of the seventies promises to be one in which they will need more blind faith than ever in the Church-as-She. Illich's metaphor of retaining faith in Her not withstanding the rigidity of the Church-as-It is the most helpful pastoral advice offered by anybody for 1970. And it seems predictable that the most genuine and committed progressives in the Church—Cardinal Suenens of Belgium and Cardinal Alfrink of Holland, Bishop Mendez Arceo and Archbishop Helder Camera of Brazil, Hans Küng, the Berrigans and, in his own ambivalent way, Ivan Illich—will never leave the Church because of their profound and mysterious faith in the Church-as-She. Their very radicalism seems to give them the courage to play the rules of the game, and to reform from the inside—notwithstanding the insults heaped upon them by the institution. Other great progressive churchmen—Cardinal Newman, Teilhard de Chardin, Yves Congar, Abbé Pierre—had helped to renew the Church after enduring similar harassment from Rome. Erasmus was much more progressive than Luther. Bishop Mendez Arceo is more radical than former Bishop James Shannon. The Berrigans and Ivan Illich are infinitely more progressive than Charles Davis. Their endurance, and the capacity of any reform-minded Catholic to remain in the institutional Church, will depend on the mystery of faith, on that intimate and often incommunicable experience of the heart, on what Ivan Illich calls "the childlike simplicity of the Christian faith."

In June 1969, due to the furor in all segments of the Catholic Church over Illich's interrogation and due to the pressure put upon the Holy See by liberal bishops of several countries, the Vatican revoked its ban on CIDOC. Pope Paul personally delivered the new ruling concerning CIDOC to Bishop Mendez Arceo during a private audience. It allowed Catholic priests and religious to resume attending courses in Cuernavaca under certain conditions: that CIDOC return to "the spirit of its foundation," and that its teaching be supervised by the Conference of Latin American Bishops. The Vatican order also invited Illich to resign from the center "within a reasonable time," and urged him to place it completely under the supervision of the Latin American bishops. In this age rife with civil disobedience in both church and state, the previous Papal ban on CIDOC had had about the same effect as a movie ban by the Legion of Decency, causing a flood of applications by progressive priests and nuns indignant over the

Vatican's treatment of Ivan Illich. The new edict made as little sense as the first. It was as if the Vatican had allowed Catholic priests to attend the New School for Social Research under the condition that its teaching be approved by Cardinal Cooke.

At the time the new ruling was made public, Ivan Illich was extremely busy planning an extensive seminar on alternatives to present educational systems, held at CIDOC in the spring of 1970, which he led with prominent educators from many countries. Illich had no observation to make on the relaxation of the ban, save that it would have no more effect than the previous ruling, since CIDOC had always been—he emphasized the words—"a secular organization."

However, Bishop Mendez Arceo did have a mordant comment on the Vatican's change of mind, which he made during his sermon one June Sunday in the Cathedral of Cuernavaca. (Bishop Mendez Arceo, like Ivan Illich, has a very cleansing sense of humor.) "I urge you to pray," he said to his flock, "for those of our brothers who considered us separated from the Church community in Mexico. Many of them have made possible the incredible interrogation by the Congregation for the Doctrine of the Faith, whose publication has resulted in the enormous good of accelerating the renewal of that Congregation."

Index

Index

Index

Index

Index

A NOTE ABOUT THE AUTHOR

Francine du Plessix Gray spent the first part of her childhood in Paris, and came to this country at the beginning of World War II. She attended the Spence School in New York City and Bryn Mawr College; she received her B.A. in philosophy from Barnard College, where she accepted the Putnam Creative Writing Award. From 1952–4 she worked as a reporter for the United Press, and later for several French magazines.

Francine Gray has had stories published in *The New Yorker* and *Mademoiselle*, interviews and articles in *Art in America* and *Vogue*. *The New Yorker* has published all three parts of *Divine Disobedience* in shortened versions. In the past year her coverage of the activities of the New Left for *The New York Review of Books* and *The New Yorker* has attracted considerable attention. Mrs. Gray lives in Warren, Connecticut, with her husband, the painter Cleve Gray, and their two young sons.